T0328132

WTO/GATS and the Global Politics of Higher Education

Studies in Higher Education

PHILIP G. ALTBACH, *General Editor*

WTO/GATS and the Global Politics of Higher Education

Antoni Verger

Routledge
Taylor & Francis Group

NEW YORK AND LONDON

First published 2010
by Routledge
605 Third Avenue, New York, NY 10017

Simultaneously published in the UK
by Routledge
4 Park Square, Milton Park, Abingdon, Oxon OX14 4RN

Routledge is an imprint of the Taylor & Francis Group, an informa business

Copyright © 2010 by Taylor & Francis.

Typeset in Sabon by IBT Global.

All rights reserved. No part of this book may be reprinted or reproduced or utilised in any form or by any electronic, mechanical, or other means, now known or hereafter invented, including photocopying and recording, or in any information storage or retrieval system, without permission in writing from the publishers.

Trademark Notice: Product or corporate names may be trademarks or registered trademarks, and are used only for identification and explanation without intent to infringe.

Library of Congress Cataloging-in-Publication Data
Verger, Antoni, 1975–
    WTO/GATS and the global politics of higher education / by Antoni Verger.
    p. cm. — (Studies in higher education)
    Includes bibliographical references and index.
    1. Education, Higher—Economic aspects. 2. Education and globalization.
3. World Trade Organization. 4. General Agreement on Trade in Services
(Organization) I. Title. II. Title: World Trade Organization/General Agreement
on Trade in Services and the global politics of higher education.
    LC67.6.V67 2009
    338.4'3378—dc22
                                                              2009019794

First issued in paperback 2013

ISBN13: 978-0-415-84866-4 (pbk)
ISBN13: 978-0-415-99882-6 (hbk)
ISBN13: 978-0-203-86667-2 (ebk)

Contents

INTRODUCTION

BLOCK I
GATS in Context

BLOCK II
GATS Results and Procedures

BLOCK III
Inside the Negotiations

Figures

Boxes

Tables

Abbreviations

AAU	Association of African Universities
ACE	American Council of Education
ACJR	Alliance for Fair and Responsible Trade, Chile
AUCC	Association of Universities and Colleges of Canada
CAUT	Canadian Association of University Teachers
CDP	Colegio de Profesores (Teachers Association)
CERI-OECD	Centre for Educational Research and Innovation
CESU	Comité Exportador de Servicios Universitarios (Export Committee of University Services)
CHEA	Council for Higher Education Accreditation
CIN	Consejo Interuniversitario Nacional (National Inter-University Council)
CNAP	Comisión Nacional de Acreditación de Pregrado (Undergraduate Accreditation National Commission)
CNTE	Confederação Nacional dos Trabalhadores em Educação (Education Workers National Confederation)
COL	Commonwealth of Learning
CONAP	Comisión Nacional de Acreditación de Postgrado (Postgraduate Accreditation Nacional Comission)
CONEAU	Comisión Nacional de Evaluación y Acreditación Universitaria (University Accreditation and Evaluation National Commission)
CPC	Central Product Classification

CRUCH	Consejo de Rectores de Universidades Chilenas (Chilean University Chancellors Council)
CRUP	Consejo de Rectores de Universidades Privadas (Private Universities Chancellors Council)
CTERA	Confederación de Trabajadores de la Educación de la República Argentina (Argentinean Republic Education Workers Confederation)
CUSFTA	Canada-US Free Trade Agreement
DIRECON	Dirección General de Relaciones Económicas Internacionales (Internacional Economic Relations Division, Chile)
DRWG	Domestic Regulation Working Group
DSB	Dispute Settlement Body
ECLAC	Economic Commission for Latin America and the Caribbean
ECOSOC	United Nations Economic and Social Council
EFTA	European Free Trade Association
EHEA	European Higher Education Area
ESIB	European Students International Bureau
EU	European Union
EUA	European University Association
FTAA	Free Trade Agreement of the Americas
FTA	Free Trade Agreement
GATS	General Agreement on Trade in Services
GATT	General Agreement on Tariffs and Trade
HCHR	United Nations High Commissioner for Human Rights
HED	Higher Education Division, Chilean Ministry of Education
IADB	Inter American Development Bank
IATP	Institute for Agriculture and Trade Policy
IAU	International Association of Universities
ICFTU	International Confederation of Free Trade Unions

ICT	Information and Communication Technology
IESALC	Instituto Internacional para la Educación Superior en América Latina y el Caribe (Internacional Institute for Higher Education in Latin America and the Caribbean)
IFC	International Finance Corporation
IMF	International Monetary Fund
INQAAHE	International Network of Quality Assurance Agencies in Higher Education
ISIC	International Standard Industrial Classification
ITO	International Trade Organization
LDCs	Less Developed Countries
LEN	Ley de Educación Nacional, Argentina (National Education Act)
LES	Ley de Educación Superior, Argentina (Higher Education Act)
LOCE	Ley orgánica constitucional de enseñanza, Chile (Education Organic Constitutional Act)
MERCOSUR	Common Market of the South
MFN	Most Favored Nation
NAFTA	North America Free Trade Agreement
NCITE	National Committee for International Trade in Education
NEA	National Education Association
NGOs	Non-Governmental Organizations
NPM	New Public Management
OBHE	Observatory of Borderless Higher Education
ODA	Official Development Assistance
OECD	Organization for Economic Co-operation and Development
PRSP	Poverty Reduction Strategy Papers
PSI	Public Services International

RWG	Rules Working Group
SAPs	Structural Adjustment Programmes
SDT	Special and differential treatment
SNA	System of National Accounts
SPU	Secretaría de Política Universitaria, Argentina (Higher Education Division)
TRIPS	Agreement on Trade Related Aspects of Intellectual Property Rights
UNCTAD	United Nations Conference on Trade and Development
UNDP	United Nations Development Program
UNESCO	United Nations Educational, Scientific and Cultural Organization
US	United States
USCSI	US Coalition of Services Industry
USTR	US Trade Representative
VSNU	Association of Universities in the Netherlands
WB	World Bank
WEI	World Education Indicators
WTO	World Trade Organization

Foreword

Susan Robertson

The World Trade Organization (WTO), one of the newest international organizations to have emerged on the global stage over the past two decades, has also been one of the most controversial. Its biennial meetings have continued to attract thousands of protesters from around the world, whilst the negotiation rounds continue to stall on what remains an intractable issue; the development of a fairer global trading system which might enable developing countries to compete on the same terms as the powerful developed nations. Paradoxical as this might sound, for many developing countries, free trade is not really free trade, but a way of enabling the powerful countries to set the terms of global trade to suit their own agendas and interests.

Formed in 1995, the WTO had a specific mandate: to promote free trade, and to regulate global trade. An innovative feature of the WTO's mandate was to also bring the services sectors, such as education, health, finance, transport, and so on, within the ambit of the global trading regime, along with goods. The General Agreement on Trade in Services, under which negotiations around education fall, has been particularly controversial. This is in large part because education has long held an unshakeable claim—to being both a public good, and more recently a fundamental human right. It is therefore easy to see how familiar referent points—like education as a public good—are challenged by ideas, such as 'trade in education services' (which is how the WTO/GATS agreement describes this activity), or 'education as an export industry' (as in the case of Australia and New Zealand, two nations with significant economic returns to selling education abroad).

Now the problem with much of the writing on the WTO and GATS is that it has tended to be caught up in the 'for' and 'against' debates, with often insufficient understanding of quite what is being traded away (if at all), how, and to what extent, and what the long term implications of this are for education in particular, but also other sectors as well.

In other words, there have been surprisingly limited close, systematic and critical examinations of the WTO/GATS negotiations and outcomes concerning education. In part this is a consequence of the strategy that was pursued of creating a new organization—the WTO—which enabled powerful nations, such as the US, the EU, Canada, Japan and Australia, to advance their interests in a new arena which was sufficiently off the radar for many researchers. It is also the case too that a new kind of literacy is required to make sense of what are highly legalistic texts and decisions. Finally, I would suggest that scrutinizing organizations, such at the WTO, and the GATS, requires careful research not only on the texts that are officially produced, but looking closely at the organization to understand better how it works.

It is precisely this kind of work that characterizes Antoni Verger's research which is the basis of this book on GATS and the Global Politics of Higher Education. Verger does not let himself get seduced by the easy rhetoric of the protester. Instead, he carefully builds up his case by looking at GATS as a mechanism of global governance, by placing GATS into the context of higher education markets, by taking us step by step though the process of negotiation and unfolding trends, introducing us to the actors and their views on the process, including two countries—Chile and Argentina.

What is clear from Verger's work is that it is not education per se, that is viewed as a key commodity to be traded in the global economy, though there is little doubt education markets in higher education continue to return significant value to those countries that are investing very heavily in a services-based economy. Rather, education is viewed as a useful bargaining chip, a pawn in a bigger game of global trade negotiations. This state of affairs is the result of the fact that trading in education services typically does not involve the Minister for Education, but the Minister for Trade. Given too that education affairs are not always conducted at the national scale, but operate in sub-national jurisdictions, it is easy to see that the Minister for Trade's position may not reflect at all that of the education constituency within a country.

The significant absences in spaces to debate the role, place and purpose of education in a democracy, the heavy handed ways in which powerful countries have advanced their own interests in the WTO meetings, the absence of capability within Geneva for developing countries to present their interests especially in a legal environment and framework that is largely foreign, all have generated significant debate about the WTO itself as an organization. However the crucial move that agreeing to the GATS rules around education would signal, is ceding a significant degree of autonomy and sovereignty to the WTO which in turn would lock in, and act on the interests of the globalizing firms, not the global polis. As Verger so brilliantly is able to show through his careful, measured and detailed unpacking of the GATS processes is something we do need to know about because of the significance of what is at stake. However the journey he takes us on leaves us wiser, and able to ultimately act in a more effective way because as they often say—the devil is in the detail. Strategic interventions can only be built from the kind of analysis this book presents to us.

Susan Robertson
University of Bristol
April 2009

Acknowledgments

This book and the research behind the book are highly indebted to numerous people. First, I want to acknowledge the advice and confidence of Xavier Bonal and Xavier Rambla. Without their support, and the opportunities they have opened up to me in the academic world, I would not have been able to carry out this research.

The long research process behind this book has been enriched through continuous exchange with my colleagues and friends in the *Seminari d'Anàlisi de Polítiques Socials* (Autonomous University of Barcelona), the *Observatori del Deute* (Polytechnic University of Catalonia) and the Amsterdam Institute for Metropolitan and International Development Studies (AMIDSt-University of Amsterdam). I do not put the names of each of them here because the list would be too long, but they already know who they are.

The research has also benefited from doing international visits in Argentina, Chile, England and the Netherlands. Thanks to Daniel Suárez (LPP-Buenos Aires), Myriam Feldfeber (Universidad de Buenos Aires), Roger Dale and Susan Robertson (Globalisation Education and Societies—Bristol University) and Mario Novelli (IS Academie 'Education and Development' -University of Amsterdam) for welcoming me to their centers. Special thanks to Olivier, Alexandra, Mónica and her friends for provide me with accommodation in Geneva when I was doing fieldwork on the WTO.

The final product has been enriched thanks to the comments of experts in the fields of comparative higher education and international development: Susan Robertson, Mario Novelli, José J. Brunner, Javier P. Hermo, Gabriela Siufi and Philip Altbach. Thanks specially to the later for accepting my work in the outstanding collection on higher education he is editing. The final version of the book has also benefited from the professional edition carried out by the Languages Service of the Autonomous University of Barcelona and, of course, thanks to AMIDSt for investing in this project and paying the linguistic edition service.

My special gratitude is for my family and friends in Mallorca, Sabadell, Barcelona and Mataró. Thanks for understanding that doing a PhD research thesis (above all on an international topic) means that is difficult *to be there* very often.

Last, but not least, my deepest acknowledgments are for Mar, for her constant support, her wise comments and for being always by my side, despite the "distance joke".

Introduction

1 GATS, Higher Education and Global Governance Studies

In recent years, higher education has been immersed in a sea of transformations and transitions of a very different nature. The commodification and the transnationalization of higher education and the increasing fluxes of cross-border provision of university services, together with the increasing role played by economic international organizations in higher education affairs, are probably the most remarkable examples of the changes currently being manifested in the field. The intensification of economic globalization has become a key causal force of these changes. On the one hand, the process of economic globalization, which promotes the territorial integration of the economy on a world scale, pressures universities to provide the means for the smooth functioning of the global economy as well as for the competitiveness of countries, corporations and persons at the international level. On the other hand, economic globalization, understood as the expansion of the capitalist economy to new spheres, places pressure on universities to modify their nature and their *raison d'être*. Thus, in addition to being a medium of the economy, universities in themselves have become objects and products of the economy. Today, universities are managed very similarly to private corporations and the operations of many of them do not differ in any significant way from those of the conventional industry that makes up the global economy: they establish branch campuses abroad, engage in mergers and takeovers, become part of stock markets and realize export activities abroad.

Furthermore, higher education is becoming increasingly embedded in transnationalization dynamics, which must be distinguished from the traditional dynamics of internationalization. The main difference between transnationalization and internationalization does not have to do so much with the scale of operations as much as with the way relationships are structured in the scale in question. 'Internationalization' structures the relationships of the universities and university members based on national borders and regulations, while 'transnationalization' constitutes exchange and trade circuits that transcend state borders and rules and in which universities, professors and students operate and circulate freely. Transnationalization materialises, for example, when a university establishes branches in different countries or buys a university from another country, issues certificates that are recognized in foreign countries by means of in-person or on-line courses, or freely employs international teaching and research personnel.

Finally, some of the most important international organizations, both regional and global (such as the European Union or the World Bank), are introducing—or placing more importance on—higher education related-topics within their political agendas and consequently becoming more influential in framing or altering national and local higher education policies. These organizations do not necessarily treat higher education as a topic, but more as a resource to deal with other topics that are more central to their agendas, such as economic competitiveness, the achievement of knowledge-based societies and, since the constitution of the World Trade Organization (WTO), the international liberalization of trade.

1.1   GATS ENTERS THE SCENE

The constitution of the WTO General Agreement on Trade in Services (GATS), which promotes the liberalization of trade in higher education, is directly related to the abovementioned transformations: the commodification, the transnationalization and the increasing presence of higher education in global politics.

The GATS is negotiated at the multilateral level by all WTO members, which represent most of the countries in the world. The agreement incorporates into its scope higher education services, as well as services related to other levels of education, and promotes trading of these services by member countries. Despite being a non-conventional element in the world of education, the GATS has become a key component of the supra-national governance of education. The commercial liberalization promoted by this trade agreement affects various areas of state education policy regulation. Its effects on the regulatory sphere will be increasingly significant because, as it is established by the GATS itself, trade liberalization advances progressively and is set in successive rounds of negotiation. Moreover, once the legal content of the agreement is fixed in the state regulatory framework, it becomes very difficult to modify. As a result, the GATS has become a key legal instrument for the establishment of a global regime of free trade in education or, in other words, for the establishment of a transnational set of rules, principles and procedures, which condition national regulations, common understandings and the behavior of countries when dealing with higher education issues.

The agreement has also highlighted and given an impulse to a new logic of commercial and competitive higher education exchange, which largely clashes with the traditional logic of internationalization, concerned with cooperation and cultural exchange (Wende 2003). Under the GATS, the international paradigm of global competition takes on a central role in the field of higher education and pushes the traditional one of cooperation into the background. Likewise, the deepening of the liberalization commitments in education in the GATS favors the constitutionalization of neoliberalism on the international education agenda, as well as the institutionalization, in Fligstein's (1993) terms, of a new transnational market for higher education.

Nonetheless, this liberalization process does not advance mechanically and in a linear manner. The GATS liberalization disciplines are not compulsory and WTO member countries are normally free to decide whether or not to adopt them in the framework of progressive rounds of negotiations. Moreover, the GATS entrance onto the education scene has led to a widespread and often passionate debate about the effects, the costs and the benefits of the Agreement for education systems (Williams 2003). For their part, major actors from the international educational community and educational stakeholders in various countries have strongly campaigned against the GATS. Factors external to the WTO system, such as national politics and priorities or the adhesion/contestation to the agreement by different actors in the world of education, may alter the trajectory and the advance of the GATS. On the one hand, they may contribute to making the regime of international trade in education promoted by the GATS more or less liberalizer. On the other hand, they could mean that the process of constructing this trade regime advances at a faster or slower rate.

It should be acknowledged that the public debate on GATS and education was much higher at the beginning of the millennium, when the Doha Round started. At the moment this book is being published, the level of public debate on GATS and education is lower. In part, this is due to the fact that the Doha Round negotiations are advancing at a slow path.[1] There have been some important periods of impasse during the negotiations, the most serious one starting after the failure of the Cancun Ministerial Conference in 2003. The slowness of the negotiations is caused, to some extend, by the too broad range of topics being covered (which include more than forty big issues such as agriculture, cotton, services, subsidies, intellectual property, dumping, regional agreements and a long etcetera). The length of the negotiation agenda, and the fact that all the topics are negotiated at the same time and in an interlinked way, makes it difficult for more than 150 countries to reach a consensus that satisfies all parties. However, another important source of problems for implementing the Doha agenda is the clear reticence of developed countries to liberalize agriculture and other strategic markets. Industrialized countries usually apply double standards on trade policies: they are very active spreading the idea of free trade in international forum, but at the same they invest a huge amount of resources to protect their national industries, as well as to promote their internationaliation. The recent world financial crisis is also affecting Doha in the sense that more and more countries are opting for protecting those sectors of their economies that generate more jobs.

However, the slow rhythm of the negotiations does not reduce at all the political relevance and the implications of the GATS for education. First, independently of the evolution of the Doha Round, the GATS is already in force and is being administered by the WTO Secretariat. General obligations, such as Most Favored Nation, and the first liberalization commitments acquired by countries in the Uruguay Round (1986–1994) have to be respected by members. Second, the Doha negotiations are advancing at a slow path, but they are advancing. Maybe the results will not be so ambitious as pro-liberalization sectors initially expected, but there will be a progression of liberalization, also in education. In fact, as we explain in detail in Chapter 5, in the context of Doha, various countries are willing to commit higher education liberalization for the first time (the US is one of them), and other countries are deepening the commitments acquired in the Uruguay Round. These figures could increase in the near future depending on a number of factors that will be explored throughout the book.

1.2   RESEARCH ON THE GATS AND EDUCATION: A BRIEF REVIEW

Since the end of the nineties, the GATS has become an important topic of research for education scientists. The topic has been analyzed from very different perspectives. One set of authors has focused on the juridical interpretation of the disciplines and rules contained in the agreement and its relationship to educational regulation (Zdouc 1999; Rikowski 2003; Kelsey 2003). Another group of scholars has expounded on the effect of the GATS on education systems from the point of view of various dimensions of impact (quality, equity, the changing role of the state, etc.) (Altbach 2004a; Nunn 2001; Kelk and Worth 2002; Robertson and Dale 2003; Saner and Fasel 2003; Knight 2002; Scherrer 2005; Sauvé 2002a). A third research line, much more descriptive in nature, is based on the monitoring of the GATS negotiations and the state of the art of education liberalization (OECD 2002; Sauvé 2002b; Sauvé and Stern 2000; Nielson 2003).

The research presented in this book, although connected to the three research lines mentioned above, has a fourth line of inquiry. Specifically, it deals with the education liberalization factors in countries participating in the WTO/GATS negotiations. In other words, it aims to identify the causes by which countries agree (or reject) to apply the liberalization rules of the WTO in the educational sector. The core research question is therefore, why is education liberalized by countries in the GATS context?

Other authors have analyzed the GATS from a very similar perspective. Not all of them share the same research question, but in a broad sense, they try to understand the rationale behind education liberalization in the GATS context. Some scholars carry out their research by considering a broad sample of countries and by modeling ideal types (Knight 2004; Larsen, Momii, and Vincent-Lancrin 2004). Others do so through empirical research in selected countries and applying case study methodology. Scholars working in this later research line, and the cases analyzed by them, are Mundy and Iga (2003), for the cases of Japan and US, Bassett (2006), US, Zhang (2003), China, Ziguras et al (2003), Australia, Vlk (2006), Netherlands and Czech Republic, and Frater (2008a), for Jamaica.

The work of these authors has been highly inspiring for the research presented in this book. However, most of the existing work attempts to understand education liberalization under the GATS from a single scale perspective, mainly centered at national level. This implies a 'methodological nationalism' bias that is very common in education sciences and comparative education research and which leads to the danger of missing important processes that take place below, beyond and above the nation state (Dale and Robertson 2007). To overcome this and other limitations, the research here engages with multi-level governance and other globalization theories.

1.3   THEORETICAL APPROACH:
THE GLOBAL POLITICS PERSPECTIVE

The analysis of the relationship between the GATS and education can be situated in the area of *globalisation and education*. This is an emerging area of studies that looks at the implications of the processes of economic, political and cultural globalisation in the field of education. As this book aims to demonstrate, the shaping of this new area does not simply mean introducing new topics onto the agenda of educational research, but rather revising certain theoretical postulations, models of analysis and research methodologies (Bonal, Tarabini-Castellani, and Verger 2007).

First, as pointed out previously, serious consideration of globalization means transcending methodological nationalism (Dale and Robertson 2007). In the current globalized environment, international actors and educational (and extra-educational) factors originating at supra-national scales are affecting national education policies, priorities and outcomes. An important part of the educational changes should be better understood, therefore, as being as embedded within interdependent local, national and global political economy complexes (Novelli and Lopes Cardozo 2008).

Secondly, although directly related to the previous point, there is a clear need to look beyond educationism (Dale and Robertson, 2007). That means that when we analyze new trends and regulatory transformations in the educational field we have to take into account that all these elements may be influenced and shaped by extra-educational structures, events, rationales and processes (such as the prevailing welfare regime, the levels of poverty and social cohesion or the economic performance in a country).

The third challenge concerns methodological statism, which implies assuming that state actors do not have the monopoly over political action and that non-state actors are also relevant political agents in the global governance of education. It also implies that states cannot be understood as monolithic units of analysis because there are different factions and struggles within the state that are all pushing for different, and sometimes contradicting, interests and agendas (Cox 1995). It should be pointed out that challenging methodological statism and recognizing the political relevance of non-state actors does not necessarily mean that the state is becoming less powerful. Rather, it means accepting that the role and functions of the state have been altered in the broad scenario of governance, that other players are actively participating at the levels of education policies and politics, and that the state is not as autonomous in relation to certain policy issues as before.

To successfully face these three challenges, and to really engage in the globalization debate, education scientists should focus particularly on the 'politics of education' level of analysis. The politics of education refers to the educational agenda and the processes, problems and structures through which this agenda is created (Dale 1994). In the globalization context, this also means considering the international processes and the cross-border power relations that contribute to structure a global education agenda.

Box 1.1   'Politics of Education' Questions

- What functional, scalar and sectoral divisions of labor of educational governance are in place?
- In what ways are the core problems of capitalism (accumulation, social order and legitimation) reflected in the mandate, capacity and governance of education? How and at what scales are contradictions between the solutions addressed?
- How are the boundaries of the education sector defined and how do they overlap with and relate to other sectors? What 'educational' activities are undertaken within other sectors?
- How is the education sector related to the citizenship and gender regimes?
- How, at what scale and in what sectoral configurations does education contribute to the extra-economic embedding/stabilization of accumulation?
- What is the nature of intra- and inter-scalar and intra- and inter-sectoral relations (contradiction, cooperation, mutual indifference?)

Source: Dale and Robertson, 2007

Analysis at the politics of education level involves research questions such as those contained in Box 1.1.

Studying the GATS and education from the politics of education perspective gives the research added value. Apart from the interest the GATS offers in itself, analyzing it from a broader perspective allows several of the elements that characterize the current educational governance scenario to be explored. For example, the scalar and sectoral division of education policymaking, the economic embeddedness of the global educational agenda and the participation of non-state actors and international organizations in defining state education policies. Therefore, analyzing the GATS from this perspective allows us to enter into broader debates and frameworks for the analysis of contemporary social science such as the changing role of the state in globalisation, the existing power relations in the pluri-scalar governance scenario, or the role of ideas in defining the agenda, the decisions and the preferences within international politics.

The following sections introduce theoretical and conceptual references to these analytical frameworks, which contribute to this particular analysis of education liberalization under the GATS.

a) Non-State Actors and Global Politics

One of the objectives of this research is to analyze the influence of education non-state actors in the GATS negotiations. Specifically, the research focuses on the role of civil society organizations involved in the education sector such as teachers unions, development non-governmental organizations (NGOs) and associations of public and private universities.

The literature on global governance points out the increasing influence in international politics of non-state actors coming from the civil society field. This literature observes the capacity of transnational NGOs, social movements and transnational advocacy networks to create international norms by persuasion (Fehl 2004; Keck and Sikkink 1998; Arts 2005), to transform the perceptions over countries' identities, and to challenge the international agenda as well as the ways in which national interests must be dealt with (Haas 2002). It also demonstrates the capacity of epistemic communities to produce and disseminate scientific knowledge that is relevant for policy-making, above all in relation to policy issues that generate uncertainty (Haas 2004; Evans 2006). However, it is always difficult to specify how, when and through what actions do non-state actors matter more.

Some interesting debates also exist about the privileged scales of political action by civil society, and whether non-state actors can affect global politics directly or whether they need to do so via the mediation of nation states. Furthermore, it remains questionable how open the current multilateral system is to civil society demands that clash with more established principles, rules and understandings within international organizations and regimes.

In this respect, O'Brien et al (2000) propose the "complex multilateralism" theory, which says that multilateralism is moving away from an exclusively state-based structure, and that private actors are currently able to play an increasingly important role in multilateral structures. One of the potential implications of this new scenario is that the international system must contemplate and encourage the entry of a new set of interests that are not necessarily linked to specific national-based interests, as was the case in the framework of traditional state-centered multilateralism. In the new multilateral context, organizations such as humanitarian NGOs and trade unions could introduce certain topics onto the international agenda from the perspective of global justice or universal rights.

Other less globalist scholars consider that local and national scales are still fundamental for understanding international politics. As a consequence, they argue that the impact of civil society in international politics is actually mediated through the interactions produced within domestic structures (Halliday 2002; Keck and Sikkink 1998) while global politics are not an end in themselves, but rather an influential medium at the state level. This is reflected, for instance, by Sidney Tarrow (2001), who considers that the re-scaling strategies activated by local social movements through international networks are principally used to project and amplify their local demands. Social movements could also take advantage of certain international agreements, such as human rights agreements, signed by their target state to legitimate their demands and to discipline the behavior of the state in question (Tsutsui and Wotipka 2004). This tactic is commonly known as the 'boomerang effect' because it permits local groups to achieve political impact at state level projecting their activity and demands on a global scale (Keck and Sikkink 1998).

Andrew Herod is another author that aims to transcend the local-global dichotomy when analyzing social movements. His analysis of trade union strategies confronted to transnational corporations shows that the successful cases are those where the scales of resistance strategies are rooted in an analysis of the specific geographies of the struggle and in the capacity of the resisting trade union to utilise its own power resources at particular scales at particular moments (Herod 2001a; Herod 2001b).

In this specific research, the above mentioned literature—mainly coming from the political geography and global governance areas—is combined with classical theories of social movements. Framing theory is particularly useful to understand how the cognitive action of non-state actors contributes to the achievement of certain political objectives (Benford and Snow 2000). The most important cognitive activities contemplated by these kind of theories are explanation (or the way the problems that social movements face are explained), motivation (to encourage the participation of people and groups in particular struggles), prognostic (solutions or alternatives proposed to the problems) and the frame alignment to link particular campaigns to other ideas, struggles or understandings of the reality. However, the success of social movements' ideas and cognitive action are also contingent to extrinsic factors. To capture the contextual constrains and opportunities for social movements, we refer to political opportunity structures and similar theories that pay attention to the political context of collective action (Tarrow 1994). This means that, to analyze social movements influence we need to take into account political and institutional variables such as the openness degree of the political system, the ideology of the governments (or other targeted organizations), how the power is distributed in the international organization or in the political system in question, the alliances with powerful actors as well as the political culture and the willingness of policy-makers to engage with civil society ideas, concerns and demands (Giugni, McAdam, and Tilly 1999).

b) The Role of Ideas in (International) Politics

A second line of inquiry of our research involves the role of ideas in politics. Dealing with ideas means dealing with human consciousness, intersubjective understandings, norms, knowledge and argumentation (Finnemore and Sikkink 2001). Scholars that pay more attention to the role of ideas usually emphasize the role of non-state actors in politics. This is due to the fact that non-state actors do not have as much material power as state actors, but they can hold "powerful ideas" that are independent of economic and military capacities (Keck and Sikkink 1998). To a great extent, the strength and legitimacy of non-state actors depends on their beliefs, scientific evidence and moral principles (Korzeniewicz and Smith 2003). That is why persuasion and argumentation are key tactics of civil society organizations in influencing political outcomes.

When investigating the role of ideas within politics, the key research question is not whether ideas matter or not, because it is assumed that human interpretation and ideas are always variables that frame political outcomes; rather, the questions are: how and when those ideas matter more (Wendt 1999)? Are ideas autonomous sources of power (Walsh 2000)? And what kind of ideas (world views, principled beliefs or causal beliefs) matter more (Goldstein and Keohane 1993)?

Scholars differ in their answers to these and other related questions. Undoubtedly, there is no common understanding of which kind of ideas matter more and how. In fact, different theoretical approaches deal differently with these dilemmas. For instance, institutionalism emphasizes the political impact of ideas once they become institutionalized. This means that ideas exert influence as elements that are embedded in institutions, regimes or policy paradigms (Hall 1993), and that actors behavior in institutional settings is mainly guided by the logic of appropriateness (March and Olsen 2005). For instance, if the logic of appropriateness predominates in an international organization, member countries will tend to act in accordance with the principles and other beliefs that have been constructed and accepted in the framework of this organization and, consequently, countries would be willing to subordinate their particular interests to the common ideas and understandings that the international organization represents.

For more rationalist scholars, ideas exert influence as lenses that focus on the best option for policy-makers to maximize their interests or as coalitional glue to facilitate the cohesion of particular groups. In this way, ideas simply alleviate coordination problems in those situations where there is no a unique possible balance (Goldstein and Keohane 1993). This approach is more appropriate to explain political outcomes in international contexts where consequentialism becomes the dominant rationale for interaction (March and Olsen 2005). Under consequentialism it is understood that actors that participate in global institutions are goal-oriented and engage in strategic interactions to maximize their utilities on the basis of given preferences (Risse 2000).

Finally, constructivism ascribes a more leading role to ideas. A core assumption of constructivist researchers is that the interests and preferences of actors are social constructions and not objectively given (Haas 2004; Hay 2002). These scholars are interested in analyzing ideas functioning as road maps for policy making. In the situations where it happens, ideas act more clearly as explanatory variables to define actors' preferences "by stipulating causal patterns or by providing compelling ethical or moral motivations for action" (Goldstein and Keohane 1993: 16). It has been acknowledged that there are more possibilities for ideas to act as road maps in periods of crisis or when policy- makers have to face new and complex problems on the political agenda that generate uncertainty (Finnemore and Sikkink 2001; Richardson 2005). For instance, the '*GATS and education*' topic would fulfill these requirements (novelty and complexity) to make ideas matter more within the context of negotiations. Constructivists consider that ideas are more than simple instruments of human action and that they have constitutive power and intrinsic forces (Blyth 2004). This scholars does not deny that ideas can act embedded in institutions, but are more interested in the processes by which ideas that were initially held by a minority become widely held and institutionalized (Hasenclever, Mayer, and Rittberger 1996). Their research focuses on the role of persuasive arguments and communicative action as independent causes of social behavior and political change. In this case, deliberation would become more relevant than consequentialism and appropriateness for understanding the behavior and decision-making processes in international forums (Risse 2004).

c)   Globalization and the Re-Scaling of Education Politics

The GATS is a perfect case for exploring the existing links between the changes in global politics/economics and the changes in national education policies. The act in itself of analyzing an international trade agreement that deals with educations issues implies challenging methodological nationalism and educationism because it means recognizing that national education systems are affected by extra-educational inputs and procedures that originated at the supra-national level.

However, the GATS is not being recontextualized in the same way in all countries. In this sense, it should be acknowledged that globalization effects at the local level are not identical in all places and that the recontextualization of global influences and forces is locally mediated. This idea is central to analyze the relationship between globalization and education, and to avoid positions of both extreme skepticism and hyperglobalism in our analysis (*see* Held 1999). So, to go beyond methodologican nationalism, but avoiding a globalist bias, a pluri-scalar understanding of phenomena is required. A pluri-scalar conception of education permits a more accurate representation of the nature of educational phenomena and events by exploring who controls what and on what scale. In the global age, scale and scalar interaction variables have important implications for understanding power relations, decision-making procedures and policy outcomes (Robertson, Bonal, and Dale 2002). That is why we will analyze the GATS and education negotiations on more than one scale and we will aim to distinguish how key elements and events are presented and articulated on each of the relevant scales.

On the other hand, in order to distance ourselves from a mechanistic analysis of the effects of globalization in state educational policies, it is necessary to understand how power relations work in the international arena. In this respect, some considerations should be done. First, the relations of domination between the global and the national political spheres are not always top-down. States are not only (or not always) passive adopters of global initiatives and processes, but they can aslo be promoters. In fact, nation-states (normally powerful states) are usually active initiators of the 'rules of the game' that are housed by international organizations. Powerful states are also, together with the international bureaucracies, very active in setting the agenda of international organizations.

Second, power relations between the global and the local do not affect so much at the decision-making level of policy processess. Nation-states remain the key decision makers in the global governance scenario and international organizations do not normally take decisions in the name of state actors (Dale 2005). However, other faces of power are affected: international organizations mark the problems that must be solved, strongly influence educational debates at the national level, introduce new topics and goals in the states policy agendas, and propose instruments to attain these goals (Martens, Rusconi, and Leuze 2007).

Finally, it should be acknowledged that some international organizations and powerful states can impose decisions, policy orientations or specific policies on states, but this is not the most common way power operates in international forums. Most of the time, external actors condition countries behavior through the activation of softer mechanisms. Roger Dale (1999) systematizes a set of mechanisms that permit a better understanding of the diversity of forms global politics influence national (education) policies. These mechanisms are: a) *imposition,* activated when international organizations or powerful states compel certain countries to adopt particular education policies, for instance, by setting conditions on their credit; b) *harmonization,* achieved when a set of countries mutually agree on the implementation of common policies, as is the case of the European Higher Education Area; *c) dissemination,* activated when an international organization uses persuasion and technical knowledge to convince countries to implement of certain policies; *d) standardization, which* occurs when the international community defines and promotes adhesion to a set of policy principles and standards that frame the behavior of countries and *e) installing interdependence* that occurs when countries agree to achieve common objectives to tackle problems that require international cooperation, such as climate change, 'education for all', etc.

1.4   METHODOLOGY FOR A PLURI-SCALAR STUDY

The research presented in this book has been organized in two different stages, which have been undertaken through contrasting methodological strategies. The *first phase* involves a quantitative analysis of the outputs of the GATS negotiations in the field of education and, using statistical techniques, these outputs have been associated with different explanatory factors. The results of this phase are explained in detail in the fifth chapter of this book. One of the main contributions of this phase is the drawing up of an index to measure more precisely the levels of educational liberalization, which I have called Edu-GATS. This stage was eminently exploratory in nature and the calculations carried out did not allow for much beyond description. A qualitative methodological approach was therefore adopted for attributing causality in the phenomenon under study.

The *second phase* aims to penetrate the 'black box' of the GATS negotiations to reveal the factors that explain its outcomes in the education sector. As theoretically justified above, multi-scalar empirical field work was undertaken in the second stage consisting on observation and interviews carried out at the global and national levels. A total of 56 interviews with key actors and stakeholders related to the GATS and education negotiations were carried out. The interviews retrieved data about the procedure of the negotiations (consultations to stakeholders, articulation of the negotiations between the global and national level, etc.), the position of certain countries in relation to the liberalization of education within the GATS as well as the rationale that grounds the position adopted. Observation was also carried out in events related to this issue.[2] The fieldwork involved international actors who directly participate in the negotiation subsystem of the GATS (trade negotiators in the WTO headquarters and WTO staff) as well as other international actors that aim to influence the GATS negotiations, either directly or indirectly, such as the Education International representatives or UNCTAD staff.

More intensive fieldwork was also carried out in relation to two countries, Argentina and Chile, where trade ministry representatives and education stakeholders (such as universities, education regulators, quality assurance agencies and teachers unions representatives) were interviewed as well. Carrying out national-based case studies was necessary to capture the multi-level nature of trade negotiations, the relevance of national politics for GATS outputs and, in short, to obtain a more complete picture of the politics of the services negotiations. The two countries in the sample, Argentina and Chile, were selected because they are two interesting cases in themselves, and also because they are comparable. Choosing comparable cases allows knowledge to be built up through each case study, and also through the comparison of the two cases themselves (Yin 1994). One of the rules of 'comparability' is that the cases must have similar independent variables and different dependent variables (Green 2003). In effect, Argentina and Chile have many common features (both are developing countries, located in the same region, with a similar institutional settings and historical trajectories), but they behave very differently in international trade negotiations. Neither Argentina nor Chile committed education liberalization during the services negotiations of the Uruguay Round that ended in 1994, but they have adopted different positions in the current Doha Round of negotiations, ongoing since 2001. Although this round has not yet finished, Argentina will not introduce education commitments into the GATS agreement since its education ministry has repeatedly vetoed the possibility. In fact, it fixed its preferences against the GATS in its last National Education Act (2006). Conversely, Chile takes a more liberal position on this topic. It did not commit education liberalization or most other services sectors during the Uruguay Round. At that time, the country opted to remain cautious. However, in the context of the Doha Round, Chile is prepared to commit education to free trade if the liberalization results of the negotiations are high and, moreover, Chile has already liberalized education in the framework of multiple free trade agreements with the main education exporters of the planet.

A final criterion for our sample selection is that most of the existing case studies on the GATS and education are focused in developed countries (see section 1.2 in this chapter) and, consequently, there is a lack of empirical work that analyzes the GATS and education negotiations in developing contexts. Moreover, it is more interesting and relevant to focus the research on developing countries because that is where the GATS raises more concerns and where it has been more contested by the educational community.[3] Hopefully, the case studies realized in Argentina and Chile will contribute to bridging this existing gap in the research on the GATS and education.

1.5.   ABOUT THE BOOK

This book is structured into three blocks. In the *first block* ["GATS in Context"] the research object is contextualized and the central concepts and elements of the GATS are defined. The two chapters that make up this block focus on the way education is inserted into the WTO regime through the GATS (chapter 2) on the one hand and the pro-market transformations experienced by higher education in recent decades (chapter 3) on the other. The implications of the GATS in the field of higher education are also explained, and the extent to which the Agreement accelerates and accentuates certain transformations already existing in the higher education field is analyzed. This first block enables a fine-tuning of knowledge for readers with different backgrounds, since this is a book that may interest those with a commercial or international relations background, and who are therefore familiar with the GATS and the WTO, but who may not be so familiar with the area of higher education studies. Conversely, most educational scientists and sociologists will probably be familiar with the content of the third chapter, but not so much with the second.

The *second block* ["GATS results and procedures"] is also made up of two chapters. The first of them (chapter 4) explains how the GATS is negotiated and questions the established idea that the WTO is a neutral and inclusive forum for negotiations. Chapter 5 explores the outputs of the Uruguay Round for higher education and compares them to other education sectors. It also analyzes how economic development and higher education variables, among others, are related to the education liberalization commitments established by the WTO members.

The *third block* ["Inside the negotiations"] contains the core of primary data produced during the research process. The block is made up of four chapters, which deal with the different pieces that form the puzzle of the 'GATS and education' negotiations and politics. The first piece consists of the debate on the GATS and education promoted in the global public domain (Chapter 6). The second one analyzes the meaning frames and the political action on GATS issues carried out by international organizations and non-state players which, acting at the supra-national level, are attempting to influence the outputs of the GATS and education negotiations (Chapter 7). Chapter 8 explores the negotiations from the point of view of the WTO staff and from the perspective of country representatives. The final piece of the block analyzes the negotiations at the state level based on the case studies carried out in Argentina and Chile (Chapter 9).

As a whole, this book aims to give a complete picture of the international emergence, the recontextualization and the response to GATS in the field of education. More importantly, it aims to explain the outcomes, the multi-scalar procedures and the external influences in relation to the transcendental political area for higher education that the GATS negotiations represent.

Block I

GATS in Context

2 Education in the WTO/GATS Context

The constitution of the GATS and the particular form adopted by this trade agreement have been influenced by the historical period in which the WTO was established. This chapter contextualizes the creation of both the WTO and the GATS in the post-cold war period and, particularly, in a moment where the idea of disembedded liberalism was becoming more and more predominant. However, as will be observed, the constitution of the GATS was not a process absent of conflict. Beyond understanding GATS merely as a historical product, the chapter explains the politics, the conflicts of interests and the debates manifested during the negotiations for the constitution of this ambitious and complex trade agreement.

Furthermore, the chapter explores how education services became part of the scope of GATS. As will be shown, education services were not a central issue in the debates between countries when negotiating the creation of this agreement in the context of the Uruguay Round. However, once the round was finalized, five education sub-sectors became affected by the new trade agreement.

In another section of the chapter, the particular content of the GATS and its legal implications for education are revealed, and the main rules and principles contained in the agreement are extensively explained. Finally, the way these rules and principles may affect the regulation of education in the WTO member countries are explored.

2.1 THE INTRODUCTION OF SERVICES INTO THE INTERNATIONAL TRADE SYSTEM

From the GATT to the WTO

The WTO began its activity on 1 January 1995 and its constitution was sealed by the Marrakesh Agreement (15 April 1994) which closed the Uruguay Round of the General Agreement on Tariffs and Trade (GATT). The WTO is the result of fifty years of evolution in the international contemporary trade regime set up by the GATT in 1947. At the same time, the WTO is the product of a historical framework which is markedly different in most aspects to that in which the initial trade agreement was created. The GATT was created in the aftermath of the Second World War in an initiative by the United Nations Economic and Social Council (ECOSOC). Initially the ECOSOC proposed the constitution of an International Trade Organization (ITO) with which to complete the design of the new world economic order based on the creation of the World Bank and the International Monetary Fund. One of the main legal instruments to be approved for the creation of the ITO was the GATT. This agreement, debated and signed by twenty-three countries in 1947, contained the basis for negotiating a system of tax reductions and the adoption of a series of trading rules on an international level. The principal meeting for the creation of the ITO was held in Havana in 1948. Despite the obvious tensions and differences at that meeting, fifty-three countries signed the final act. However, the process of creating the ITO was blocked when many of the signatory countries, including the US, did not ratify the Havana Charter in their parliaments. Consequently, the ITO could not be constituted and, of the entire negotiation process, the only tangible result was the GATT (Wilkinson 2000).

The GATT evolved over the years and the number of countries signing it increased significantly. However, the process entered a process of stagnation which was accentuated by the economic crisis of the seventies. The response to the crisis by many countries was to adopt protectionist measures, which contradicted the liberalization commitments agreed under the GATT (Ruggie 1982). Parallel to this, the extension of the agreement was cut back due to the adoption of sectoral exceptions such as those presented by the Multifibers Agreement in the textile sector. Furthermore, the GATT had no authority over the sectors that were becoming most significant in international trade such as agriculture, services and other non-manufactured goods (Millet 2001). In the new round of the GATT negotiations which began in 1986, these and other problems had to be faced. That round, known as the Uruguay Round, ended in 1994 after eight years of intensive negotiations.[1] Curiously, despite the fact that the creation of an international organization was not considered on the original agenda, the main result of the negotiations was the setting up of the WTO. One question, which is not devoid of political implications, is that this new organization, unlike the plans in the forties for what the ITO should have been, was created outside the United Nations system.

The material scope of the WTO, its functions and its capacity for influencing the behavior of its members are considerably greater than those of the GATT'47. Firstly, the GATT was only a trade agreement and the WTO has its own legal status as an international organization. Secondly, the WTO has a more efficient system for resolving differences than the GATT (WTO 2004).[2] Thirdly, a much wider range of negotiations takes place at the WTO than under the GATT. While the latter only included trade in manufactured goods, the WTO has authority over all kinds of services, agricultural products[3], biodiversity, intellectual property, etc.

Another important difference between the GATT and the WTO is located in the political-ideological domain. The GATT was created in the context of the cold war, in a bipolar world in which the capitalist bloc was having to legitimate its status in the face the hegemony acquired by the socialist bloc, both internally and in the eyes of third-party countries, among them the southern countries. Mainly for that reason, the original GATT subscribed to the model of embedded liberalism,[4] i.e. a model that envisioned a balance between free trade objectives and the capacity of states to achieve their legitimate social purpose (Lang 2006; Ikenberry 1992). The WTO, on the other hand, was established during the 1990s, at a time when the breakdown of the socialist bloc had become symbolized with the falling of the Berlin Wall and when neoliberalism was the dominant ideology. This ideological context is evident throughout the principles and aims of the WTO and encourages the new commercial regime to rid itself of social questions (Ford 2002; Wade 2005; Ruggie 1994). The WTO regulates the trade relations of its members oriented by the principle of "progressive trade liberalization". So, as recognized by the WTO itself its main objectives are "to help trade flow as freely as possible" and to "help producers of goods and services, exporters, and importers conduct their business" (WTO 2005a, 9–10).[5] Free-trade therefore became the principal milestone of the new system of agreements drawn up by the WTO, while other goals such as sustainable development and the development of southern countries, while featuring in the preambles to the agreements and in other declarations of principles, are not so clearly tied into the text of the agreements. Other issues, such as labor standards and human rights are completely missing from the new international trade rules. As we shall see, these absences have served to fuel criticism from civil society of the new regime being promoted by the WTO, and in particular criticism from the educational community.

Barriers to Trade in Services

Commercial agreements administrated and negotiated within the framework of the WTO constitute contracts between the states which oblige them to maintain their trade policies within defined limits. The three central areas of trade covered by the WTO agreements are goods, intellectual property and services. The agreements that deal with each of these areas are, respectively, the General Agreement on Tariffs and Trade (GATT), the Trade Related Aspects of Intellectual Property Rights Agreement (TRIPS) and the General Agreement on Trade in Services (GATS). This later agreement, the GATS, is considered to be "the most important achievement ever recorded in the multilateral system of trade since the GATT came into existence in 1947" (WTO 1999, 1). This section describes how the GATS was created and the particular way in which it has included education in its scope.

Decades ago services were not seen as tradeable goods. One of the reasons for this lies in the technical difficulties associated with the import and export of services. Trading in services is more complex and abstract than trading in goods for a number of reasons. Firstly, services are produced and consumed simultaneously, and tend to be consumed in the place where they have been produced (Francois and Wooton 2000). The exchange of goods, on the other hand, does not require direct interaction between producers and consumers since they can be easily stored (WB 1994). Secondly, services are less transportable than goods (WTO 2000) or, rather, their "transportation" is very different to that of goods. Setting up trade in services sometimes even requires foreign direct investment (FDI) by the supplier. Finally, the nature of services is such that they are less tangible and less perishable than goods (WB and UNCTAD 1994), to the extend that some refer to trade in services as "invisible trade" (White 2002). The Economist graphically illustrated this particular aspect when it described services as being "something you can buy and sell but cannot drop on your foot" (Drake and Nicolaidis 1992, 46).

Another aspect that made it difficult to conceptualize trade in certain service sectors was the active participation of governments in their production, distribution and regulation. State intervention in the service sector has been traditionally justified because services fulfill a series of basic functions (as promoters of welfare, employment, training, communication, economic development, etc.) (Kelsey 2003). When the public sector predominated in service provision, trade and the internationalization of services did not carry the same importance that they do today. This is due to the fact that, unlike the private sector, the public sector does not tend to seek profits nor does it aspire to territorial expansion to secure new markets. In addition, a sovereign state may be more reticent to allow its services to be managed by a foreign state than by a multinational corporation, especially in the more strategic areas such as energy, communications and finance.

Nevertheless, the main reason why services were not considered within the international trade system is probably because decades ago the economic importance of the sector was much smaller than it is today. At one time, services were not even considered to constitute a "productive activity". Adam Smith himself considered service activities to be unproductive work (Moos 1951). Nowadays, however, the role of services and their growing importance in the world economy is not questioned, and they have come to represent 30% of work and 20% of trade (WTO 2005a). Services in developed countries, which are often included in the "tertiary" sector, represent 70% of GNP (Sauvé and Stern 2000). In fact, as we shall see below, the inclusion of services on the trade agenda is closely linked to the fact that the richest countries and their industries are becoming aware of the growing importance of the sector, as well as the competitive advantage enjoyed by them in the world services market.

Brief History of the GATS

In 1972 the OECD invited a group of experts to study the long-term perspectives for trade in the context of what they called "the new industrial structures", and therefore contribute to frame the Tokyo Round agenda of the GATT, which was about to take place. The report produced by the experts mentioned the term *trade in services* for the first time, although at that time they did not give a specific definition of what it meant. The group limited itself to suggesting that service transactions were susceptible to being considered in the area of international trade and that the same principles and rules could be applied to them as to trade in goods.[6]

The first country to show an interest in this subject was the US, due to its clear comparative advantage in most of the service sectors. The US Congress made a significant contribution to ensuring that the trade in services proposal prospered by including it in the *Trade Act* which was sanctioned in 1974. Among other matters, the *Trade Act* stipulated that the US trade negotiators should seek to remove barriers to trade in services. Furthermore, the US Department of Trade opened up a consultation period with the national service industry to identify its interests and allow it to participate in the strategy (Feketekuty 2005).

The US delegation tried to introduce the areas of services in the Tokyo Round agenda, but the proposal met with opposition and reticence from most countries. European countries were skeptical about the possibility of applying the principles and rules of traditional trade to services. Moreover, they were unsure about their international competitiveness in this area. Meanwhile, most southern countries refused outright to introduce the item onto the agenda as they were convinced of their lack of competitiveness in the sector (Chanda 2003). It should also be remembered that production and trade in services are clearly marked by the north/south divide. Almost 80% of world trade in services originates from the EU, North America and East Asia (Karsenty 2000). The southern countries also suspected that the subject of services was a distraction device presented by the US to avoid talking about matters such as the agricultural protectionism of wealthy countries. In any case, with the exception of the US, the signatory countries of the GATT were still not familiar with the subject matter and did not see themselves capable of discussing it in a round of negotiations (Drake and Nicolaidis 1992).

Despite the fact that the matter was not included in the Tokyo Round, the debate had begun. Since then, academic activity dealing with trade in services has become stronger. Consequently, the small epistemic community that had discussed the subject at the beginning of the nineteen seventies grew. This was the logical result of an increase in the demand for information and analysis of trade in services from the political field. Most countries wanted to know more about the subject and commissioned studies to help them define their own positions and interests. The southern countries turned to their trade reference in the UN system: the United Nations Conference on Trade and Development (UNCTAD). The first papers from the UNCTAD were very critical of international trade in services. They questioned its viability, warned that the winners in the new regime would be the big transnational corporations, and alerted that the trade in services proposal would mask as trade operations those that really formed part of FDI (Drake and Nicolaidis 1992).

For their part, and with ideas that opposed those of the UNCTAD, the US Trade Representative (USTR) launched a strong campaign to success-fully introduce services onto the international trade agenda. The intellec-tual leader of this campaign in the previous years and during the Uruguay Round was Geza Feketekuty, who also coordinated the US strategy in the Tokyo Round.[7] Feketekuty himself affirmed that the campaign counted on the invaluable support of the main service companies in the US (among which *American Express* played a particularly important role), of the OECD and think tanks such as the Trade Policy Research Center. These actors published studies and articles in prestigious academic journals, organized seminars, produced materials for the press and carried out lob-bying activities aimed at promoting the incorporation of services in trade agreements (Feketekuty 2005). The big service companies in the US and the UK created lobbies such as the USCSI (US Coalition of Services Industry) and the Liberalization of Trade in Services Committee, for the purpose of ensuring that the service negotiation agenda responded to their interests (Susan Robertson, Bonal, and Dale 2002).

For tactical reasons, the arguments used by the pro-liberalization sectors to justify the goodness of the proposal could not be based on the economic benefits trade in services would bring to industry in rich countries. That would not have helped to ensure that the international community, and in particular the southern countries, accepted it. It was necessary to legitimate the proposal using different arguments, in a way that all parties would be able to see the benefits of liberalizing trade in services. Thus, it was gener-ally argued that, albeit on a sectoral scale the suppliers in wealthy coun-tries had a certain competitive advantage, the service providers in southern countries would benefit from liberalization as consumers of other services (for example, banks are consumers of telecommunications, advertising and transport services).

The members of the epistemic community dealing with trade in services had a lot in common as far as *causal beliefs* were concerned, although there were certain discrepancies in the field of *principled beliefs*. Specifi-cally, they could not agree on what the ideal balance should be between trade liberalization objectives and the capacity for state regulation. In this debate of principles some participants pushed for more market control by the states, while others wanted to restrict the political space of the states as far as possible to guarantee free trade.[8]

According to Drake and Nicolaidis (1992), most governments changed their way of thinking about trade in services and redefined their interests as a result of the influential analysis carried out by the epistemic commu-nity. However, it is worth emphasizing that if the idea of trade in services became so successful it is due also to the resources and the power of the promoters of this idea. Whatever the reasons, many countries that opposed the subject in the Tokyo Round of the GATT were more prepared to discuss it during the Uruguay Round. Even leading Third World countries, such as Brazil and India realized that there were certain opportunities in the service sector for them at the regional level. Some of the southern countries also saw that they could obtain certain economic benefits from the liberalization of trade in services if the northern countries opened the doors to their workforces as a result. These countries considered the export of "individuals service providers" to be a form of trade as valid as any other. However, the Third World countries were opposed to the fact that the FDI was accepted as a service trade mode. They also maintained that the liberalization of trade in services should only go ahead if it was compatible with pro-development principles and policy measures.[9]

The European countries had been working on the question since the Tokyo Round and had identified some "offensive interests" in different service sectors.[10] Their main concern, as seen in the communications issued by the EU during the Uruguay Round, was that government *policy space* should be respected and that the advancement of free trade in services should be compatible with the right of the states to regulate according to their political priorities.[11]

The US, on the other hand, was the country that put the most radical proposal on the table: it simply wanted to extend the GATT to the service sector, without introducing any kind of differentiation between services and other types of goods (Pardos Martínez 1994). Moreover, in their initial communications, they proposed to suppress any kind of state subsidies to service providers, to dismantle state monopolies and to remove discriminatory state regulations, such as certain accreditation procedures for service suppliers. Nor did they mention the development needs of the southern countries. However, in order to ensure that the subject of services was introduced into the international trade regime, they had to moderate some of their initial plans. They therefore accepted keeping the subject of services outside the GATT and adopting more flexible rules for the liberalization of the sector. They also guaranteed support for developing countries demands on the question of liberalizing trade in agricultural products, as long as they agreed to negotiate the liberalization of services (Mundy and Iga 2003).

The new agreement, in which the rules for liberalizing trade in services would take place multilaterally, was called the General Agreement on Trade in Services (GATS) and it was described as being the "most ambitious and complicated commitment to liberalization of all the Uruguay Round agreements" (Weiss 2001, 271). During the Round itself, the structure and content of the GATS was negotiated, almost in parallel to the establishment of the first commitments to liberalization in the area of services. However, despite the fact that the round lasted eight years, members were unable to agree on a series of chapters and the agreement could not be completed.[12]

The GATS resolved some of the main technical problems that were making the conceptualization of trade in services more difficult, such as the problem of the interaction between producers and consumers. To solve this problem, the Agreement distinguishes between four different modes of services supply (see Article I.2.a of the GATS). First, the Agreement considers that services can be exchanged internationally, even though the producer and the consumer may remain in different territories. This mode of supply is known as 'cross-border supply' (mode 1), and bears more relation to goods trading than the other modes. A second mode consists of consumers moving into foreign territory to acquire a service while the producer remains immobile (mode 2—consumption abroad). Another possible situation is where the service provider is mobile while the consumers remain in their own territory. In this case, if the service provider is a natural person we refer to the mode called 'presence of natural persons' (mode 4) and if the provider is an organization or company to 'commercial presence' (mode 3). In this last case, as decided in the Uruguay Round, the commercial operation may include foreign direct investment operations. The southern countries accepted in Uruguay that FDI could be accepted as "trade" in exchange for the inclusion in the Agreement of the Mode 4 (Drake and Nicolaidis 1992).

2.2   THE ARCHITECTURE AND CONTENT OF THE GATS[13]

The GATS is a multilateral international agreement that ranks as an international convention. This implies that, for the member countries, the content of the agreement and, in particular, the commitments acquired within the framework of the agreement are binding and must be complied obligatorily.[14] However, the content of the agreement is divided into two main parts: one that is obligatory for all signatories (*General obligations and disciplines*), and another whose fulfillment is conditioned by the commitments established individually by members (*Specific commitments*).

Scope and Definition of the Agreement

The objective of the GATS is "to establish a multilateral framework of principles and rules for trade in services with a view to the expansion of such trade under conditions of transparency and progressive liberalization and as a means of promoting the economic growth of all trading partners and the development of developing countries" (GATS preamble: 305). Through the GATS it is hoped to achieve the specific objectives of guaranteeing conditions of competition, reinforcing transparency, eliminating trade barriers and price distortions and avoiding divergence between considerations of private and social efficiency (WTO 2008).

Part I of the GATS *(Scope and definition of the Agreement)* states that the agreement is applicable to measures adopted by member countries that affect trade in services, which include also those adopted by local governments (Article I: 305–6). The sectoral scope of the agreement is very broad as well. It affects "any service in any sector except services supplied in the exercise of governmental authority" (Article I.3.b), which are defined at the same time as "any service which is supplied neither on a commercial basis, nor in competition with one or more service suppliers" (Article I.3.c). Because of its high degree of ambiguity, this definition has been the subject of much academic debate about the real scope of the GATS. The ambiguity is bigger since in certain service sectors traditionally owned and provided by the state, competitive provision and trading activities have been partially introduced in recent decades. This is for instance the case of public services such as health and education, where quasi-markets or joint management policies convened by the state with the private sector have been applied in many countries.

The services classification included in the GATS was inspired by the United Nations *Central Product Classification* (CPC). This classification includes twelve different service sectors: 1. Business services; 2. communication services; 3. construction and engineering services; 4. distribution services; 5. educational services; 6. environment-related services; 7. financial services; 8. health services; 9. tourism and travel services; 10. leisure, cultural and sports services; 11. transport services; 12. others. These sectors are divided into approximately 160 subsectors. The fragmentation of services into such a large number of sectors and subsectors introduces a certain complexity into the negotiation process, although it also means that the adoption of commitments is more flexible. However, the present classification of services is confusing, since some of the subsectors either overlap or it is not clear which of them are included in certain categories. The classification of the services is therefore permanently under discussion (MITC 2004). In the words of the former trade representative for the Philippines this confusion makes it difficult for the negotiations to move forward as the countries "may be more comfortable if they knew that what they are actually offering is exactly what they meant to offer" (Khor 2005, 5). Even the US was apparently victim of the prevailing confusing categories when it established commitments in mode 1 of the recreational services subsector. The US government was trying to restrict the activity of numerous lotteries and casinos online operating from abroad that meant a significant drain of US capital. However, this was contradicting the liberalization commitments acquired by this country in recreational services within the GATS. The US trade representatives justified the existence of trade barriers against casinos on line and related services by arguing that they did not specifically liberalize these kind of services. However, this argument was not strong enough and the WTO Dispute Settlement System obliged the US to modify federal and state laws to permit this gambling activities operating in its territory (UNCTAD 2005).

General Obligations and Disciplines

The establishment of liberalization commitments within the framework of GATS is something that has to be negotiated progressively by the WTO member countries. At the same time, the agreement also contains a series of "general obligations and disciplines" that are "non-negotiable" and which apply to all members and all sectors horizontally. These obligations and disciplines are found in the second part of the agreement and many of them are similar to those in the GATT (WTO 1999). The most important are:

a) *Most Favored Nation treatment (MFN)* (Article II): this stipulates that each member shall immediately and unconditionally treat the service providers of a WTO member state in a way which is no less favorable than that given to service providers of any other member state. The aim of this obligation is to ensure that there is no discrimination between member countries and, thereby, to accelerate the process of trade liberalization. Although the MFN is one of the pillars of the agreement, exemptions may be made, but only once and for a maximum of ten years. Exemptions can be made to avoid 'free-rider' behavior by other members or in cases where some countries are drawing up trade agreements or economic integration processes on a regional scale[15]. Regional projects will be allowed if they have a "substantial" sectoral cover and are carried out within a "reasonable" time frame (Article V, on Economic Integration). Exemptions are reviewed every five years by the Council on Trade in Services which decides whether the conditions that led to the original exemption prevail (García López 1999).

b) *Transparency* (Article III): the aim of this obligation is to guarantee free access for transnational service providers to key information related to the services field in each member country. Specifically, the article refers to information on the regulatory framework of countries affecting the development of economic activities in the services sector such as administrative rules or license procedures. According to the WTO, where this information is not available or accessible, services companies could be relegated to a less advantageous position. Members are therefore asked to create the appropriate instruments to be able to respond to requests for information about their service markets and to notify the Council on Trade in Services about the new rules, laws or directives that could affect trade in services.

c) *Recognition* (Article VII): in this article members are asked to recognize the academic—or other—qualifications of service providers from other countries. It adds that the requirement for academic qualifications must not fulfill protectionist ends.

d) *Monopolies and exclusive services providers* (Article VIII): a monopolistic provider must not act in a way that is incompatible with the obligations of members in terms of the MFN treatment or in terms of the specific commitments acquired. It does not specify whether this obligation extends to public providers.

e) *General exceptions* (Article XIV): a member may omit certain obligations assumed within the framework of the GATS where they pose a danger to the protection of public morals, or the protection of human, animal or plant life. Exceptions because of national security reasons can be also established (Article XIV bis)[16]. The text reiterates that these exceptions may not be adopted for protectionist reasons.[17]

f) *Increasing participation of developing countries* (Article IV): this article is the only one dealing with development issues. It stipulates that members should especially attend those market access demands coming from poorer countries. At the same time, members should give special consideration to Less Developed Countries (LDCs), which should not be too pressured to establish liberalization commitments. It should be pointed out that this is not a huge concession since the services markets in LDCs are not generally very attractive for transnational providers.[18]

General Obligations and Disciplines "under construction"

The GATS is an incomplete agreement (WTO 1999). It was not possible to specify a key series of questions at the Uruguay Round and they are still under negotiation (Nielson 2003). At the beginning of the Doha Round two working groups were set up to try to specify them. The first is the working group on domestic regulation, whose remit is to develop Article VI of the GATS. The other is the working group on rules, in the context of which Articles X, XIII and XV are discussed:

a) *Domestic Regulation Working Group (DRWG)*. Article VI of the GATS establishes that domestic regulations must not block the "benefits derived from the GATS". The article mandates members to develop disciplines so that certain types of rules (mainly requirements and procedures) are non-discriminatory and do not constitute unnecessary barriers to trade in services. The working group on domestic regulations covers this mandate. Its task, which should be finalized during the Doha Round, is centered mainly on the five areas of regulation. These are: *i) qualifications or aptitude requirements:* requirements relating to the competence that has to be demonstrated by each provider wishing to become authorized to provide a service in a specific territory. One of the main areas covered by these requirements is academic qualifications and other credentials that guarantee the ability of a provider to offer a specific service; *ii) qualification procedures:* administrative rules relating to the administration of qualification requirements; *iii) license requirements:* requirements for obtaining authorization to provide a service; these can be related to sensitive issues such as consumers protection or access to services by disadvantaged people; *iv) license procedures:* administrative rules relating to the award of licenses; *v) technical standards:* measures which establish the characteristics of a service and the way in which it is provided. The same area includes processes related to the reinforcement of standards. Normally, this kind of regulation aims to guarantee the quality of the services.

In short, the DRWG oversee the establishment of disciplines which guarantee that members' regulations are not more onerous than strictly "necessary" to warrant the quality of the services. To ensure that members respect the disciplines adopted in the areas of regulation covered by the DRWG, some countries have proposed the introduction of a polemic system of necessity tests. If accepted by the working group, these tests will mean that a member country that wants to introduce a certain regulation that is considered by another member country too restrictive for trade will have to demonstrate that this new regulation is absolutely necessary to achieve a legitimate objective. Necessity tests have been applied to resolve some service disputes and on each occasion they have worked against the regulator (South-Centre 2006).

b) *Rules Working Group (RWG).* The remit of this working group includes developing three of the GATS articles: *i) safeguard mechanisms* (Article X): these mechanisms would allow member countries to establish a liberalization trial period for different service sectors. If the member were not satisfied with the liberalization in a certain sector and could justify this convincingly, withdrawal of the commitment could be speeded up. The southern countries are most keen to see an advance in this sort of measures (Jawara and Kwa 2004); *ii) government procurement* (Article XIII): the principles of the MFN, and the commitments relating to national treatment and market access are not currently applicable to the government procurement of services for official ends that do not involve commercial sales. However, the RWG aspires to include public contracting operations in the system of GATS rules to permit foreign suppliers to benefit from this mode of contracting. In this case, the northern countries would be most enthusiastic about the adoption of this kind of disciplines; *iii) subsidies* (Article XV): the GATS considers that public subsidies could have the effect of distorting trade in services. The RWG aims to develop multilateral disciplines to avoid any distorting effects of subsidies on trade. The obligation for national treatment, which will be discussed in the next section, stipulates that foreign providers should benefit from the subsidy regimes of the host countries.

Specific Commitments

Despite the importance of what is being discussed in the two above-mentioned working groups, the bulk of the GATS negotiations consists of the adoption of *specific liberalization commitments* (that is why this important part of the negotiations is normally known as the 'liberalization negotiations'). Unlike general obligations, specific commitments are adopted by member countries on a volunteer basis and in successive rounds of negotiations. These commitments are fixed in liberalization lists which are annexed to the text of the GATS when the round ends (WTO 1999). According to what is established in Part III of the agreement, specific commitments are adopted with respect to two questions: market access (Article XVI) and national treatment (Article XVII):

a) *Market Access (MA).* MA refers to the entry by foreign service providers in national markets and the difficulties these providers encounter when trying to enter them. These difficulties (or barriers) tend to be related to the dense regulations that the service providers are subjected to. Members may adopt independent market access commitments according to the different service sectors and subsectors, and according to the different modes of supply. The six barriers to MA, which members may eliminate during the GATS negotiations, refer to: *i)* the number of service providers allowed in a certain territory and sector; *ii)* the value of service transactions or assets; *iii)* the total number of service operations or the total number of services produced; *iv)* the total number of natural persons that may be employed in a sector or by a specific provider; *v)* specific legal or juridical designations of providers; *vi)* specific percentages for foreign share capital or the total value of foreign investments.

b) *National treatment (NT).* Commitments in this area mean that foreign companies benefit from a treatment that is no less favorable than that received by national companies from the host country. This is one of the most characteristic areas of the GATS negotiations and it is not present in WTO agreements such as the GATT. In practice, when a country allows national treatment it is allowing market access. As in the Market Access case, NT commitments can be adopted in the different sectors and trading modes independently. However, there is no specific number of limitations to be eliminated but an indefinite number. The Secretariat of the WTO describes eight possible limitations: i) taxes and tariffs; ii) subventions and subsidies; iii) other financial restrictions; iv) nationality requirements; v) residency requirements; vi) qualifications, licenses, standards; vii) registration requirements; viii) authorization requirements (WTO 2000). Clearly, many of the questions currently covered by NT coincide with those being discussed in the Domestic Regulations and Rules Working Groups. Consequently, once both groups have defined the final disciplines, NT questions will not be as central to the GATS negotiations.[19]

Trade Liberalization: A One-Way Street

Trade liberalization is the core principle of the WTO and, consequently, of the GATS. Clearly, the GATS aims to speed up trade liberalization in the services area and make it more far-reaching. In line with this principle, the agreement contemplates the possibility that, at any time, countries may introduce new commitments in their lists—irrespective of the stage of the negotiations underway. In contrast, the agreement contains hurdles to the withdrawal of commitments already established. With regard to this question, Article XXI of the GATS establishes that: a) The members may not withdraw their commitments until three years after their undertaking, b) The modification has to be notified at least three months in advance, and c) the members affected by the modification may file a lawsuit by means of which it may be ruled that a country modifying a list has to compensate those parties affected. Under these rules, the GATS effectively locks in those who sign up to them (Robertson and Dale 2003). Consequently, democratically elected governments can find themselves in a position where their policy options and regulatory capacity is conditioned by decisions taken by previous governments when the GATS was negotiated.

2.3   (HIGHER) EDUCATION IN THE GATS

The Sui Generis Inclusion of Education

The GATS was not created to promote trade in educational services as a primary objective; rather other sectors were under the scope of the forces pushing for the liberalization of services and for the creation of a services trade agreement at the multilateral level. For instance, the education industry was not among the industrial groups that pushed for the inclusion of services in the area of competence of the GATT. On their part, international organizations such as the UNCTAD and the OECD also ignored the education sector in their sector analyses of the commercialization of services published previously and during the Uruguay Round. In the context of this negotiations round, the situation was very different for other service sectors, such as transport, financial services, tourism or telecommunications that generated a big quantity of meetings, debates and documentation. The WTO Documents Services Data Base reflects very clearly this contrast. During the Uruguay Round, 292 documents dealing with transport services were published, 369 dealing with telecommunications and zero with educational services.

Neither the first liberalization demands[20] nor the classification proposals launched by members in the services working group of the Uruguay Round considered educational services.[21] In some documents the "courses and conferences" sector was mentioned ambiguously, but at no time was it central to the discussion.[22] However, member countries decided to adopt the *Central Product Classification* (CPC) drawn up by the Statistical Division of the United Nations as a criterion for the classification of the services to be considered in the agreement on trade in services.[23] According to what arose from the debates on this matter at the Uruguay Round, among the advantages of the CPC was the fact that it focuses on products instead of activities or transactions, making it easier to distinguish between goods and services, and it recognizes a broader range of services than other options.[24] One of the service sectors included in the CPC is education. As a result, once the member countries adopted this list, education was included within the competences of the GATS and the WTO in general.

Some services representatives reacted quickly enough when they realized that their respective sectors were included on the agenda of the Uruguay Round of negotiations. Groups of professionals from areas such as aeronautical services successfully pressed for the exclusion of their sector from the negotiations.[25] This was not the case for the education sector. During the Uruguay Round, most of the educational world was unaware that education formed part of the GATT negotiations (Scherrer 2005; Vlk 2006). Some members of the educational community reacted only once the agreement had been ratified and when many member countries of the WTO had already acquired liberalization commitments in this area (Frater 2008b).

In short, there was not a great deal of interest shown initially in the inclusion of education in the global free trade system, but for "technical" reasons concerning services classification, education became part of the WTO material scope and, since then, of other regional and bilateral free trade agreements. However, since the Uruguay Round the perception of education as an export industry has changed drastically. For instance, many developed countries have realized that the export of educational services has a very positive effect on their trade balances. The economic weight of educational services in the world economy has grown constantly since the 1990s. In 1999, the value of trade in educational services was already at 30 billion dollars (Saner and Fasel 2003). Also, many public and private universities exploit more and more their services in the international field as a means of reaching non-governmental sources of financing. New Zealand is a paradigmatic case to reflect on the new role acquired by education and, specifically, higher education in world trade. In fact, this country has become one of the first countries to center its multilateral trade strategy on the educational sector.[26] As stated in a document issued by the Ministry of Foreign Affairs of the New Zealand government to its negotiators before the WTO Ministerial Conference in Hong Kong:

"Trade in Education is currently one of New Zealand's fastest growing industries, and second largest services export, with an estimated contribution of $2.2 billion dollars to the New Zealand economy. New

Zealand education providers are keen to see GATS deliver improvements in access to offshore markets for education".[27]

Furthermore, the Ministry of Foreign Affairs promotes the exportation of educational services though its "New Zealand brand" campaign, which promotes such diverse products as wine and tourism as well as education. On their part, the education industry of the country has created the "Education New Zealand" platform, with a mission "to empower New Zealand's Education Exporters". As can be deduced from this, New Zealand has "offensive interests" in education services and, consequently, it is especially active when it comes to promoting educational liberalization in the framework of the WTO service negotiations. To realize these interests, this country is leading the *friends group* of education in the WTO context[28] and has coordinated the unique plurilateral demand on education in the post-Hong Kong negotiations cycle.[29]

The GATT/WTO staff initially did not pay special attention to the education sector either, but since the end of the nineties it has made public some statements about the importance of introducing education into the GATS. The WTO Secretariat considers that the increase of students abroad, the growing international links between teachers and faculties, and the increase in the number of branch campuses are indicators of the growth of international trade in educational services. The main factors that contribute to trade in education pointed out by the Secretariat are the new methods of education provision motivated by the introduction of new technologies, the educational reforms applied in many countries that have introduced competition and secured greater autonomy for educational institutions (allowing them to get closer to the needs of business), as well as the public investment cuts that have forced public universities to trade their research services and to attract foreign students who pay higher fees (WTO 1998). For its part, the WTO Council on Trade in Services justifies the importance of having education under the GATS scope by the growing private capital share in the sector and the increase in education demand by young people and adults (WTO 2000).

Educational Levels Covered

As in many other sectors, the liberalization of educational services is not negotiated in a single block. Specifically, five educational subsectors can be offered and demanded independently: 1) *primary education*. This includes both primary and pre-school education; 2) *secondary education*. This includes post-obligatory secondary education (e.g. high school, special education and first grade vocational training); 3) *higher education*. This includes university education (undergraduate and postgraduate) and post-secondary vocational training; 4) *adult education*. Education offered in centers for adults or similar institutions that includes courses from basic literacy to more technical training; 5) *other services*. This is the most ambiguous category and it includes educational services that do not appear in the previous categories, which may include private academies for the preparation of competitive examinations, language courses, tutorial services, etc. This category may also include language level testing services, study abroad services and quality assurance and evaluation of educational programmes and centers (GATT Secretariat 1991).

The problems and general ambiguity in the classification system of services adopted by the GATS are especially noticeable in the education sector, particularly in higher education, adult education and the "others" categories. According to declarations by some delegations, this uncertainty inhibits their governments when it comes to establishing liberalization commitments on education (WTO 2005b). Moreover, certain subsectors, which are not currently included in any of the categories or educational services, do, in fact, constitute educational services. This is the case of some cultural services, recreational services (such as sports education services) and professional services.

Delegations from other member countries are also pressuring for the incorporation of new sectors in the educational services classification. New Zealand, for example, proposes the inclusion of community education, services for student recruitment, as well as the advertising and the marketing of educational services (WTO-NZ 2001). Meanwhile, the US also considers that services for recruiting foreign students should be included, as well as educational testing services (which include the design, the implementation and the analysis of evaluation tests applied to students and course materials) (WTO-US 2000).

Does the GATS Affect Public Education?

One of the questions that has generated most debate is whether the state education system is affected by the GATS, or if it only affects the private sector. To answer this question, first it has to be acknowledged that the GATS does not use categories of 'public' and 'private' when referring to its scope of competence. Specifically, it states that it does not cover services "supplied in the exercise of government authority". In other words it does not cover the service sectors that are not provided on commercial basis or in competition with one or several service providers (Article I.3). Nevertheless, most higher education systems fulfill at least one of these conditions and are therefore affected by the agreement. For instance, it is increasingly usual for educational systems to include private centers with public financing, public centers with private funding and public centers that offer courses at market prices and compete with private centers for students and non-governmental financing. The following diagram shows the types of education covered by the GATS, using information from Article I.3. It can be seen that the options of educational sectors to remain on the edge of the competitive field are highly limited. In her interpretation of Article I.3, Kelsey (2003) concludes that "very few 'public services' as traditionally defined come within that narrow window" (p. 274).

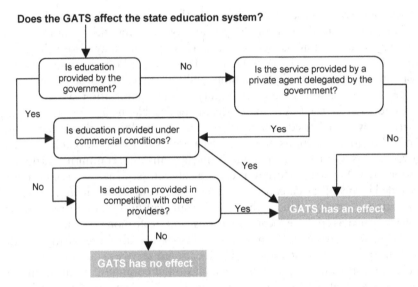

Figure 2.1 State education in the GATS. Source: Adaptation of Fidler et al (2005).

The only communication on education from member countries that deals directly with the public/private dilemma comes from Switzerland (WTO-Switzerland 2005). Switzerland considers that private agents, whether domestic or foreign, that fulfill the conditions fixed for education by governments (such as respecting basic curricula) could form part of the public education system and thereby provide a public service. This communication has been used as a reference by the WTO Secretariat to try to resolve the debate on the coexistence between the public and private sectors in the educational field (WTO 2005b).

On the other hand, the GATS also affects the regulatory actions of local and regional governments. Article I of the GATS specifies that the agreement applies to the measures adopted by members which affect trade in services and that among them are the measures applied by "(i) central, regional or local governments and authorities; and (ii) non-governmental bodies in the exercise of powers delegated by central, regional or local governments or authorities." So, in countries where educational systems have been decentralized, local educational regulators have to obey as well the obligations and commitments existing in the context of the Agreement.

Principal "Barriers" to Trade in Educational Services

When analyzing the barriers to trade in educational services two questions should be considered. Firstly, educational services may be traded according to four different modes of supply, and the types of barrier may vary according to the each mode. Secondly, barriers to trade in services are normally different from those of trade in goods since they are not based on tariffs and are incorporated in very diverse local and national regulatory frameworks (Berlinski 2001).

The following table (Table 2.1) shows the main barriers to trade in educational services according to the various modes of supply contemplated by the agreement. As we shall see, some of the measures considered are of a sectoral nature (i.e. they are educational measures), while others are more transversal in nature and cross various sectors (migration policy, rules for foreign investment, employment regimes, etc.). We can also see that most of the trade barriers identified are fixed by the importer, although some of them are measures adopted by the exporter countries themselves (such as the visas requirements for foreign students).

Table 2.1 Trading Modes for Educational Services, Types of Service and Main Barriers

Trading Mode	Examples in Education	Main Barriers
1. Trans-border provision	· Distance education · E-learning · Testing services · Text books and other educational materials	· Lack of opportunity for accreditation as an institution capable of awarding qualifications · Requirement for a local partner · Legal barriers · Restrictions on the importation of educational material
2. Foriegn consumption	· Study abroad	· Visa requirements · Recognition of foreign qualifications · Fees for foreign students · Working restrictions during the study period · Recognition of qualifications in the country of study · Limitations to currency withdrawal from countries
3. Commercial presence	· Educational branch centres abroad · Association agreements between local and foreign centres · Franchises with local institutions	· Prohibition of service provision to foreign entities · No access to a licence for awarding a recognised qualification · Restrictions to contracting foreign teaching staff · High subsidies to local institutions · Obligatory exams controlled by professional organisations or states · The existence of state monopolies
4. Presence of natural persons	· Lecturers, teachers and researchers working abroad	· Immigration or residency requirements · Recognition of qualifications · Employment regulations

Source: author and Mundy and Iga (2003), García-Guadilla (2003) and Robertson et al. (2002)

The communications on educational services issued by the delegations of Australia and the US point out that the main barriers to educational services as perceived by those countries. The US communication placed more emphasis on measures affecting the profit rates of the education providers such as discriminatory taxation or obstacles to the repatriation of capital (WTO-US 2000). It is interesting to note that the barriers identified by the US in its communication are identical to those identified previously by the National Committee for International Trade in Education (NCITE)—an industrial education group and powerful *lobby* on the definition of the trade negotiation strategy in the US (Mundy and Iga, 2003; Bassett, 2006).[30]

2.4   EDUCATION, ALSO IN REGIONAL TRADE AGREEMENTS

The GATS is the unique multilateral agreement dealing with trade in education services at a multilateral scale, but there are numerous regional and bilateral trade agreements (RTA) that also contemplate the liberalization of education.[31] Despite this book focus on the GATS, it is important to pay attention to these "other" agreements because of various reasons. First, the number of existing RTAs is very high, and it is increasing constantly. Second, they have a direct impact into the WTO/GATS negotiations and, recently, the WTO is becoming more and more concerned about the relevance acquired by these agreements. Third, RTAs normally favor a more aggressive liberalization pattern than GATS. These three issues are developed below.

Smaller Scale, But Huge Presence

To date, there are 184 RTAs in force that have been notified to the WTO. However there are also regional agreements in force that have not been notified to the WTO, agreements signed but not yet in force, agreements currently being negotiated, and those in the proposal stage. If we consider all of them, the number of agreements to be implemented by 2010 is close to 400.[32] The high number of RTAs, and the fact that numerous WTO members countries have subscribed to various of them, have generated a "spaghetti bowl" of agreements that overlap between them and with the WTO system of rules (WTO, 2004).

Most RTAs have been created after the WTO has been constituted (there were around 125 in year 1995, and this number tripled within a ten years period). The WTO itself recognizes that the numerous impasses that the multilateral negotiations are suffering could be the cause of this outbreak of RTAs (WTO, 2004). In fact, the US and the EU are embarked in a sort of race to capture new markets through these trade initiatives since the Doha Round is not advancing at the expected path. Thus, rich countries have adopted a two-track strategy, i.e. they actively promote trade liberalization at the global and bilateral level at the same time. Moreover, these countries prefer RTAs because for them it is easier to impose their preferences at smaller scales (Wilkinson, 2004), above all since developing countries are increasingly organized and empowered at the multilateral level.

However, it should be acknowledged that the relevance of South-South agreements (those conformed between developing countries leaving rich countries apart) is also growing in number and political relevance (Muhr 2008).

The Spaghetti Bowl Concern

Since its creation, the GATT allowed the existence of regional custom unions and other forms of trade agreements (see GATT, art. XXIV). The new WTO agreements (GATS and TRIPS) also recognize and accept this co-existence. However, since the number of RTAs is rising so drastically, the coexistence is becoming more problematic. The WTO is concerned about the RTAs because they violate the non-discrimination principle, affecting transparency and previsibility of the system of international trade (OMC 2001). In fact, in occasions, the WTO refers to the 'RTAs problem' in a sarcastic way:

> What has been termed the "spaghetti bowl" of customs unions, common markets, regional and bilateral free trade areas, preferences and an endless assortment of miscellaneous trade deals has almost reached the point where MFN treatment is exceptional treatment. Certainly the term might now be better defined as LFN, Least-Favored Nation treatment (WTO, 2004: 19).

To manage this problem, the WTO has created a RTAs Committee to examine the compatibility of the multilateral and regional rules—although members almost never reach a consensus over these issues in the context of this Committee (WTO 2005d). Furthermore, in the framework of the Doha Round, the Working Group on Rules is trying to improve the WTO disciplines to be applied to regional agreements. For instance, this Working Group has created a transparency mechanism for RTAs that, in Pascal Lamy's words, "is an important step towards ensuring that regional trade agreements become building blocks, not stumbling blocks to world trade."[33]

The WTO is increasingly concerned about the growing number of existing RTAs because the content of these agreements contradicts very often the WTO rules. However, the WTO is also concerned because RTAs weaken the multilateral negotiations space. For instance, numerous countries are giving political priority to bilateral negotiations and allocate their best negotiators in these forums instead of in the WTO (WB 2005). On the other hand, the behavior of countries in the WTO negotiations is affected by their participation in RTAs. For instance, as we will observe in chapter 9, the Chilean's bargaining capacity in multilateral negotiations is clearaly undermined by the high liberalization commitments Chile has adopted in numerous free trade agreements. In the case of Argentina, the country's strategy and position in the GATS context would be probably different if it would not participate in MERCOSUR.

GATS-plus: Regional Agreements Specificities

Following UNCTAD, regional trade agreements conduct to a deeper liberalization of services than GATS (UNCTAD 2005). This is, in part, due to the fact that RTAs negotiations advance faster than multilateral negotiations. However, this is also due to the different nature and content of the two types of agreements. Albeit the articles and rules contained in GATS and RTAs are very similar, RTAs (above all north-south Free Trade Agreements) are usually less flexible and less development friendly than GATS. Because of this, some scholars qualify RTAs as GATS-*plus* (Abugattas 2005; Teitelbaum 2004). Specifically, various elements make RTAs to be perceived as more liberalizers than GATS. First, RTAs thematic scope is broader. For instance, numerous RTAs include government procurement disciplines, while GATS does not do it yet. Second, some RTAs do not allow exceptions to the MFN principle (for instance, the EU–Mercosur association [Berlinski 2001]) and others consider national treatment as a general obligation (this was, for instance, the case of the FTAA). This way, members do not count with the possibility of maintaining certain restrictions in terms of national treatment. Third, the RTAs system for the acquisition of commitments is the *negative list*. This way, countries have to list the services sectors that do not want to open to trade and it is assumed that all sectors that are not included become liberalized. Finally, some RTAs, such as NAFTA, contemplate the 'like investor to state' norm. This norm permits to private actors (normally transnational corporations) to make use of the dispute settlement mechanism of the trade agreement without the mediation of any state (Teitelbaum 2004).

2.5   CONCLUSIONS

The GATS has become one of the pillars of the WTO system of rules. Free trade is the core principle of the GATS and, as a consequence, the promotion of this particular system of trade in the services sector is the key objective of the agreement. However, the tension between free trade and the right of the states to erect trade barriers to prosecute the social purpose is still under discussion in the context of WTO committees such as the rules working group and the domestic regulation working group. Furthermore, the ongoing negotiations on market access and national treatment commitments (normally called 'liberalization negotiations') will determine how far are the member countries disposed to open their services sectors to trade.

When the GATS was designed during the Uruguay Round, the education sector was not a central topic in the discussion. Moreover, the education community was totally absent of the discussion. However, since then, trade in higher education services flows have become increasingly significant and education has gained centrality in the trade strategy of those developed countries interested in gaining access in education markets abroad.

As the WTO negotiations advance, the GATS rules, obligations and disciplines are becoming more relevant pieces for the global governance of education and for the deepening of transnational education markets. Something similar happens, although at a smaller scale, with the growing number of RTAs that also promote education liberalization (normally in a more aggressive way than the multilateral agreement).

In the following chapter, the evolution of the GATS is situated in a broader context of transformations recently experienced within the higher education field. The contribution of the trade agreement to the intensification of some of these transformations is also analyzed.

3 GATS, Markets and Higher Education

The WTO considers that the introduction of education services into the ambit of the GATS makes a lot of sense in the current context, in which great transformations are taking place in the field of education and especially in the field of higher education. Generally, the WTO is referring to transformations such as the growing involvement of the private sector in education, the major competition between education providers, the increase in demand for education at all levels, the growing presence of international students in many university systems, a rise in the number of branch campuses abroad, the introduction of new technologies in education at a distance provision, and the reduction in public investment in higher education systems (WTO 2000; WTO 1998). This chapter will expand on the vision of the transformations experienced in the field of higher education offered by the WTO and, more importantly, will explain how the GATS actually contributes to accentuating many of the trends outlined by the organization.

3.1 GLOBALIZATION, COMPETITIVENESS AND HIGHER EDUCATION

The GATS is being negotiated in an environment of education commodification (i.e. creation of educational markets) that is acquiring a global scope. Privatization and liberalization policies are key factors in this process of education commodification. These kinds of policies are being adopted and implemented by states in numerous points of the planet since the nineties. As Brunner (2006) says, the states are the principle operating agents when it comes to adopting measures for creating educational markets[1]. However, beyond the individual will of the states, there are deeper causes behind the global tendency towards educational commodification. The argument here is that the pro-market policies and trends currently being experienced in higher education are driven by the economic globalization process and, specifically, by one of the main points of tension that this process has generated: the tension between the expanding demand for higher education and the contraction of direct state intervention in the sector.

Educational systems are affected, directly and indirectly, by processes of economic globalization and liberalization. Globalization intensifies economic competition at all levels—between companies, regions, states, cities, etc. (P. Brown and Lauder 1997). Within this context, education and knowledge have become key factors for competitiveness, to the point where many countries and regions aspire to becoming "knowledge economies or societies" (S. L. Robertson 2005; Burton-Jones 1999; Jessop 2000)[2]. Even the Lisbon Treaty of the EU is centered on the strategic objective of making Europe "the most competitive and dynamic knowledge economy in the world before 2010."[3] Today, "knowledge economies" have become a powerful political and economic imaginary that frames many of the development strategies in both developed and developing countries (Naidoo 2007). In fact, higher education is at the center of strategies for economic development in many countries, especially in areas of workforce training, applied research and technological transfer (P. Brown and Lauder 1997; Barrow, Didou and Mallea 2004). On the micro level, individuals also feel under more pressure to compete with each other in different economic spheres, and in particular in the labor market (Brown and Lauder 1997). Higher education is therefore also under the spotlight of individual positioning strategies in the labor market (Marginson 2004). From all this, we can deduce that higher education is perceived more and more as a profitable investment, both for states and for individual citizens. The logical consequence of this is that there has been a major increase in the demand for education goods. According to estimates by some authors, the growth in demand for higher education is currently a worldwide phenomenon that has never before reached such high levels (Johnstone 2004; Newman 1999).

However, at the same time, the economic globalization itself makes it more difficult for the states to respond to the task of responding to this increase in education demand on their own. The causes of this are, again, related to the current competitive economic climate and not only affect the educational sector but also broader changes taking place in the public sector (Dale 1999). Economic globalization alters the relationship between the state and education in different manners. At least, three impact dimensions can be identified: the priorities, the capacities and the functions of the state in the higher education sector. Firstly, competitiveness alters the *priorities* of nation-states in the area of public services. The "competition state", or the state that wants to become competitive, actively promotes business initiatives, innovation and profit generation, in both the public and private sectors. These new objectives compete with the traditional welfare objectives of the Keynesian states (Cerny 1997). Universities are not at the margin of this change in the order of priorities of the state and face an increasing pressure to adapt their research and teaching activities to the market demands. Secondly, the *capacity* of countries to provide public services is altered. Governments that have liberalized their economies rely on smaller amounts of income from taxes and tariffs and the race between countries to attract foreign investment means that fiscal pressure on capital is modified yet further. Consequently, governments have to cut back or rationalize public investment and reduce public debt (Dale 1999; Green 2002). This pressure has directly affected higher education and, on many occasions, has resulted in cutbacks in public funding in this area (Aronowitz and De Fazio 1997; Carnoy 1999a; Marginson 1999). Thirdly, globalization affects the *function* of the state in the education field. Countries that want to become more efficient and competitive are pressured to modify their role in the area of public services. Specifically, they tend to provide fewer public services directly (Mundy 1998) opting instead for models based on *partnerships* with the private sector and/or local governments, and indirect control of services through different forms of regulation (Kwiek 2001).

Liberalization and Privatization of Higher Education

It has been seen that states find themselves having to respond to a growing demand for higher education, while having to reduce their capacity for intervention in this area. This contradiction has a major effect on the higher education agenda and policies in most countries. Very often the solution applied is to introduce liberalization and privatization measures for higher education.

Liberalization may be defined as the introduction of competition and other principles, rules, logics and market values in educational systems (Reid 2005). The states can encourage competition through more competitive financing policies (results-based funding policies, for example), forcing education centers to seek external financing, applying methods of business management to public services or promoting decentralization and financial autonomy for university systems. In a more competitive environment, universities have to decide on their priorities, obtain independent financing and set out strategies for attracting clients (Henry et al. 1999). Some governments introduce competition into the university system as a simple way of overcoming the effects of the so-called 'fiscal-crisis' of the state. Others have done so not only for instrumental reasons but because, guided by neoliberal beliefs, they are convinced that "more competition" within the system will lead to improvements in educational quality, productivity, responsibility and innovation in the university world (Olssen and Peters 2005).

Liberalization policies mean the reformulation of the relationship between education and the state. The 'evaluative state' concept clearly condenses the essence of this reformulation. The evaluative state represents a shift of the state responsibilities in higher education from direct provision to the evaluation of the system. In this new setting, the state establishes standards for content and performance and evaluates whether the universities are achieving their objectives efficiently. According to the results of the evaluations, the state may choose to penalize or reward the centers

(Neave 1988). Evaluation allows the state to retain control of university systems even when they have washed their hands of the direct provision and management of educational services. Some authors therefore consider that the evaluation mechanisms allow the state to control higher education "remotely" (Mollis and Marginson 2002).

Privatization is the second political node in the current higher education scene, although is retrospectively fed directly by liberalization policies. Privatization is basically centered on two areas of educational policy: education provision and funding. In both policy areas, the main causal force for privatization is the restriction in higher education public supply and public funding, in a context of increasing demand of university services. In fact, the OECD itself considers that the growing demand for educational services can only be met by more private investment in the education sector (OECD 1996). In its report *Educational Policy Analysis* (1997), among other recommendations, the OECD states that "the privatization of financing is imperative in a period marked by the intensification of budgetary pressures" (Laval 2004, 63). Public spending restraints mean that universities are increasingly forced to diversify their financing (Porter and Vidovich 2000), increase their fees and replace grants with loans (Carnoy 1999b; Santos 2004). It is not surprising, therefore, that private financing of higher education is rapidly gaining ground. This trend can even be seen in the more wealthy countries. In fact, public spending on higher education in OECD countries, which in 1995 represented 81.2% of all spending on education, had dropped to 76.2% by 2003 (OECD 2006), and all the indications are that this downward trend will continue.

Fortunately for many governments, the new common sense of 'education as a key factor for competitiveness' means that there are increasing numbers of people willing to pay for access to higher education. In a labor market that is clearly two-tiered, competitive and that, in some countries, displays precarious work and high levels of unemployment, individuals perceive university diplomas as key instruments for reaching a good labor position (Apple 1997). Education has therefore taken the form of a positional good much more intensively than in previous decades. Consequently, the individuals, in line with their economic means and ambitions, will try to gain access to the most prestigious higher education centers. The fact that more people are prepared to pay for their education undoubtedly opens the doors to educational privatization and to the creation of university markets. One can therefore consider that education for competitiveness would be a key mechanism, from the point of view of the demand, for understanding the emergence of educational markets -and/or new niches in the existing education markets.

From the point of view of the supply, some governments are actively promoting privatization through measures such as tax subsidies or incentives for private higher education centers, or restricting access to public universities (for example by setting higher entrance grades requirements)

(Carnoy 1999b; Johnes 1995). However, governments do tend to encourage the private provision of higher education by omission. This means that if they remain passive in the face of the growing demand for higher education, they are indirectly preparing the ground for the emergence of new private universities and education centers.

The New Private Providers

In recent years, new non-conventional private agents have appeared in the higher education sector. These new higher education providers have characteristics that markedly differentiate them from traditional private centers. Firstly, their activities are focused on teaching—therefore they do not assign as many resources to research and knowledge creation (Knight 2007). Secondly, they are profit-orientated and it is precisely this objective that principally marks their academic activity, the range of programs they offer and other university policy options (Van Damme 2003). According to Rodríguez Gómez (2003) these institutions also count on private capital investments and governing structures that are similar to those of conventional private companies (for instance, in terms of the control mechanisms of their shareholders); their teaching content is eminently practical and includes little theoretical content, often offering two year programs without the option of obtaining a degree. The main objective of many of these centers is to "sell qualifications and diplomas", often via educational services of dubious quality, which has generated criticism among the traditional academic community (G. M. Brown 2005; Bhushan 2006; GUNI 2006). The number of for-profit higher education institutions grew considerably in the 1990s.[3] According to estimates by Merryl Linch, market growth for this kind of centers in 1999 was 15% compared with 6% for traditional public institutions (Merrill-Lynch 1999).

There are two other types of private providers that have recently entered with force in the higher education scene and that also break with the more traditional forms and rationales of education provision. These are the *corporate universities* and the *virtual education centers*. Corporate universities are educational centers that offer specialized training to workers or potential workers for a large company. These centers depend directly on the company and are a key component of their production strategy as well as a loyalty-building element among their workforces (Meister 1998). Currently, 40% of the most powerful corporations have educational services of this kind (Rodríguez Gómez 2003). It is estimated that there are some 1,600 corporate universities worldwide (Larsen, Martin, and Morris 2002). A list with the names of the most known corporate universities can be checked in Box 3.1. Until now, these institutions did not award university titles and were not officially accredited as higher education centers. The programs they offered were designed to cover the needs of the company in a more focused way (Meister, 1998). However, these centers are rapidly evolving and many have started to obtain accreditation and open themselves up to broader markets, enabling them to meet a larger demand beyond their own workers. In fact, approximately 25% of corporate universities are already attracting students who do not have any links with the company. This is the case of Microsoft, for example, which has approximately 1,700 professional training centers (Larsen and Vincent-Lancrin 2002). Corporate universities are also becoming more international as they establish centers that are embedded in the transnational branches of the companies they are linked to. This is the case of Cisco Networking Academy, which offers distance learning and runs 10,000 academies (on a partnership basis) in 150 countries.[4]

The *distance education centers* are also gaining a greater presence, partly because they can afford to extend their educational activities at lower cost (López Segrera 2003; Carnoy 1999). Their profitability lies in the fact that the building maintenance cost is low and the cost of transporting materials and communication has been reduced thanks to the Internet. Sometimes the cost of their teaching staff is lower than that of in person education centers.[5] In 2001 there were 1,180 distance education centers (TFP 2002). Box 3.2 contains the names of some of the most successful of them. These centers cause the same distrust among the traditional academic community as the for profit institutions, largely due to the confusion that exists in the regulatory frameworks to which they must conform (Brown 2005).

Box 3.1   Corporate Universities

The list of the main corporate universities includes companies in the production sector (General Electric, General Motors, Land Rover, Shell), consumer good sector (Coca Cola, Marlboro, Mc Donalds), commercial sector (Wal-Mart, Eddi Bauer, Best Buy, Home Depot, Target Stores), financial sector (American Express), entertainment sector (Disney, Universal) and, above all, the computing and telecommunications sector (Apple, AT&T, Microsoft, Xerox, Motorola, Sun, Oracle)

Source: (Rodríguez Gómez 2003)

Box 3.2   Virtual Universities

The most successful distance university attracting foreign students is the University of Phoenix, which has some 100,000 students and 100 centers in the US, Puerto Rico, Canada and Holland. The International University ("the university of the web") also has a major presence. In Latin America some of the most important distance universities are: Universidad Virtual de Centro-Oeste (Brazil); Universidad Red (Argentina, Brazil, UK, Israel); Red de Información Iberoamericana (Argentina, Brazil, Colombia, Costa Rica, Cuba, Ecuador, Mexico, Peru, Venezuela and Spain).

Source: (García-Guadilla 2003)

Finally, another set of new service providers that has made a strong entrance into the higher education market is made up of the following (Rodríguez Gómez 2003; López Segrera 2003): a) *IT skills certification centers.* These are companies that award certification for computer skills and they also tend to operate via Internet and on a transnational scale; b) *distance education software companies,* with close ties to the expansion of virtual learning environments. Some examples are Webct, Blackboard and Shells adhoc; c) *brokering companies,* which match supply to demand in the virtual learning sector, such as the Globe Wide Network Academy, and the Electronic University Network; d) *corporate centers* that assess knowledge of languages; e) *education evaluation and quality assurance agencies.* In many countries these are state-operated, but in others they are private. Some are even transnational companies offering an international service.

3.2   COMMERCIALISM: BUYING AND SELLING EDUCATION ON AN INTERNATIONAL SCALE

Changes manifested in the education field do not only concern to aspects of organization or to the distribution of educational goods. Profound changes into the traditional conception and functions of higher education are manifested as well. So, currently, in addition to providing means for the smooth functioning and competitiveness of the capitalist economy, universities and the services they offer are, in themselves, objects and products of that economy. Universities have therefore become companies that produce value through the sale of educational and research services. This characterization of universities as an economic end is clearly seen in the growing sector of private universities on the one hand, and in the tendency for public universities to behave like private companies, on the other. Public universities are increasingly behaving as autonomous business units that aim to sell services in an increasingly liberalized system. Consequently, they feel under pressure to restructure themselves institutionally to become better adapted to the economic system they have become part of and in which they will have to compete with increasing ferocity. As developed in this section, this structural transformation of the university system is directly connected to the intensification of trade flows in educational services, which are being developed more and more on an international scale.

Trading University Services

Currently, the educational sector has a direct role in two types of operations that constitute the globalization of the economy: foreign trade and foreign direct investment (FDI). Both private and public universities are involved in both types of operations. If the volume of trade and FDI flows in education is insignificant in most countries (at least if we compare it with other sectors) it has increased drastically since the 1990s[6]. Many countries, and especially those with the largest comparative advantage in educational trade, have started to recognize that educational services is an knowledge-intensive export industry that can contribute positively to their trade balance (Barrow, Didou-Aupetit, and Mallea 2004). As a consequence they actively promote their systems of higher education in the international field through international development aid, migration and visa policies, grant programs for foreign students, policies for quality assurance and the recognition of qualifications, or directly through their trade policy in forums such as the WTO (Larsen, Momii, and Vincent-Lancrin 2004).

As reflected in the negotiations for the liberalization of services being carried out by the WTO, the countries with more "offensive interests" in terms of exportation of educational services are Australia, the United Kingdom, New Zealand, Canada and the US. As mentioned in the previous chapter, the most aggressive among them is New Zealand, whose massive interest in liberalizing educational services can be understood at a quick glance of Figure 3.1 (see below), which shows that the volume of exports in educational services there has increased by 1000% in the past five years. However, European countries also tend to align themselves to this more aggressive model. In fact, one of the main objectives of the constitution of the European Higher Education Area (EHEA) is strictly commercial. According to Dale (2003), the EHEA prepares European universities for international competition and the traditional European universities therefore have to become global universities and export their educational services around the world. Indeed, European education ministers have proposed to make the European higher education systems the "the most-favored destination of students, scholars and researchers from other world regions" (EC 2002, 5). It should be pointed out, however, that this EU strategy also involves a defensive element, since it is not only an attempt to secure brains from other regions, but also to avoid the migration of its own brains to the US.[7]

Beyond the strategies adopted by the countries in trade forums, many universities, either individually or within the framework of university associations, have launched programs to encourage trade for their services—especially the sale of undergraduate and postgraduate degree courses. By doing this, they pretend to diversify their financing and obtain non-state resources, which, as we have already mentioned, is one of the main priorities for higher education institutions in the current context of economic globalization (Santos 2004; Ziguras, Reinke, and Mcburnie 2003).

Some Facts About Trade in Educational Services

Despite the difficulties in assessing the exact volume of trade flow that educational services represent (Saner and Fasel 2003), the indications are that trade in education has grown in all the four modes of services supply.

Below we can see how each of these modes functions in the specific case of education:

a) Mode 1 (cross-border supply): consists of providing an educational service in one country to another, with no physical contact between the producer and the user. This is the case with e-learning and other distance education programs.

b) Mode 2 (consumption abroad): clients go to a foreign country to consume a service. The clearest example of this is when students move from one country to another to study. In this case, the country providing the courses exports a service to the student's country.

c) Mode 3 (commercial presence): this is the most complex mode of the four, and involves the physical displacement of the supplier to the importing country. Sometimes this mode goes beyond trade as it involves FDI operations. This happens when the exporting company establishes branches abroad or sets up local centers. Jane Knight has systematized a series of operations that involve FDI and those that do not. Those that involve FDI are (Knight 2007):

- Establishment of campuses/branches in a country by a university from another country. Qualifications are awarded by the investing provider, and are therefore the qualifications of the country of origin.
- Creation of an independent institution: a foreign institution sets up a university in a certain country, which then operates as a local university and therefore awards qualifications according to the regulations of the host country.
- Takeover/merger: in this case the foreign center buys all or part of a local education center. The functioning of the center and the qualification will probably conform to the regulations of the host country.

There is another set of trading operations in the framework of mode three that does not involve FDI, but is channeled by associations and networking between centers on an international level. Some examples of this are franchises (a prestigious centre in one country grants a franchise to a centre in another country) and twinning of centers or programs from different countries. Many of these initiatives run the risk of simply being marketing strategies that do not translate into the quality education that they promise. Many franchises offer programs with infinitely lower levels of quality than those offered at the main centers. In Latin American countries, many low quality local private universities form associations with second-rate Spanish universities with the strategic aim of attracting clients (they are aware of the fact that Latin-American students are often attracted to study programs that are jointly organized by a 'European' university). Most countries still do not have the necessary instrument to assess these new forms of transnational provisions and there are frequently cases of fraud and the students can be seriously disadvantaged (Garrett 2005).

d) Mode 4 (presence of natural persons): supply of services in one country by natural persons from another country. This is the case of academic staff contracted to carry out research or teaching in foreign universities. In this case, the lecturer's country of origin is considered to be the exporter of the educational service.

Of the four existing modes of supply, most data exists for mode 2 (students who study abroad). In 2005, there were 2.7 million higher education students registered in a foreign country, which represents a 61% increase since 1999 (OECD 2006). The OECD countries (i.e. the most highly developed countries in the world) are most competitive when it comes to attracting foreign students. In fact, the OECD area receives 85% of all international students. These flows are concentrated in just a few countries. The US, the UK, Germany, France and Australia attract 65% of all overseas students in the world (Verbik and Lasanowski 2007). The main exporter of educational services in the world is the US. This country earns over 13 billion dollars per year in the form of foreign student enrolment (Basset 2006). However, whereas the US is the main exporter of education in absolute terms, in countries such as Australia and New Zealand educational services exports represent a much higher percentage of total exports. For example, the economic input in Australia in 2000 in the form of foreign students amounted to 5.6% of all exports. After coal and iron ore, education was the most exported asset of this country (Olds 2008).

The following figure (Figure 3.1) shows details of the main exporters of higher education between 2000 and 2005. For all countries involved, export activity can be seen to have increased greatly over the period, and especially in the case of New Zealand. Despite an absolute increase in the number of students, some countries (specifically, UK, US and Germany) have seen their overall market share for foreign students decrease. The country where this reduction was most drastic was the US (26.1% in 2000 and 21.6% in 2005). Many analysts attribute this fall to difficulties in obtaining students visas following the 9/11 attacks (Sirat 2008).

The other side of trade flows are the importers of educational services (that is, the countries of origin of students studying abroad), among which certain Asian countries, such as China, India, South Korea and Japan, are particularly significant (OECD 2004).

Curiously, the main recipient countries for international students are those that set the highest fees. This is for instance the case of the US, the UK, Australia and New Zealand, where university fees are much

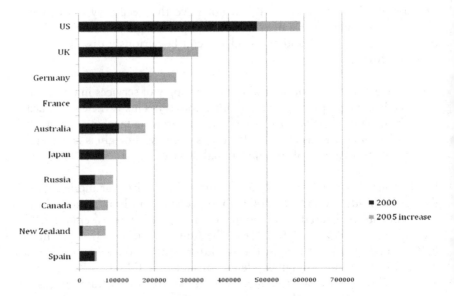

Figure 3.1   Main exporters of higher education (mode 2).
Source: author; data from OECD (2007)

higher for international students than for national ones. The subject of tariffs, therefore, does not appear to be an inhibiting factor for studying abroad. Those who do choose to study abroad seemed to be influenced more strongly by factors other than the cost of the courses. Many choose to do so because higher education is more accessible in the host countries than in their own, whether this is because the entrance requirements are lower, a higher number of students is admitted or a greater range of courses is offered. Students from poorer countries are particularly inclined to go abroad to study when their own country does not offer a particular specialization. In fact, sometimes the governments even encourage their student population to study abroad as they are aware of the limitations of their own education offer (Larsen, Momii, and Vincent-Lancrin 2004).

There are also students who go abroad for extra-academic reasons, such as escaping from oppressive political regimes, to gain experience of living in a different country and familiarize themselves with a new culture and for learning languages (Altbach 2004a). In other cases, there is a certain prestige attached to foreign qualifications, especially if they are obtained from prestigious universities. Therefore, although it is not always easy to obtain official recognition of some qualifications awarded in foreign higher education systems, the students know that employers value the fact that the qualification was obtained from a foreign university

(WTO 1998)[8]. There are also many people studying abroad with the intention of working in the destination country (Vinokur 2006). Studying abroad is also perceived as a way to acquire the skills and abilities needed for working in transnational companies, or generally to open up the number of opportunities in an increasingly globalized labor market (Didou 2006).[9]

Trade flows for modes 1 (distance education) and 3 (creation of universities abroad and others forms of commercial presence abroad), have also increased in recent years. Mode 1 represents approximately 6% of international students' registrations in higher education, and this percentage experienced constant increase during the nineties (Larsen and Vincent-Lancrin 2002). Cross-border distance education also increased with the advances in electronic communication and the erosion of temporal and spatial restrictions that this produced (Jessop 2001). The so-called virtual universities are also attractive because mobility costs are almost non-existing, and these costs are especially high for people studying physically abroad (Marginson 2004).

Mode 3 is, again, predominated by the territorial expansion of the British, Australian and US universities. Many of them offer their services through associations with local universities in the host countries, although often they create new campuses and institutions. The Australian campuses abroad receive 29% of all foreign students in the higher education system in Australia while international British campuses receive around 140,000 students (Larsen and Vincent-Lancrin 2002). One of the usual strategies for the international expansion of universities consists of buying private universities abroad. This is the case of the North American consortium Sylvan Learning Systems, which has bought private universities and business schools in Mexico, Chile, France, Spain and Switzerland (Aboites 2004).

It is worth pointing out that some countries actively promote direct investment by foreign universities in their own territories as a way of abating the lack of resources in their own educational systems, and sometimes in order to minimize the brain-drain problem (Zhang 2003). Other countries do it to attract foreign students and, by doing so, to generate a profitable export activity and to raise their political profile and influence in the region (Verbik and Lasanowski 2007). For their part, the universities opt to set up foreign branches as a way of diversifying their markets and becoming less reliant on local student numbers, in order to take advantage of partnership opportunities with other universities or with local industry, or simply as an income generator (Verbik and Merkley 2006).

Trade in higher education contributes to the convergence of national education markets within an international education market. In this new scenario, the dynamics of competition are accentuated still further as the local universities, whether public or private, also have to compete with providers from other countries. At the same time, the governance of higher education systems becomes more complex due to the fact that state governments have to coordinate the activities of the new stakeholders (foreign universities, international accreditation agencies, etc.) operating in their territories.

3.3   UNEQUAL EXCHANGE IN EDUCATIONAL TRADE

The direction of trade flows for educational services is one more indicator of the imbalance in the world economy. Most of the less developed countries are net importers of educational services, since their education industry is not competitive enough in the emerging global education market. Consequently, the balance of trade in the education sector is negative in practically all developing countries, even in the main exporting countries. Figure 3.2 shows data for imports and exports of education for the ten developing countries with the greatest export capacity (with reference to mode 2). It can be seen from these figures that the only countries with a positive trade balance are Cuba, South Africa and three countries in southwest Asia. Furthermore, if we compare the figures in this graph with those in Figure 3.1, we can see that the export capacity of developing countries is much more limited that that of developed countries. Specifically, the 10

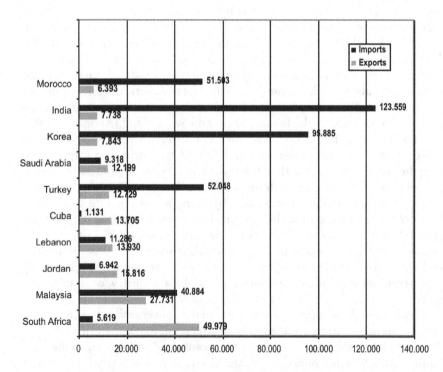

Figure 3.2   Trade balance for developing countries with the largest education exports. Source: author; data from UNESCO (2006)

developing countries included export only around 8% of that exported by the 10 rich countries in Figure 3.1.

Developing countries that export education, on the other hand, generally work within the limits of regional markets rather than in the context of the global market (Verbik and Lasanowski 2007). This is a characteristic trait of the semiperiphery since semiperipheral countries are central in their own regions, but peripheral in the world system (Wallerstein 1979). The table below (Table 3.1.) shows trade relations in education for three regional powers: South Africa, India and Brazil. The center/semiperipheral/peripheral relationships can be clearly seen here because none of the countries included export educational services to central countries and they only do it in the region. On the other hand, they only import education services from the centre.

The causes of this imbalance in trade exchange for educational services between northern and southern countries are related to the precariousness of university systems in most developing countries. Students from these countries tend to emigrate to more central countries, either because of the limited offer available in their own countries or for the prestige associated with studying at a university in a developed country. This idea is clearly expressed by Max-Neef (1991:98) when he says "if as a Latin American economist I wish to become an expert in Latin American development problems, it is necessary to study in the United

Table 3.1 Semiperiphery and Trade in Educational Services (Mode 2)

Developing countries education exporters	Main destination of exports (origin of foreign students)	Imports of higher education services in the region (destination of their students)	Main origin of imports (number of students abroad)
Brazil	South America (70%)	South America (±6%)	USA (7,566), France (1.846), Portugal (1,796), Germany (1,776)
India	Asia (57.4%) Africa (24.46%)	Asia (2.25%) Africa (0%)	USA (79,736), Australia (15.742), United Kingdom (14.625) Germany (4,237), New Zealand (1,205)
South Africa	Africa (72.96%)	Africa (0%)	USA (1,971), United Kingdom (1,408), Australia (643), Cuba (340), Germany (196)

Source: produced by the author with data from UNESCO (2006) and OECD (2006)

States or in Europe to be respectable in the eyes of both my Southern and Northern colleagues"—cited in Ball (1998, 123). When the direction of trade is from southern to northern countries, however, the reasons tend to be different. According to Altbach, for example, the few students from the US who study abroad (around 0.2% in total) do so for the cultural experience it represents. It should be acknowledged that western universities are not only the most prestigious because they have more material resources, but also because they dominate the curriculum and the scientific discourse (Altbach 2004b).

As far as the other modes of supply are concerned, the north/south divide is very similar to that described for mode 2. Universities from rich countries are, in the main, those with the capacity to set up branches abroad. In a study published by the OBHE in 2003 about the most internationalized education companies in the world, it is shown that 50% of the biggest companies are from the US. In contrast, only 6% of them come from developing countries such as India, South Africa, Malaysia and Singapore. No other exporting developing countries are identified in this OBHE research (OBHE 2003). Something similar happens with branch campuses abroad: 53% are linked to a US institution and only 12,2% to developing countries institutions. Furthermore, as happens with student mobility, developing countries establish university branches in neighbor countries of the region, but never in rich countries (Verbik and Merkley 2006).

The only mode of supply in which some developing countries are competitive is mode 4. Many developing countries promote the commerce of persons because they want a part of their population to move abroad to work in the services sector, earn high salaries and send money back home as remittances. Developing countries also could benefit from sending professionals and students to the developed countries so that they can receive a good education and, in the mid-term, return with knowledge about the latest technological advances (Carnoy 1999a). Even so, it should be remembered that this trade modality accentuates the problem of brain-drain and, as a consequence, a valuable "human capital", in which several years of training have been invested by the state, vanishes.

In short, trade flows for higher education services clearly benefit rich countries. The education industry in developed countries can easily open up markets in the less developed world thanks to the gaps in state provision and the prestige associated with studying at a university—or a branch of that university—from a developed country. Moreover, the policies imposed and disseminated by the World Bank and the IMF, both sectoral—centered on higher education—and economic—condensed in the Structural Adjustment Programs—have traditionally limited the public spending on higher education in developing countries. Consequently, this has encouraged the developed countries to become global higher education providers (Barrow, Didou, and Mallea 2004). In effect, the current state of trading in educational services may become a new dependence mechanism between the north and the south.[10]

3.4 THE GATS IN THE GLOBAL GOVERNANCE OF EDUCATION

The GATS feeds into many of the trends in higher education explored in this chapter, specially, privatization, liberalization and commercialization, but it is not the only driving force of these trends. The GATS contributes to the accentuation and sedimentation of these processes, but they had already started before the existence of the trade agreement.

However, the GATS has also direct implications for the educational field. The fact that the logic and rules of free trade penetrate the education sector means that education becomes circumscribed to new production and consumption relations, as well as to new regulatory frameworks and procedures for political decision-making and political action. That is why we can consider the introduction of education into the framework of free trade agreements has spilled over into a new wave of transformations in the field of higher education, which has not been sufficiently explored yet from the viewpoint of educational sciences. Specifically, we are referring to the following: *a*) deepening supranational structures for the governance of education; *b*) the consolidation of a global market for higher education, through the blocking of new regulatory frameworks; *c*) the introduction of educational transnationalization dynamics which transcend the dynamics of internationalization itself.

Deepening Global Governance of Education

The GATS reinforces global structures for educational governance. This means that the GATS rules make that certain aspects of education governance that were traditionally situated at state level are relocated on a supranational scale (Robertson and Dale 2006). Global governance is defined as a new method of governance in which the power, functions and authority of nation states are reconstituted, based on the extension of international jurisdictions and institutions for global governability that are juxtaposed with the state ambit (Held, 1999).[11] The global governance of education is equivalent to a complex multilevel system of division of activities and functions in educational policy. This new method of governance involves international organizations, international NGOs, big corporations and other non-state actors in key education policy areas such as funding, provision, ownership and regulation (Dale, 2003). This pluri-scalar method is captured in the following figure:

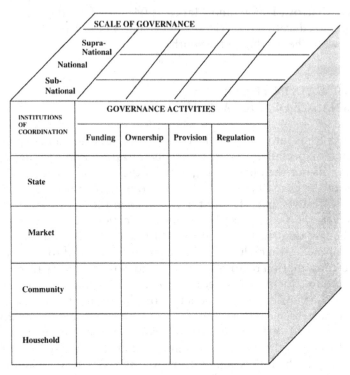

Figure 3.3   Multiscale governance of education.
Source: Dale (2003)

Since the nineties, the WTO and the GATS have been embedded in this scheme of multilevel governance and have acquired more influence, directly or indirectly, in the mentioned areas of educational policy and, as developed below, specially on education regulation aspects. The phenomenon of the global educational governance emerged much earlier than the GATS. Since the 1950s there have been important international organizations such as the World Bank, UNESCO and the OECD, that have influenced national educational policy (Mundy 1998; Mundy 1999). However, the presence of the GATS involved a series of substantial changes with respect to the previous state of governance. Years ago, the international organizations influenced the states by framing their education agendas and through the diffusion (and sometimes imposition) of specific policies. The main areas of education policy where international organizations were involved were funding, policy advice and policy framing in general. But with the exception of a few UNESCO conventions, education regulation was realized at the state level. Currently, the irruption of the GATS has meant that the state has also lost its monopoly in the field of educational regulation (Robertson, Bonal, and Dale 2002). In this new scenario, certain decisions have become centralized on a supranational scale and the states cannot intervene as autonomously as before. The trade agreements therefore take on a formal sovereignty in certain aspects of state education policy (Robertson and Dale 2006). Many of the regulatory elements in the GATS are fixed by the general obligations of the agreement, while others are in the process of being fixed. As we have seen, the establishment of these new elements is negotiated in three different fora: *a*) Periodic negotiations to establish liberalization commitments (market access and national treatment); *b*) working group on rules; *c*) working group on domestic regulation.

The process of re-scaling of education governance driven by GATS, beyond formal and procedimental aspects, also deals with the content and the political orientation of education policy. Several authors agree that the trade regime promoted by the GATS is markedly neoliberal in its policy orientation (Altay 2006; Kelsey 2008; Robertson, Bonal, and Dale 2002; Scherrer 2007; Schugurensky and Davidson-Harden 2003). According to neoliberalism the best thing for efficient economic functioning and the distribution of welfare is market integration and the opening of national economies. The GATS favors a 'neoliberal' sort of education governance since it promotes deregulation and the opening up of national markets to trade and competition, accentuating the use of market mechanisms in the supply of services and limiting state intervention. As Stephen Gill has stated, the WTO and its agreements promote the *constitutionalization of neoliberalism*, i.e. they favor neoliberalism to be institutionalized in the quasi-legal structure of the state and in the form of international policies (Gill 2003).[12]

The content of the GATS overlaps, and to a certain extent contradicts, the content of other instruments for the supra-national governance of higher education which are based on no-market logics, such as the 1998 worldwide declaration on higher education by UNESCO—in which the moral and prescriptive principles of the functions of higher education were defined (UNESCO 1998)—or the OECD and UNESCO guidelines on the cross-border provision of quality higher education (UNESCO 2005a). These and other instruments may be neutralized by the WTO system since they do not contemplate the capacity to fix binding rules which must obligatorily be complied with by the signatory countries, which is something that the GATS does. The only global legal instrument that could eclipse the GATS in terms of higher educational transnationalization would be an UNESCO convention, but UNESCO members have never approved a global convention on this matter. As a result, on a global scale, the GATS is unrivalled.

However, on a regional scale there are other education internationalization experiences and instruments that could clash with the GATS rules and that, unlike the free trade agreement, are driven and promoted by planners, politicians and stakeholders from the educational field. For example, the regional conventions on the recognition of qualifications promoted by UNESCO on different continents,[13] initiatives to integrate standards by the higher education accreditation agencies in the regional sphere, and initiatives for the integration and/or coordination of higher education systems such as MERCOSUR-Educativo and the European Higher Education Area.

Stabilization of a Global Higher Education Market

Free trade agreements are not necessarily the cause of the emergence of educational markets at the international level. In this chapter we have seen how the commercialization of education is promoted and carried out in the first place by the states at the margin of trade forums and trade agreements, and sometimes by the university centers themselves by using their own autonomy. The GATS and other trade agreements, however, are related directly to the stabilization and consolidation of educational markets on a global and/or regional scale.

According to Fligstein (1993), the institutions necessary for shaping the markets are ownership rights, governance structures, rules of exchange and conceptions of control. The last of these four elements has become a fundamental factor in the stabilization of the markets. By *conceptions of control* we are referring to the agreements that structure perceptions of how a particular market behaves, thus enabling the different actors in the market to interpret their own environment and act accordingly to control the situations that arise. Conceptions of control also allow business to interpret actions of others and understand the market structure (Fligstein 1993). Free trade agreements affect all the elements that shape the markets, according to Fligstein, but they particularly involve conceptions of control, and they do so in three ways. First, by reinforcing the principle of transparency. Article III of GATS forces countries to make available and public all kind of information related to the provision of services in their territory. Second, they bring *harmonization* and *standardization* of the regulatory frameworks of certain policy areas, and by doing so they order and unify the wide range of existing multinational regulations. It should be acknowledged that the existing regulatory 'melting pot' affecting services in different territories tends to be viewed as a real obstacle by transnational services providers. Third, as we saw in the previous section, free trade agreements are very effective when it comes to *fixing* and *blocking* new transnational rules to which national goverments become obliged. As set out in Article XXI of the GATS, it is very difficult for states to modify their liberalization commitments individually and at their own discretion. This guarantees respect for the principle of previsibility and the transnational service providers know that they can act within an environment that is legally stable. These three elements indicate, at the same time, that in the first place the GATS bestows and guarantees new rights to (transnational) capital, while presenting new obligations and responsibilities for the states.

Transnationalization of Higher Education

Educational internationalization is not an exclusive effect of free trade agreements. In fact it is by no means a recent phenomenon. One of the first waves of internationalization of universities took place during the colonial period, when empires such as Spain, France and Britain introduced higher education systems and institutions in their colonies. The commercialization of university services on an international scale is not new either. An example that also comes from the past is that the European medieval universities were already used to registering significant numbers of foreign students (Brock 2006).

The main novelty that free trade agreements cause in terms of foreign relations in the field of education is the acceleration of dynamics of transnationalization. The main difference between the internationalization and transnationalization of education lies not so much in the scale on which the different stakeholders are operating as in the way in which the relations between them are structured in the scale in question. The internationalization of higher education was traditionally carried out through cooperation and foreign trade relations. Universities exporting services on an international scale, or those that cooperate with universities in other countries, tended to do so within international frameworks in which the relationships are established and designed according to state borders. As van der Wende (2001) points out, internationalization entails an *interconnection* between state education systems, and is implemented in such a way that the borders and the authority of the state are not questioned. As a result, the states and, specifically, state regulations play a key role in mediating international education relations.

Transnational relations, on the other hand, are developed *through* the nations. Transnationalization consists of a series of exchange circuits for the consumption and selling of university services independently of state borders and other conditioning factors, in which the universities, lecturers and students circulate freely. In the educational field transnationalization may take place through the capacity of a university to establish branches in different countries without restrictions, to issue certificates that are automatically recognized abroad or to freely contract international teaching and research staff. The GATS is the supranational treaty that is able to exert most pressure in favor of educational transnationalization. It promotes the redefining of territories and infrastructures related to the production and consumption of services. Its system of rules also promotes independence and convergence between different state education systems, as well as shaping the common regulatory frameworks in different areas of educational policy. This means that the role of the states and of the state borders is diminished in some areas since part of the education policy regulations, which traditionally were under their scope, have become reterritorialized.

3.5 CONCLUSIONS

The GATS promotes free trade in all kind of services through the introduction of substantial changes in national and sub-national regulations. Like other bilateral or regional agreements, the GATS introduces a new regulation to the area of services, which favors free market operations and encourages new relational patterns between states and the services sector. These changes are framed in a broader transformation of the role and priorities of the state in the higher education sector, evidenced in the new scenario of economic and political globalization. By removing barriers to trade in services, the GATS contributes to higher education trends such as privatization, liberalization and commercialization.

On the other hand, the GATS promotes what we consider a new wave of transformations in the higher education field. Table 3.2 summarizes these new transformations in higher education associated with the advance of the GATS. The trade agreement is not always the only causal force acting in the different dimensions of change identified, but it is a key factor in terms of deepening their scope of influence.

Table 3.2   Education and Free Trade: A New Wave of Transformations

Higher Education Scenario	Transformations		
	Supranational educational governance	*Education markets*	*Foreign relations*
Without GATS	External influence on national education policy	Emergence of education markets	International dynamics
With GATS (and other trade agreements)	Areas of education regulation fixed on a global scale in a new international regime of educational trade	Consolidation of educational markets Conception of control (Previsibility, transparency and harmonization)	Transnational dynamic Dissolution of state borders in the production and consumption of educational services

Source: Author

Block II

GATS Results and Procedures

4 Negotiating the GATS
A Multi-Level System

The GATS negotiations are conducted under a specific set of norms, rules and procedures. In practice, they unfold in various negotiation "subsystems" ranging from local to global. The GATS negotiations are primarily a two-level process, i.e. global and national. In cases such as the European Union, the regional level is also significant due to the definition of a common negotiation position between European countries (Barton et al. 2006). At the global level, negotiations are conducted in what is called the "participant subsystem". The participant subsystem integrates the organs, procedures and actors that directly depend from the international organization. Specifically, in our case study, the subsystem is lead by the representatives from the WTO member countries that are assisted by the WTO Secretariat. The negotiations within the WTO participant subsystem are more intense and attract more media attention when General Councils or Ministerial Conferences are being held. The most significant decisions and the trade commitments of the WTO negotiation rounds are adopted in those forums. However, the negotiations at the WTO are carried out in Geneva day after day in the framework of numerous trade committees, working groups, etc.

On their part, each WTO member country constitutes a "representative subsystem" that interacts with the global participant subsystem. In the country-based representative subsystem, national preferences, interests and positions are identified and defined. In theory, trade negotiators at the WTO level will have to represent and promote these preferences, positions and national interests in the context of the principles and core beliefs represented by the international organization. The representative subsystem is conformed by country trade negotiators and trade representatives (usually coming from the trade, foreign affairs or equivalent ministries) and key stakeholders of the sectors in question (e.g. service sector regulators, service providers associations, trade unions). These actors are supposed to meet within the representative subsystem to set out national positions on various issues related to the GATS negotiations.

In the context of the GATS negotiations, additional subsystems can be identified for specific areas and at different territorial scales. For instance, in the case of education services negotiations, the international educational community (e.g. UNESCO, Education International and other education-related organizations and associations) forms a loosely-structured subsystem that also aims to influence the GATS negotiations. This indicates that international politics go beyond the sum of interactions between country subsystems and that emerging global actors, without the mediation of states and national representative subsystems, also aim to directly influence international politics. The newly acquired relevance of autonomous transnational actors means a shift from international politics to global politics. In this new recent shift in the conception of politics, the emergence of transnational civil society movements stands out. Global civil society organizations and movements are increasingly independent of national politics and borders, as maintained by the complex multilateralism theory mentioned in the introduction to this book.

As previously noted, the final decisions and agreements in the GATS context are made within the WTO participatory subsystem. However, events within the WTO are markedly influenced by interactions with other subsystems representing a broad range of often competing interests. The role of the various representative and sectorial subsystems with respect to the participatory subsystem complicates the understanding of the GATS negotiation process. Therefore, the events in each of the subsystems, as well as the interactions between the subsystems themselves, could be viewed as independent variables that are relevant to gaining an understanding of the GATS outcomes and, specifically, of the adoption of education liberalization commitments by member countries. As a consequence, taking into accounts what happens in each of the subsystems is a necessary precondition for scholars aiming to provide a comprehensive analysis of the GATS implications in the various sectors covered by the negotiations.

In the following sections that compose this chapter, we will explore each of the negotiation subsystems involved in the GATS and education negotiations. For each subsystem, the most significant stakeholders, as well as specific norms, rules and procedures that conform the agreement will be described.

4.1   GATS NEGOTIATIONS AT THE NATION-STATE LEVEL

As previously mentioned, the WTO negotiations have important ramifications and are multi-level. They are not exclusively global, as some literature seems to suggest. Key events influencing the outcomes of the negotiations occur beyond the negotiation centre in Geneva. In fact, preferences and positions on certain issues covered by the negotiations are largely defined at the national level. Among other implications, this means that the Geneva-based trade negotiators are not autonomous actors. They are "country representatives" and are tasked with carrying out nationally defined mandates. Depending on the countries involved, these mandates may be less or more flexible in relation to certain aspects of the negotiations than to others.

National mandates are theoretically defined through consultations at the state level, normally conducted by the trade ministry (or equivalent). The principal consulted parties are state representatives and regulators of the sectors affected by the liberalization negotiations. These consultations may also involve private stakeholders (e.g. businesses, service provider associations, workers representatives). This set of actors, and the relations between them, comprise what we refer to as the "representative subsystem" of negotiations at the national level. However, the political influence of this subsystem varies depending on factors such as the level of economic development. Thus, the national representative subsystem is normally less relevant in the less developed countries (LDCs). This is because the LDCs' scant skilled human resources are usually concentrated in the WTO headquarters. Moreover, their negotiators may not receive clear and strong national mandates and their connections and level of coordination with the national trade ministry are usually weak. Consequently, they have more autonomy to define their country's preferences and positions within the WTO negotiations than other countries' negotiators do.[1]

Consultation at the national level is a tedious process because, if conducted rigorously, a large number of sectorial meetings must be coordinated and very different demands and inputs must be processed. The GATS negotiations cover 12 broad service sectors, each of which represents an area in which official regulators, private providers, interest groups, trade unions and quality assurance agencies interact. Those actors may present conflicting demands and concerns in relation to the GATS. These contradictions may be intersectorial, but may also emerge within the sectors themselves. For instance, a country's education ministry may be interested in opening up the higher education system to attract foreign investment and expertise, while an association of private universities may oppose such measures in an attempt to avoid competition with foreign private providers.

Nevertheless, the consultation process is usually completed by means of "shortcuts," partly because the negotiators do not have sufficient time or human resources to develop a more in-depth process encompassing all sectors and stakeholders. As one trade negotiator from a developing country pointed out:

> [Negotiating services] is just horrible. Our team is very small and we have to participate in a lot of meetings. So it is not easy [. . .] Everybody expects you know everything; when I attend a meeting of computing services, I am supposed to understand everything and that is impossible [. . .] Most of the countries have to do more internal work because we are not doing it properly [. . .] And the world of services is so complex than nobody understands anything. In Chile, there are only 10 people who really know what the services negotiations are about (Interview Trade negotiator 17, Santiago, 2006).

Consequently, the consultation process is not as comprehensive as it was intended to be. However, a lack of resources is not the only reason for this. On occasion, the process is less participatory due to political bias and preferences. As a result, some actors are consulted more extensively ore more often than others. In fact, negotiators usually avoid consulting trade union representatives (or do so reluctantly), since the latter are normally resistant to liberalization policies, whereas tend to have closer and more harmonious relations with employers and national industry representatives. This was a common pattern detected in almost all the countries studied. Furthermore, in some cases, trade negotiators helped to organize the national services industry and taught their representatives how to structure their demands within the framework of the GATS negotiations.

Another common shortcut pertains to the rationale of the consultation. Two types of consultation rationales may be distinguished. In the first, stakeholders may be asked if they want their sector to be opened up (or to be more open) to trade within the GATS. This is referred to as "strong" consultation because stakeholders have an opportunity to address the key decisions surrounding the definition of the country's preferences. In the second, stakeholders may be asked how certain technical and regulatory aspects should be modified if trade liberalization commitments are made. In that case, the decision would be made by the trade ministry, while the decision-making power of stakeholders would be limited to secondary matters. This is referred to as "soft" consultation because the level of stakeholder participation in the core decision is low or virtually nil. In other words, the final decisions and the definition of preferences can either be centralized within the trade ministry or delegated among various interested parties.

This also means that the influence of the education ministry and other education stakeholders, such as teachers unions or university representatives, can vary significantly depending on the country and on the consultation procedure used there. In short, the procedure for defining a mandate at the national level is, in itself, a variable that may alter the outcome of the negotiations. Therefore, the level of openness (or otherwise) during the consultation process is, to paraphrase Tarrow (1994), a political opportunity that will affect the ability of education stakeholders to influence the GATS negotiations. However, it should be noted that non-state actors could also open windows of opportunity, act strategically and force the trade ministry to promote, albeit unwillingly, a more open and transparent consultation procedure.

4.2   GLOBAL CIVIL SOCIETY AND THE WTO

Participation in international networks may be useful for civil society organizations seeking to present and amplify certain demands (Tarrow 2001). As mentioned in the introduction to this book, social movements can also take advantage of certain international agreements signed by their target country, such as human rights agreements, in order to legitimize their demands and influence state behavior (Tsutsui and Wotipka 2004). This tactic is commonly known as the "boomerang effect" because local groups can have a political impact at the national level by presenting their activities and demands on a global scale (Keck and Sikkink 1998). Another group of scholars has noted that the impact of civil society on international politics is actually mediated through interactions within domestic structures (Halliday 2002).

However, a more innovative argument holds that civil society may influence global politics without the need for state mediation. Based on a recent UN classification, non-state actors are able to become active political players within international organizations in a variety of ways (UN 2007): a) dialogue; b) advocacy; c) private fundraising; d) information and learning; e) operational delivery and creation of partnerships.[2] To some extent, this classification is related to the complex multilateralism model, which maintains that multilateralism is moving away from an exclusively state-based structure and that private actors are playing an increasingly important role in multilateral structures. Indeed, this classification shows that international organizations must become more open to civil society organizations (such as NGOs or trade unions) and interact directly with them, without state mediation.

One potential implication of this new scenario is that the current international system provides for and encourages the participation of a new set of interests that are not necessarily linked to the specific national interests that predominated within the former multilateralism framework. For instance, in this context, organizations such as humanitarian NGOs and trade unions attempt to place certain topics on the international agenda from a perspective of global justice. Some also try to challenge hegemonic understanding and generalized principles such as the primacy of free markets, which are predominant within the traditional multilateral organizations (O'Brien et al 2000).

The Power of Non-State Actors

The fact that some windows of opportunity have been opened for non-state actors to influence multilateral institutions does not mean at all that these actors have attained the same status as traditional international leaders, such as governmental representatives and the staff of international organizations (Cox and Jacobson 1972). In fact, most of the modes of civil society participation contemplated in the above-mentioned UN classification do not relate to decision-making. However, decision-making capabilities are merely one face of power and, in occasions, not necessarily the most relevant one. Other faces of power consist on the agenda settlement, the settlement of the rules of the game and the definition of preferences (Lukes 2005). In the international arena, civil society actors can bring their power and influence to bear on the preferences of actors who, within the framework of international organizations, make decisions at the political level (normally the representatives of member states) or at the operative level (normally the staff of international organizations). Civil society actors can also place new topics on the organization's agenda; in so doing, they influence the decision makers' behavior and frame their policy options.

Global Civil Society Within the WTO/GATS Structure

Initially, the WTO preferred to operate as anonymously as possible in order to be more effective and to avoid expending resources on public information and public relations policies (Jiménez 2004). Nevertheless, the intensification of the protests against the organization forced it to reinforce its relations with NGOs and to become more transparent (Scholte 2000). Some authors maintain that the "Battle of Seattle" marked and inflection point and clearly forced the WTO to adopt a strategy aimed at improving its overall image (Wilkinson 2000). However, the relationship between the WTO and civil society was already contemplated in various provisions of the Marrakesh agreement prior to Seattle'99. These provisions were laid out in the "Guidelines for Arrangements on Relations With Non-Governmental

Table 4.1   WTO Relations with Civil Society

Participation form	Devices and instruments permitted and authorized by the WTO
Dialogue	· NGOs can attend ministerial conferences and annual public symposia held in the WTO headquarters. · Other spaces for NGOs are also available: lunch dialogues, electronic forums, talks with WTO representatives, etc.
Advocacy	· The WTO allows NGOs to meet with country representatives to advise them, to lobby for certain policies or to gather information on the status of the negotiations. · NGOs can distribute position papers on trade issues among the delegations or via the WTO website.
Private fundraising	· Ministerial Conferences are funded by private donors, normally large transnational corporations.[1] · Some NGOs raise private funds to help Southern countries' delegations to take part in the negotiations or certain disputes.
Information and learning	· NGOs can distribute research papers on trade issues among the delegations or via the WTO website. · The WTO organizes seminars and workshops and publishes an information newsletter for civil society organizations.
Operational delivery	-------------------------------

[1] For instance, the Seattle Ministerial Conference was entirely funded by corporations such as Microsoft and Boeing (Barlow and Clarke 2003).
Source: author

Organizations" approved in 1996. In Table 4.1, we apply the UN classification on civil society participation to the 1996 Guidelines and to other mechanisms for NGOs to interact with the WTO.

Table 4.1 shows that most of the forms of NGO participation established by the UN are recognized in the WTO participatory subsystem. The NGO participation opportunities created by the WTO could make us to conclude that the organization's transparency level is high. Nevertheless, as set out in the WTO Guidelines, there are some limitations on NGO participation. For instance, NGOs cannot be directly involved in negotiation meetings and obviously have no decision-making power with respect to the functioning of the organization (WTO 1996). In addition, much of the information relating to the negotiations is not available to NGOs because negotiators may need to maintain confidentiality for strategic reasons (WTO 2004). This could be the case for certain documents pertaining to demands and offers made by countries during the GATS negotiations.

Other authors see another limitation to the participation of Southern NGOs in the fact that most of the participation mechanisms proposed by the WTO fall under the heading of information and communication technologies (Wilkinson 2002b). However, it should be noted that traveling to Geneva to participate directly in the proceedings is a more expensive proposition for southern NGOs. Moreover, and more significantly, the WTO does not welcome all kind of NGO. On various occasions, the Director-General of the WTO and other high-level representatives have publicly voiced disapproval with NGOs that do not subscribe to the core principles of the WTO (Jawara and Kwa 2004). For instance, Peter Sutherland, GATT/WTO Director-General from 1993 to 1995, expressed the following opinion in the report marking the 10th anniversary of the WTO he coordinated:

> While many NGOs are well informed and a good number have the expertise and the interest to be constructive commentators or advisors on WTO issues, others do not. (. . .) Certainly, the Secretariat should be under no obligation to engage seriously with groups whose express objective is to undermine or destroy the WTO in its present form" (WTO 2004, 41 and 48).

In addition, Mike Moore, WTO Director-General from 1999 to 2002, once publicly stated:

> The people that stand outside [protest movements] and say they work in the interests of the poorest people. . . they make me want to vomit. Because the poorest people on our planet, they are the ones that need us the most.[3]

Both quotations reflect the WTO structural and discursive selectivity in relation to civil society participation. They also reflect that, albeit is not really surprising, actors that held very different views on which principles should govern the international regime on trade are systematically excluded by the WTO. Therefore, it seems that the WTO is open to holding discussions with civil society organizations on procedural issues or on how the current international regime should address trade-related issues; however, it does not recognize civil society organizations' right to challenge the WTO constitutive rules and core principles.

4.3 THE WTO PARTICIPATORY SUBSYSTEM: A SELECTIVE CONTEXT

The WTO professes to be a neutral forum for negotiating trade issues in which member countries make decisions autonomously. In response to critics who say that the WTO is at the root of the world's problems, the WTO representatives maintain that this kind of analysis is wrong because "essentially, the WTO is a place where member governments go to try to sort out the trade problems they face with each other" (WTO 2005a, 11). A WTO sympathizer was even more explicit during a debate in the media, saying that the WTO should not be problematized or blamed because "the WTO is [just] a table. People sit round the table and negotiate. What do you expect the table to do?" (WTO 2005a, 11).

However, the WTO is much more than a table or a neutral forum for negotiations. It is an institution and, as such, is able to shape the behavior, the ideas and the preferences of its members. Moreover, the WTO does not provide a level playing field for interacting and negotiating; at the very least, it is more level for some countries than it is for others. In actual fact, as already said in relation to civil society participation, the WTO is a selective context that prioritizes certain strategies, discourses and actors. In a nutshell, the outcomes at the WTO—such as the results of the GATS negotiations—are mediated by rules, procedures and hierarchies that prevail in the organization itself.

The WTO as a System of Rules

The trade in services negotiations within the WTO are developed within the framework of a strict system of rules that pushes for certain outcomes in pursuit of "possible and desirable" results, while ruling out results that are deemed unacceptable. The most important WTO rules for negotiating services are contained in the GATS itself, more specifically in the "Progressive Liberalization" section. Article XIX of this section reads as follows:

> Members shall enter into successive rounds of negotiations, beginning not later than five years from the date of entry into force of the WTO Agreement and periodically thereafter, with a view to achieving a progressively higher level of liberalization. Such negotiations shall

be directed to the reduction or elimination of the adverse effects on trade in services of measures as a means of providing effective market access.

Article XXI (also in the "Progressive Liberalization" section) sets out significant impediments to prevent countries from reneging on established liberalization commitments. Reading these articles reveals that the GATS rules of the game are not only about trade; they rather pertain to the promotion of a specific system of international trade: free trade. Thus, the constitutive rules and principles of the WTO/GATS seek to promote free trade on a global scale and this particular trade system is presented as a "natural kind of capitalism" that all countries must embrace (Wade 2005). There are other principles that theoretically orientate the WTO role and content, but none of them are as well established as the free-trade principle.

The methodology of the services negotiations constitutes another important set of rules that frame the GATS outcomes. The specific methodology is not fully developed within the GATS; member countries must reach a consensus on this at the beginning of each negotiation round. In the two services rounds (Uruguay and Doha), the demand-offer method was adopted. This means that each round consists of bargaining sessions in which countries make demands and offers. First, a country calls on the other countries to open up the various services sectors it is interested in. The other countries then respond to these demands by presenting lists of offers concerning the sectors they are prepared to liberalize. These lists are provisional and can be modified later on, depending on the status of the negotiations. The round concludes when all the member countries present their final and definitive lists of offers. These lists specify whether the countries will introduce liberalization commitments, as well as in which services sectors and to what degree. Until now, liberalizing a minimum number of services sectors or subsectors at the end of the round has not been compulsory, although the EU unsuccessfully attempted to change this rule at the WTO ministerial conference in Hong Kong in 2005 with a view to accelerating the liberalization process. Specifically, the EU pushed for the introduction of quantifiable benchmarks under which member countries would have been required to adopt liberalization commitments in a minimum number of subsectors each round (Khor 2006). In the end, the members merely agreed to reinforce the plurilateral approach, which enables a group of countries with common interests in a specific sector to make joint demands (Knight 2007).

It is important to note that education and the other services sectors are not negotiated independently or "one by one." They are negotiated in relation to all topics covered in the negotiation round. To provide an indication of the scope and complexity of the WTO agenda, the topics covered in the current Doha Round, in addition to services, include the following: implementation issues, non-agriculture market access, rules, intellectual property, dispute settlement, textiles, agriculture, investment, government procurement, trade facilitation, environment, electronic commerce, small economies, debt and finance, technology transfer, technical cooperation, less developed countries, special and differential treatment, subsidies, etc. (WTO 2005a). Negotiating all of these topics simultaneously and contingently is known in trade jargon as the "all-unique method." This means that offers on one topic are contingent on the average "level of ambition" of the round. From a development point of view, the all-unique method, compounded by the introduction of issues such as services, intellectual property and investment (i.e. areas in which developing countries are not very competitive), weakens the negotiating position of poorer countries. This is due in part to the fact that new negotiating fronts are opened and the poorest countries may struggle to allocate their scarce human resources. More importantly, however, the scope of the negotiations broadens and the agenda becomes unbalanced: there are more issues on the table that will require new concessions if poorer countries wish to obtain liberalization concessions from developed countries in the traditional areas where they are more competitive (such as agriculture and raw materials).

It should also be noted here that, as seen in section 4.1, the behavior of the country delegations in the WTO participatory subsystem is restricted by negotiation guidelines established at the national level. The related mandate may be more rigorous or more lax. In the latter case, the mandate is more open to the interpretation and subjectivity of the trade negotiators. However, certain sectors are deemed out-of-bounds by the countries (in the negotiators jargon, a "red-line" is drawn on these sectors). Consequently, the trade negotiators definitely know that they cannot offer this sector during the negotiations. In fact, countries such as Argentina, Brazil and Venezuela have drawn a clear red line over education during the Doha Round. As the trade representative of one of these countries stated:

> We received the plurilateral demand on education coordinated by New Zealand [in 2006], but we received the instruction from the capital [Ministry of Trade of the country] that we should not even attend the meeting. The topic has been absolutely vetoed for us" (Trade negotiator 02, Geneva, 2006).

Other Rules Affecting the Services Negotiations

Another important set of rules is not contained in the GATS itself, but may also affect the services outcomes. These are: the WTO accession rules, the dispute settlement system and the trade policy exams.

The *WTO Dispute Settlement System* is very powerful and much more effective than that of the United Nations organizations (WTO 2004). It is a key mechanism used to bring state behavior into line with free-trade prerogatives. The Dispute Settlement Body (DSB)—the main component of the WTO Dispute Settlement System—does not force members to establish liberalization commitments, but may contribute to the reinterpretation of existing commitments with a view to broadening their scope. For instance, this is what happened to the US in the gambling services case (Ortino 2006). This well-known dispute was triggered because American federal and state law restricted the economic activity of "on-line casinos" for moral reasons, as well as in an attempt to prevent compulsive gambling and to avert a monetary drain to other countries. Antigua and Barbuda, an important exporter of this kind of services, maintained that the US was reneging on its liberalization commitments and asked the DSB to create a panel to resolve the dispute. In its defense, the US initially argued that it did not liberalize this type of service. However, the panel ruled that the US GATS schedule includes specific commitments for gambling and betting services, which fall within the subsector entitled "Other recreational services (except sporting)."[4] Consequently, the US federal government and some state governments had to modify their regulations to permit this type of economic activity and services. Interestingly, this case is well remembered and has made trade negotiators very cautious when carrying out the schedules of commitments.

Global inequalities also affect the way the DSB works. For instance, some developing countries cannot initiate proceedings within the framework of the DSB because it is too expensive or because they lack technical expertise in trade dispute resolution (Kapoor 2004). For the same reasons, developing countries do not usually participate as third parties in dispute settlement proceedings. Moreover, rich countries that lose a dispute can avoid liberalization sanctions by compensating the other parties. In other words, rich countries can buy their obligations (WTO 2004), while poor countries that lose a dispute must open up their markets to trade; usually, they have no other option. Most importantly, however, North-South inequalities affect the relevance of the sanctions that are applied. If a powerful country loses a dispute against a country with a small economy, the effect of the sanctions may be negligible if the small economy is simply allowed to raise tariffs on the powerful country's exports. In contrast, if the powerful country wins and, consequently, raises the tariffs on the small country, the latter's exports could be seriously undermined.

Until now, the DSB has not dealt with education issues. In the 10-year period since the WTO was established (1995–2005), sixteen demands invoked GATS articles, although none related directly to education services. Despite the fact that there have been no education-related disputes, several interviews show that the powerful DSB is a source of concern for country representatives who are considering making commitments in services sectors that are deemed sensitive, such as education (Interviews Trade Negotiators 07 and 11, Geneva, 2006).

The WTO accession rules only affect new and prospective WTO members. Under the accession rules and procedures, prospective members must agree to extensive liberalization of services, as well as in other economic sectors. As we show in the following chapter, the accession rules have a direct bearing on the liberalization commitments of member countries. The developed countries are not affected by these rules because they are all founding members of the WTO. The new members thus lose negotiating power within the WTO because they must adopt deep liberalization measures to be granted full membership. As a result, they may have no service sectors left to bargain with.

Lastly, *trade policy reviews* are another important WTO source of influence. All member countries are subject to periodic reviews of their trade policies in all areas, including services. Once again, the evaluation criteria are oriented toward free and open trade, as well as by the previsibility principle and other guarantees for foreign providers and exporters. These criteria may influence the behavior of member countries that hope to score well on a trade policy review or, at least, to avoid being publicly denigrated (Henderson 1998).

Power Inequalities Between Countries

The WTO is aware of the internal economic inequalities of its member countries. The organization usually classifies countries based on their level of development, using the following categories: developed countries, developing countries and less developed countries (LDCs).[5] On occasion, the "transition countries" category is applied to former Communist countries, particularly in Eastern Europe.

The level of economic development conditions the negotiation process itself, as well as its potential outcomes. A number of authors have confirmed this phenomenon in relation to various aspects of the negotiations, as well as in relation to different sectors (James Smith 2004; Narlikar 2001; Hoekman and Will Martin 2001). This is in fact the case for the education liberalization negotiations. As explained in the following chapter, there is a strong correlation between the level of economic development and the establishment of liberalization commitments in the education sector under the GATS. Indeed, the development variable also has a bearing on the countries preferences and positions. This way, countries may have offensive or defensive interests within the education sector depending on their level of economic development. While LDCs usually have offensive interests in exporting primary and agriculture products, they do not in the area of education due to their lack of competitiveness in the international higher education market. For their part, developing countries usually identify interests in specific service sectors such as tourism or agricultural services or in transversal issues such as Mode 4, but not usually in education. Some developing countries are competitive in education exports at the regional level, but rarely at the multilateral one. Lastly, developed countries are interested in advancing liberalization in all services sectors, including education, because, compared with most countries, they have a clear comparative advantage in this area of the GATS negotiations.

Other authors have noted that economic inequalities between members shape the way the WTO participatory subsystem works. Within the framework of the WTO, almost all decisions are made by consensus. Apparently, this decision-making procedure is much more democratic and egalitarian than that of the World Bank or the IMF, where countries' voting power is proportional to their economic contributions to these organizations. Officially, all member countries, regardless of their economic status, have the same power within the WTO and the level of inclusiveness within the organization is high (Koenig-Archibugi 2002). However, consensus-based decision-making *per se* does not guarantee equity, internal democracy or inclusiveness. This is because not all parties have the same consensus-building capacity. Within the WTO, less developed and developing countries do not have extensive human and economic resources to defend their interests during the negotiations. For instance, only one-third of the LDCs have a permanent representative in Geneva, while the others have small delegations that are overstretched by virtue of the fact that they must take part in WTO negotiations while also representing their country in Geneva-based UN organizations and agencies (Robertson and Dale 2003, Nunn 2001). By contrast, the average number of representatives for the WTO Quad countries (US, Japan, Canada and the EU) is 16.75 (Jawara and Kwa 2004). Southern countries' delegations are struggling to keep up with the intense pace of negotiations in the current round, which covers seventeen areas, most of which are technically complex and time-consuming. In 2002, a total of 5,224 meetings were held within the framework of the Doha Round (IATP 2003). Even though these meetings were open to all members, countries' representatives of poorest countries clearly could not attend all of them.

Global inequalities also crystallize in direct power relations between member countries. Scholars have documented various common power practices, including the following:

a) Coercion and "consensus buying": When negotiations are blocked, rich countries have the option of obliging poor countries to accept certain deals by buying their preferences. For instance, rich countries may offer Southern countries access to credit, debt relief or preferential trade agreements on the condition that they support certain positions within the framework of the negotiations. In high-tension situations, blackmail and threats are commonly used by powerful countries (Jawara and Kwa 2004; Kapoor 2004; Bello 2002).

b) Exclusion: Poor countries are systematically excluded from various decision-making forums and opportunities. All WTO negotiation spaces are open to all members. However, some parallel spaces are created with the objective of speeding up decision-making on certain matters. Some of these spaces include "Green Room meetings" or mini-ministerial conferences (IATP 2003; Wilkinson 2002a). Poor countries are not usually invited to these gatherings, and developed countries are consistently over-represented.[6]

Because of reasons as these exposed here, Kapoor (2004), building on Habermas's speech act theory, concludes that the WTO does not provide a forum for an "ideal situation of speech" (i.e. conditions that would enable genuine and open deliberations between the member countries, based on equity, inclusivity, non-coercion, etc).

The Role of the WTO Secretariat

Having gone this far it seems clear that the WTO is not as neutral and inclusive as some authors and the WTO itself maintain. This section, by dealing with the role of the Secretariat, addresses another common belief about the WTO: the supposed "low level of delegation" existing within this international organization.

Following Koenig-Archibugi (2002), the level of delegation of member countries in the WTO seems to be low for two reasons. First, political decisions are made by member countries on a consensus basis. The level of delegation in an international organization is considered higher when decisions are made by a majority of votes (i.e. countries that vote against a certain decision have to accept to delegate on the policy issue affected by the decision despite this means renouncing their specific preferences and interests). Second, the WTO staff members have very restricted powers. Member states are the only stakeholders that can modify agreements and make political decisions. The staff members have no political decision-making authority; officially, they only make operative decisions and administer the countries' political decisions. This is in stark contrast with other international organizations in which bureaucrats have a higher political profile, as in the case of the IMF (Payne 2005) or the World Bank (Heyneman 2003). The WTO itself takes a favorable view of this fact:

> The WTO is different from some other international organizations such as the World Bank and the IMF. In the WTO, power is not delegated to a board of directors or the organization's head (. . .). This is quite different from other agencies whose bureaucracies can, for example, influence a country's policy by threatening to withhold credit (WTO 2005a, 101).

However, the WTO and more specifically its staff are also a source of power, much more autonomous and influential than normally stated. The WTO bureaucrat with the most responsibility and influence is the Director-General. Within the framework of the trade negotiations, he plays the role of mediator. As the rest of the staff, he does not make decisions relating to the agreements and cannot impose criteria on country members. He is supposed to be impartial, but his role is also highly political. Acting as a broker in the context of the negotiations situates him in a privileged position to push for certain agendas or to benefit certain interests. Indeed, if the Director-General only played a purely administrative role, there would be less rivalry between member countries when lobbying for candidates during the Director-General selection process.

The other Secretariat members, such as the Services Division bureaucrats are supposed to be impartial as well. Indeed, on occasions when they have issued documents that are viewed as biased by certain member countries, members have criticized them for attempting to influence the negotiation process and outcomes. Interestingly, this is what happened with a document focused on education services, as we will see in Chapter 8.

However, this does not mean that the WTO bureaucrats do not seek to influence the course of the negotiations. Far from this, the WTO staff members, who are constantly in touch with countries' representatives in Geneva, seek to proactively frame the existing debates. Because of this reason, some trade delegations have even described the Secretariat as a "third party in the negotiations" (Jawara and Kwa 2004). And, following Barton el al (2006)'s analysis, day-to-day power tends to shift between the richest member countries and the WTO staff. But, what are exactly the sources of power of the Secretariat? First, it should be acknowledged that the Secretariat provides the basic information used by members to interpret their own and their trading partners' trade practices. It also provides the institutional memory for country delegates and panel participants (Barton et al 2006). This is especially relevant in the case of developing nations with no permanent trade delegation in Geneva; for them, the Secretariat becomes the more direct source of administrative support and information.

Second, the Secretariat has more intellectual capital (information and knowledge) than most negotiators. Its knowledge and influence are activated through mechanisms such as technical assistance, training courses (normally attended by developing countries' delegations and policy-makers) or through the publication of reports, studies and other documents for the general public (press releases, newsletters, booklets on the WTO, etc.).

Third, the Secretariat's influence is brought to bear in non-formal spaces and in day-to-day practices in which subjectivity and interpretation are even more relevant than in formal spaces. For instance, its influence is exerted when they develop (or directly write) the responses and arguments provided by the various WTO councils and committees chairs, in the preparation process for most of the documents the chairs of these councils and committees sign, in the formulation of recommendations in OEPC reports, in the preparation of the Director-General's speeches, etc. However, it should be acknowleged that the influence of the WTO staff is greatest when the members' interests are not clear-cut or when the country delegates have a lower level of expertise.

In summary, the Director-General and the other WTO staff members have limited direct authority. However, they have the power of persuasion and are key information brokers during the negotiation process. In fact, it could be considered that they act as a pro-liberalization epistemic community faction embedded within the WTO itself, which gives them greater capacity and legitimacy to disseminate ideas and to teach norms on relevant political actors.

4.4   CONCLUSIONS

The GATS negotiations complex is conformed by various subsystems that are organized at different territorial scales. The WTO is one of the central subsystems of the negotiations, but not the only one. Global civil society, and national interests organized at the state level are also framing the GATS negotiations and to trying to influence their outcomes.

In this chapter we have exposed that the WTO is not a neutral forum. It is rather a selective structure and system of rules that is biased towards certain ideas, strategies and stakeholders. It favors pro-free-trade actors and ideas and discriminates against actors that view labor standards, human rights, environmental concerns and the right of states to pursue social objectives as more legitimate than trade liberalization. These rules affect both member countries and civil society organizations trying to influence the negotiations.

At the same time, global inequalities, which are not effectively addressed within the WTO system, make it easier for certain countries to defend their interests within the organization than for others. The power imbalance between member countries is clearly evident in the WTO day-to-day workings and decision-making processes. Global inequalities condition as well the interests and the positions of member countries in the different sectors being negotiated. For instance, it is unlikely that a developing country identifies market access to higher education as one of its priorities in the GATS negotiations.

Despite its small size and budget and its lack of decision-making authority, the WTO Secretariat has acquired more influence than was officially intended. The WTO staff expertise and their knowledge of the institution are key mechanisms for framing state representatives' debates and preferences during the trade negotiations. However, the Secretariat's influence is more relevant in relation to less developed countries and smaller economies.

5 State of Play and Trends of the Negotiations

Liberalization commitments are the principal outputs of the GATS negotiations. During the negotiations, the WTO members make various liberalization commitments in services sectors, which are expected to become more ambitious with each successive round. Once a negotiating round is finished, a list setting out the liberalization commitments adopted by each country (known as the "list of commitments") is appended to the GATS text and thus becomes part of the WTO Agreement.

The first commitments on education liberalization were made during the Uruguay Round (1986–1994). Currently, new service negotiations are being conducted as part of the Doha Round, which was launched in 2001 (the specific service negotiations began in 2000). Until now, many WTO members have availed themselves of the flexibility principle during the service negotiations and have not made any education-related commitments within the GATS; until 2006, only 47 of the 149 member countries have made such commitments.[1] In the wake of the Doha Round, this scenario is likely to change because several countries have announced plans to make higher education liberalization commitments. Thus far, three countries have offered to open up their higher education sectors for the first time, while three more are "improving" the higher education commitments made during previous negotiations.[2]

In this chapter, the outcomes of the negotiations for education service liberalization are analyzed and a number of tentative explanations are offered concerning the rationale behind the commitments. Using quantitative analysis, the factors relating to the number and level of the commitments are explored. More specifically, causal factors such as the member countries' degree of development or the requirements, structure and other features of their higher education systems are addressed.

We will begin by providing an overview on interpreting the lists of commitments. This is a necessary first step because the lists of commitments are the principal data source for quantitatively analyzing education commitments. Based on the structure of the lists, we have designed a new liberalization index, known as Edu-GATS, which quantifies and compares the higher education commitments made by the WTO members. Edu-GATS is also used to compare the liberalization status of higher education with that of other education subsectors.

5.1   LISTS OF COMMITMENTS AND CALCULATING EDU-GATS

The lists of commitments provide information about the degree of trade openness agreed to by the member countries in each service sector and sub-sector. In particular, the lists specify the limits that will be maintained or eliminated in the area of national treatment and market access. Additional commitments may be made, although thus far no country has done so in the education field. Moreover, commitments and limits are expressed based on the four modes of trade (cross-border supply; consumption abroad; commercial presence; movement of natural persons).

The lists are complex, not only because of the number of items they contain, but also because the logic of the various headings differs. On the one hand, the column for the service sectors uses a "positive" logic (method of positive list), i.e. the lists set out all the names of the sectors and sub-sectors that the countries have decided to liberalize. On the other hand, the columns for market access and national treatment follow a "negative" logic (method of negative list): liberalization is complete if a box is empty or an entry reads "none". On the other extreme, if an entry reads "not binding," no commitment has been acquired. However, liberalization is not "all or nothing"; it can occur gradually. If countries wish to place certain limits on liberalization, this should be specified clearly in the list. Finally, the lists include an initial heading entitled "horizontal commitments" that encompasses transversal limits, i.e. that apply to all sectoral commitments. It should be noted that the technical complexity of the liberalization commitments—compounded by confusion with respect to the WTO service categories—has led some delegations to make commitments with respect to services they never intended to liberalize (Gould 2004).

To illustrate how this logic is put into practice, Table 5.1 shows a section of a hypothetical list. Country X liberalizes its primary education subsector as follows: a) market access: no commitment in mode 1 or mode 4; total opening up in mode 2; in mode 3, it is stated that domestic capital

Table 5.1   Partial List of Commitments (Example)

5. Education services (Country X)		
	Market access	*National treatment*	*Additional commitments*
A. Primary education (Country X)	1) Unbound 2) None 3) 25% of the capital must be domestic 4) Unbound	1) None 2) None 3) None; Unbound for subsidies 4) Unbound	

Source: Author

should comprise at least 25% of the investment; b) national treatment: total opening up in modes 1 and 2; opening up in mode 3, although the foreign provider will not be entitled to receive public subsidies; no commitment in mode 4. Additional commitments are not made.

Once the logic and the structure of the lists of commitments are understood, the degree of liberalization can be calculated. As mentioned in the introduction, this calculation is used to measure and compare the higher education liberalization commitments made by the WTO members, as well as to compare the status of higher education liberalization in relation to that of other education subsectors.

This calculation also makes it possible to gauge the relevance of the above-mentioned liberalization factors at two analytical levels. At the first level, we will examine the correlation of certain explanatory factors (such as national economic development, education system characteristics and WTO accession date) with the existence—or lack—of education commitments made by the member countries. At the second level of analysis, we will examine the correlation between the same explanatory variables and the degree of commitment to education liberalization. In this regard, we will only analyze countries that have actually made commitments in the education sector. The second level also involves measuring the level of the commitment accurately. Precisely, the lack of data existing at this level led to the production of the Edu-GATS index.

Calculating Edu-GATS

When calculating Edu-GATS, the following elements are considered: a) the education subsectors in which commitments have been made; b) limits in market access and national treatment, which may vary depending on the subsectors and the four trading modes; and c) horizontal commitments, which apply to all sectoral commitments. The basic premise is that the greater the number of limits included in the lists of commitments, the lower the degree of trade liberalization.

As shown in Chapter 2, six limits may be included in terms of market access by member countries. So, according to this, the formula for calculating Edu-GATS establishes that six is the maximum of limitations. Therefore, for each subsector (y), $MAx=(6-L)/6$ (where x equals each trade mode and L is the number of limits established, including those in the horizontal commitments). Additionally, we consider that there are eight possible limits in national treatment, so $NTx=(8-L)/8$. Edu-GATS thus corresponds to the sum of both factors (see equation below). The weighted value ranges between 0 (totally closed) and 1 (totally open).

$$EduGATS = \Sigma_y(MA_x) + \Sigma_y(NT_x)$$

were $MAx=(6-L)/6$ and $NTx=(8-L)/8$

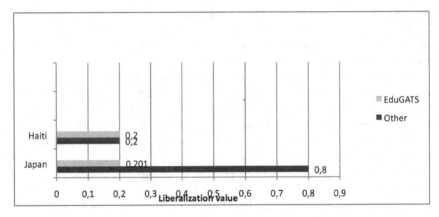

Figure 5.1   Comparison between the WTO/ OECD and the Edu-GATS method.
Source: Author

As regards the level of liberalization, Edu-GATS is a more accurate measure than the indexes used by the WTO and the OECD. In their reports on the GATS negotiations, those agencies usually refer to the number of subsector commitments as the main indicator (OECD 2002; WTO 2005c). The imprecision of this criterion becomes clear when we examine the lists of commitments from Japan and Haiti, to take one example. Japan has made commitments in four education subsectors and Haiti in one. Therefore, the WTO and OECD reports conclude that Japan's commitments are much more extensive, by a ratio of 4:1. However, Japan has included many limits in each subsector; according to our calculations, Japan's level of commitment in education has a value of 0.201. Haiti has only one commitment in the list, but it has no limit; the value of its commitment is thus 0.2. Contrary to the conclusions of the WTO/OECD, the level of commitment of the two countries is very similar (see comparison of the results of both methods in Figure 5.1).

5.2   STATUS OF HIGHER EDUCATION LIBERALIZATION

Higher education is the subsector that is facing the highest pressure to be liberalized in the GATS context. For instance, during the Doha Round, the sole multilateral request on education was focused on "Private Higher Education and Other Private Educational services."[3] This was also the only education subsector requested by the European Community during the same round (specifically, their demand was addressed to the US). However, this trend is not reflected in the current liberalization commitments

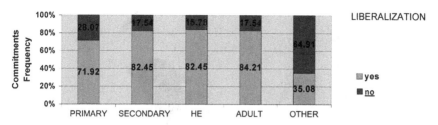

Figure 5.2   GATS and education subsector commitments.
Source: Author

undertaken within the GATS. To date, 57 WTO members have included at least one education subsector in their lists of commitments, while 48 of them have made commitments in higher education.[4] Figure 5.2 shows the percentage of subsectors liberalized by these 57 countries. As can be seen, higher education is liberalized as often as secondary education and slightly more than primary education. The "Other Educational services" category is not liberalized as extensively, probably because, as noted in Chapter 2, it is not entirely clear what types of educational services are contemplated in it. Finally, "Adult Education" is slightly more liberalized than "Higher Education."

When Edu-GATS is used to measure the level of liberalization commitments, it emerges that the level for higher education is slightly higher than the average level for all education sectors. This is the usual pattern in most of the member countries and does not depend on the level of economic development (see Appendix 1).

In the following maps, the general Edu-GATS calculation is compared with the higher education calculation for all WTO member countries. The maps show which countries have liberalized education (Figure 5.3) and higher education (Figure 5.4) within the GATS, as well as to what extent. The exact Edu-GATS value for each country is also provided in Appendix 1. The maps show that the northern countries usually have more extensive and more numerous liberalization commitments in higher education, as well as in the other education subsectors. This north-south gap is explained in more detail in the following section.

The Edu-GATS values can also be compared in terms of modes of supply and education subsectors. In this regard, as Table 5.2 shows, trade liberalization is quite constant from subsector to subsector, but not so constant among the various modes of supply. More specifically, with respect to mode 4 (movement of natural persons), commitments are less extensive than with the other modes. This reflects the fact that, within the GATS negotiations, member countries (above all richer countries) usually reject commitments that would require amendments to their immigration rules, visa requirements and other regulations relating to the international mobility of workers.

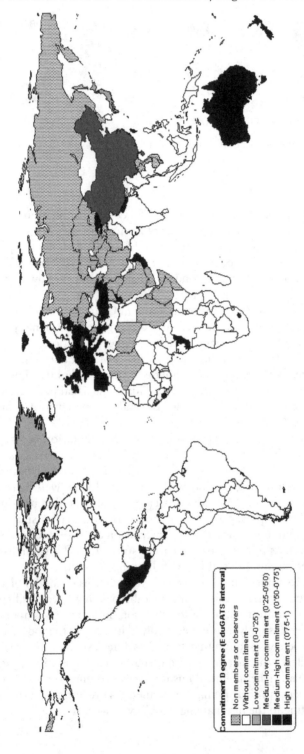

Figure 5.3   Edu-GATS for higher education.
Source: Author

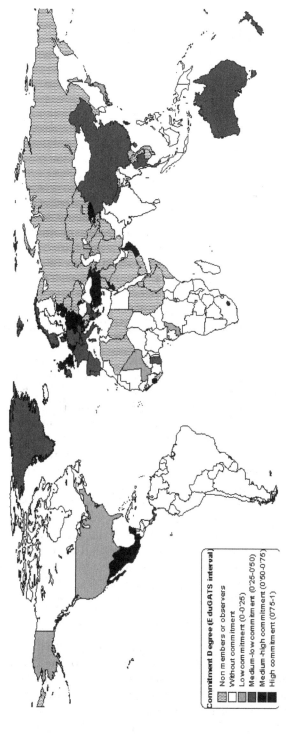

Figure 5.4 Edu-GATS for all sectors.
Source: Author

Table 5.2   GATS Education Commitments and Supply Modes (Edu-GATS Values)

	Primary	Secondary	Higher Education	Adult	Other
MODE 1	0.54	0.64	0.71	0.72	0.32
MODE 2	0.63	0.73	0.73	0.76	0.34
MODE 3	0.44	0.50	0.51	0.56	0.22
MODE 4	0.17	0.21	0.20	0.23	0.12

Source: Author

5.3   THE RATIONALE FOR LIBERALIZATION: A PRELIMINARY EXPLORATION

Most WTO members have not yet liberalized higher education and other educational services within the GATS. More specifically, after health care, educational services are the sector in which the WTO members have established the fewest liberalization commitments. The situation is very different in other service sectors under the WTO Agreement, such as the highly liberalized sectors of tourism and travel services (with commitments by 129 member countries) or financial services (with commitments by 107 countries).[5]

To understand why liberalization in education advances more slowly than in other sectors, we would do well to remember that education, health care or water supply, for example, are sectors in which the state normally plays a dominant role; they are also essential to the effective implementation of various social rights. Consequently, within the GATS negotiations, these sectors are known as "sensitive." Nevertheless, despite the fact that there are common anti-liberalization elements in all member countries, the results of the education service negotiations vary widely between them. As part of our examination of variations in the behavior of countries during the GATS negotiations, we will analyze various factors associated with the liberalization of higher education and other educational services, focusing on three factors: a) the characteristics and needs of national education systems; b) the degree of economic development; and c) the WTO accession date.

a)   Influence of Education System Characteristics

In this section, the influence of specific characteristics of national education systems is contrasted with the number and level of the liberalization commitments. This relationship is referred to occasionally in the existing literature (see Knight, 2002; Larsen et al, 2004; Mundy and Iga, 2003). More specifically, the variables we will consider are the private funding of education (e.g. family outlays); state subsidies to the private sector; the private sector's enrolment share; and foreign student flows (i.e. import rates of higher educational services within mode 2). The data and indicators used to measure these variables are derived from the OECD (2001) and UNESCO (2006).

Based on our statistical analysis, only two of the aforementioned variables correlate to some degree with liberalization: the private sector's enrolment share and state subsidies to the private sector. This correlation is only identified in the area of higher education; there is no correlation for the other education levels. As shown below, both factors are associated with the number of education commitments. However, they do not correlate with the degree of these commitments.

As shown in Figure 5.5, the greater the private sector's relative importance, the fewer the education commitments. This could be because governments believe that domestic education supply (public as well as private) is sufficiently high and thus feel it unnecessary to facilitate the participation of foreign suppliers in their national education systems within the GATS. Another plausible explanation is that, due to its relative importance, the private sector can lobby governments not to liberalize education within the GATS, thereby minimizing competition with foreign suppliers. In this regard, (Mundy and Iga 2003) and Bassett (2006) have noted that private universities in the US constitute a very active and effective lobby group, particularly when it comes to exerting pressure on the US Trade Representative not to liberalize the higher education sector.

As shown in Figure 5.6, countries that provide more subsidies to the private sector make fewer education commitments. This correlation may indicate that countries that heavily subsidize their domestic private sector

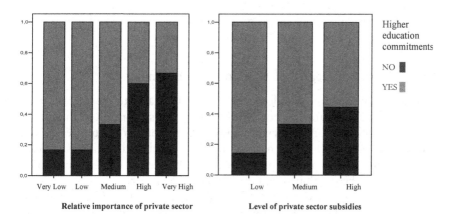

Figure 5.5 Commitments in relation to the relative importance of the private sector.

Figure 5.6 Commitments in relation to state subsidies to the private sector.

Source: Author

are not willing to apply the same standard of generosity to foreign institutions. Again, pressure might be brought to bear if the private sector is biased towards non-liberalization because it is unwilling to share state funding with foreign suppliers.

On the other hand, no correlation exists between imports of higher educational services and liberalization commitments within the GATS. Some countries facilitate multilateral education flows because they have adopted a strategy of capacity-building by attracting expertise and knowledge from abroad. They could thus use the GATS and other trade forums to reinforce this capacity-building process. This seems to be the case for China and Malaysia (Larsen et al, 2004; Zhang, 2003). Nevertheless, our statistical analysis shows that this policy or intention could not be attributed to most of the countries. The implementation of this strategy may be more frequent in developing countries, although we found that the lack of correlation between education imports and GATS commitments is found in all countries, regardless of economic development level.

Moreover, private education funding does not appear to be statistically related to the level of education liberalization in the countries studied. This is at odds with the findings of Mundy and Iga (2003), who maintain that there is an inverse relationship between education liberalization within the GATS and public education spending. They explain this apparent paradox by observing that countries with higher liberalization commitments (which are, very often, developed European countries) are "relatively confident of their national ability to buffer dislocations to educational systems caused by the liberalization" (pp. 312). However, when Edu-GATS is applied, this statistical relationship is not as significant in relation to the education sector in general or to higher education in particular. This divergence from Mundy and Iga's findings stems from the different methods used and, more specifically, from the way of liberalization commitments were measured.

b)   Influence of Degree of Economic Development

The degree of economic development is strongly related to the liberalization commitments of countries, both in the education sector and in the higher education subsector. As shown in Figure 5.7, the Southern countries, which encompass both developing nations and less developed countries (LDCs) are less willing to establish commitments in the area of higher educational services than the developed and transition countries are.[6]

As previously noted, the GATS could be perceived by Southern countries to be a suitable mechanism for attracting direct investment and expertise to their education systems, especially higher education, which is usually under funded by the state. In other words, the GATS could become a "market solution" aimed at solving state investment and

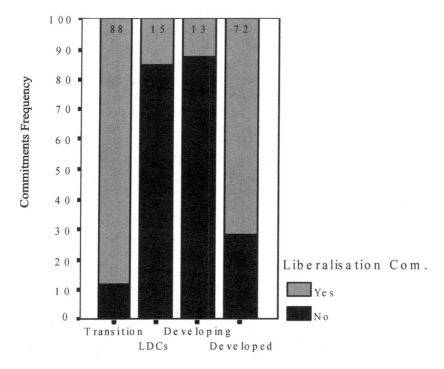

Figure 5.7 Higher education commitments in relation to economic development.
Source: Author

expertise in higher education. So why are southern countries much more reluctant to make liberalization commitments for higher education and other educational services than northern countries are? Various factors could account for this. Based on GATS and education literature, it could be argued that southern countries perceive that opening up their education systems is associated with threats and drawbacks rather than benefits.

First and foremost, it should be noted that the developing countries are almost always net importers of higher education (OECD 2002; OECD 2006). Consequently, education institutions in many of these countries not only have great difficulty accessing global education markets, but trade liberalization may also shut out of their own markets due to foreign competition (Aboites 2004; Rodríguez Gómez, 2004; Barrow et al, 2003). Additionally, southern countries should be aware that trade liberalization as envisaged in the GATS may introduce considerable complexity into the area of domestic regulation and education financing (Malo 2003), in addition to imposing limitations to state regulation. In fact, developing countries do not usually have suitable legal and technical mechanisms in place to evaluate the quality of international (or domestic) higher educational services. The internationalization of education in many southern countries has led to the proliferation of "diploma mills" (Carnoy 1999a; García-Guadilla 2002), indicating the low quality of the services provided. Furthermore, some southern countries associate GATS commitments with a potential exacerbation of their ongoing "brain drain," a problem that is usually more acute for poor countries than for rich ones (Knight, 2003; Wende, 2003). These and other arguments on the implications for development of the GATS are addressed in detail in Chapter 6.

Nevertheless, developing countries are not always less reluctant to embrace trade in the education sector. If Edu-GATS is combined with the "modes of supply" and the economic development variables, it emerges that mode 4 (movement of natural persons) is the only one for which the developed countries are less "open to trade," as shown in Figure 5.8. This is largely due to the fact that rich countries view mode 4 commitments as incompatible with their existing immigration policies (Saner and Fasel 2003). In contrast, mode 4 is precisely where many southern countries would like to see more progress: they view their comparative advantage in the trade in services as lying primarily in exports of "human resources" (UNCTAD 2005). More specifically, the interest of southern countries in this trade mode stems from the income they receive from foreign remittances (Shashikant 2005).

However, in the wake of the Doha Round, the existing North-South gap in the liberalization commitments may diminish. Even though this Round is ongoing, most of the WTO member countries have submitted their initial offers in the services area. Based on these offers, a number of developing countries such as Pakistan, Korea, India, Peru, Colombia, Singapore and Bahrain appear willing to open up their higher education sectors to global trade.

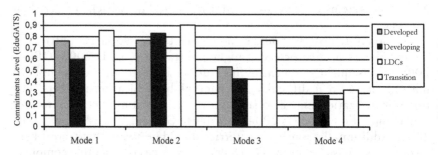

Figure 5.8   Edu-GATS in relation to modes of supply and economic development.
Source: Author

c) WTO Accession Date

Most of the WTO member countries with existing education liberalization commitments made them during the Uruguay Round, which was the first round of negotiations contemplating services. In that Round, 28 countries opted to liberalize their education sector to a greater or lesser extent. At present, although the second round of service negotiations is still ongoing, 47 countries have made liberalization commitments in education. This increase may be due to the fact that, at any given moment, member countries may add new commitments to their lists, regardless of the outcome of the negotiations. Nevertheless, we must also bear in mind that the number of WTO members was lower during the Uruguay Round than it is today. More specifically, only 76 countries were WTO members on the day it was founded (January 1, 1995), while the number of members currently stands at 153 (July 23, 2008). Therefore, membership has doubled over the past 13 years.

These data made us aware of the fact that the countries that joined the WTO after the Uruguay Round have liberalized their education sectors more extensively than the founding members have. And, indeed, once the calculations were done, it could be observed that the countries that joined the WTO at a later date have made more (and more intensive) education commitments.

This correlation is due to the fact that, under the WTO accession rules, countries that wish to become full members must agree to apply a large-scale package of liberalization measures. Article XII of the Marrakesh Agreement states that any state (or customs union) "may adhere to this Agreement in conditions that are considered appropriate by the WTO." In

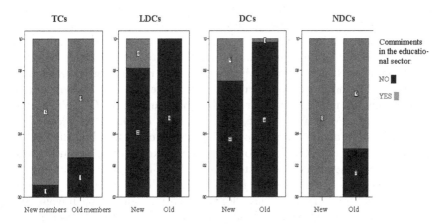

Figure 5.9   Number of commitments in relation to WTO accession date.
Source: Author

practice, this means that when a country applies for full WTO membership, a working group is set up to evaluate its trade policies and to specify the sectors that must be liberalized. This working group is made up of delegates from existing member countries. Normally, these delegates pressure the candidate country to liberalize sectors in which their own countries have offensive interests. Hence, the accession process is not established *ex ante*, but as almost all of the activity at the WTO boils down to negotiations. Once negotiations have been finalized between the candidate country and the working group, a draft accession protocol is submitted to the WTO Ministerial Conference, which has the competences to accept or reject the application (Suranovic 2005).

In short, under the WTO accession rules, most new members, at the time of joining, were externally pressured to liberalize various sectors of their economy, particularly services.[7] So, based on this statistical analysis, it seems that liberalization in the education service sectors depends as much on institutional and extra-educational factors (e.g. the WTO accession rules) as on education-related strategies of countries.

5.4 CONCLUSIONS

In this chapter, we have determined that, within the GATS framework, higher education has been liberalized at a very similar level as the other education sectors have been. Trade flows are largest in the higher education subsector and, consequently, that is where trade liberalization pressures and demands are more intense. Nevertheless, until now, these pressures have not been reflected in the number or in the level of the liberalization commitments by member countries.

This chapter also proposes a number of preliminary responses to our core research question. More specifically, we have explored the correlation between several factors (e.g. public spending on higher education, relative importance of the private sector, national economic development) with the GATS results in the education sector. As regards liberalization factors, three main conclusions emerge. Firstly, contrary to common assumptions in the GATS and education literature, certain features of higher education systems are not statistically related to the results of the GATS negotiations (at least not in a way that can be globally extrapolated). Secondly, the north-south divide is an important factor for understanding the GATS education outcomes. Rich and poor countries alike perceive common risks in liberalizing their education sectors under the WTO Agreement, although developing countries most likely face additional threats. This may explain why so many southern countries adopt a defensive attitude when negotiating education liberalization and why there is a significant gap between the commitments of northern and southern countries in this regard. However, and thirdly, factors that are apparently unrelated to the discussion over education issues have a significant correlation with the liberalization of education, particularly the WTO adhesion rules.

Still, many questions remain to be answered. In the chapters that conform the following block, we will provide a more complex and comprehensive explanation of education liberalization within the GATS. In meeting this challenge, we will need to analyze new data and, most importantly, penetrate into the "black box" of the negotiations.

Block III

Inside the Negotiations

6   GATS and Education
The Passionate Debate

The GATS has generated an intense and passionate debate in the education field (Williams 2003; Birtwistle 2006). A review of the existing GATS literature shows that the education service sector has generated the most controversy within the WTO. The education stakeholders in the debate (university associations, teachers unions, education researchers, etc.) have adopted critical positions accusing the trade agreement of interfering in education policy. Although these stakeholders remained silent when education was brought into the new international trade regime during the Uruguay Round, they finally spoke out during the Doha Round. Despite this delayed reaction, they have played a key role in carrying the "GATS education debate" into the public sphere.

One of our research objectives is to determine whether this debate has influenced the participatory subsystem of the GATS negotiations at the WTO level and, consequently, whether it has had any impact on the GATS outcomes. However, gaining an understanding of the debate (i.e. its core issues and content) is a first and necessary step toward determining its political relevance. That is why this chapter focuses on systematizing the ideas, arguments, causal beliefs and principles that shape the GATS education debate.

6.1   THE MAIN FOCUSES OF THE DEBATE

In our exploration of the GATS and education debate, we identify a broad set of ideas. These ideas provide keys to understanding competing positions in the education liberalization negotiations that, to some extent, could contribute to the definition of interests and positions of countries negotiating the GATS. First and foremost, the ideas under debate could help policy-makers assess the costs and benefits of education liberalization by establishing causal relations between the GATS and its consequences for education systems. This sort of ideas is kown as causal beliefs (Goldestein and Keohane 1993). However, political and public debates are also shaped by somewhat less objective than causal beliefs or scientific ideas, such as principled beliefs. Principled beliefs are usually influential when are associated with certain doctrines or political ideologies. For instance, in case of uncertainty over a new policy issue, the criterion for a political party to make a decision or to adopt a position over this issue could be to adopt the position/decision that resounds better in its broader ideological corpus.

The GATS and education debate, like most political debates, has two main dimensions: one is explanatory and the other is proposal-oriented. The issues identified within the explanatory focus are as follows: a) the right to regulate; b) education and development; c) education access; d) education quality; and e) education concepts. The proposal-oriented or prognostic dimension offers recommendations on how to address the issues perceived as problematic (Della Porta and Diani 1999). Each issue is addressed from different "meaning repertoires." Meaning repertoires can be defined as patterns of explanation that emerge within the processes of production of meaning and become key elements for individuals seeking to understand the world and assign a meaning to reality (Parker 1992). Usually, at least two meaning repertoires are identified for each issue in the GATS and education debate. One is critical with respect to the implications of the GATS for education, while the other provides a positive interpretation of the effects of the Agreement.

Relevant data sources to do this analysis include articles in academic journals, as well as reports, newsletters and websites produced by international organizations and civil society groups.

6.2   EXPLANATORY DIMENSION: HOW THE GATS AFFECTS EDUCATION

The Right to Regulate

According to Gilpin, one of the core issues of the international political economy is the persistent clash between the increasingly interdependent international economy and the efforts of the states to maintain economic independence and political autonomy (Gilpin 1987). States, including free-trade proponents, are often forced to manage this contradiction since they know that promoting trade liberalization means having to give up some of their political autonomy. This tension is particularly relevant to the liberalization of services because state regulations must be modified or eliminated to a much greater extent than in other economic sectors; limits are also placed on the ability of the states to bring in new regulations covering a broad range of policy issues. Within the GATS negotiations (in both the liberalization and the domestic regulation negotiations) this is known as the "policy space" dilemma.

a) Policy Space Restriction

The critical literature emphasizes that the GATS drastically restricts ability of the states to regulate education and, in particular, to promote social and equity policies within the education field.

> From the point of view of education policy, these so-called obstacles to trade are more appropriately understood as domestic policy instruments that could reasonably be required to meet legitimate educational policy objectives. Regulations governing joint partnerships and local hiring, for instance, could be required to ensure that programs have an appropriate level of Canadian content (. . .) Negotiating GATS rules to remove and reduce these 'obstacles' as the US proposes would increasingly restrict the ability of governments to regulate in the educational sector. (Grieshaber-Otto and Sanger 2002, 81).

The most commonly cited GATS article within such critical literature concerns domestic regulation (Article VI). By some accounts, the results of the Working Group on Domestic Regulation may be especially intrusive in several areas of education regulation. Jane Kelsey (2003) contends that Article VI initially states that the GATS guarantees "the right of members to regulate," even though its content paradoxically focuses on the negation of this right. Education International, that is the biggest international federation of teachers unions, has been one of the first agents to denounce the implications of these disciplines for state policy space:

- Proposed domestic regulation disciplines would unduly interfere with the right of governments to enact regulations governing the provision of education. It is simply not acceptable that judgments about the quality of education be subject to second-guessing by WTO dispute panels.
- In general, applying a necessity test to domestic regulations ignores the reality of how educational regulations and regulations in all sectors are developed. Rules and standards are developed through compromises that impose neither the greatest burden nor the least burden on service providers. Requiring all regulations to be the least burdensome would limit both the content and the process for democratic decision-making.
- Requirements that regulations be based on objective criteria also raise important concerns. That's because many legitimate regulations are often based on "subjective" judgments about the quality of a service (EI 2006, 4).

Other observers focus their criticisms on the potential implications of Article VII of the GATS concerning recognition. For instance, van Ginkel and

Rodrigues Dias (2006) maintain that this article means a step backwards in the traditional system of equivalencies that establishes that each university, wherever they may be located, provide diplomas based on programs with identical content and structure worldwide. Moreover, the equivalency standards set out minimum requirements, thus fostering mediocrity rather than excellence in addition to undermining creativity and innovation (van Ginkel and M. A. Rodrigues Dias 2006). A similar concern has been raised by regional university associations, which belief that GATS could contravene regional recognition agreements established within the framework of UNESCO (EUA 2002).

Another concern relates to the GATS ability to block liberalization commitments. This means that, after adopting this sort of commitments, a specific government education policy could become a permanent state policy (Fredriksson 2004). The WTO's powerful dispute settlement system and other disciplinary mechanisms, such as necessity tests (a focus of ongoing debate), are also called into question because of their interference in states' regulatory capacity:

> The problem is that the possibility for government to regulate service activities is considerably reduced by the GATS. Governments' measures that affect trade in services are subject to a strict necessity test that will apply to a wide range of domestic regulations. Therefore, under the GATS, certain public policies aimed at the promotion of social or educational objectives would be prohibited because they "affect trade" and are not strictly necessary to the maintenance of the education system. The real issue is that the GATS has operated a transfer of democratic governmental authority from the state to the WTO. Indeed, the burden of the proof lies on the government. If a governmental measure is challenged in the WTO system, the government will have to demonstrate that the measure was strictly necessary, and that it does not constitute a barrier to trade. Then, "the delicate responsibility for balancing the public interest with commercial considerations" would be transferred "from elected governments representatives to appointed tribunals or WTO panels." (Devidal 2004).

b)   GATS Upholds Regulatory Capacity of Countries

In various occasions, the WTO services division has rejected the above-mentioned criticisms of policy space issues:

> Commitments to liberalize do not affect governments' right to set levels of quality, safety, or price, or to introduce regulations to pursue any other policy objective they see fit (WTO 2001, 35).

The GATS preamble recognizes the "right of Members to regulate, and to introduce new regulations, on the supply of services within their territories in order to meet national policy objectives and, given asymmetries existing with respect to the degree of development of services regulations in different countries, the particular need of developing countries to exercise this right." Indeed, scholars who are skeptical with respect to the policy space implications of the agreement usually cite the preamble:

> This concern [GATS effects on policy space] does not take into account the fact that the rights to regulate in order to meet national policy objectives are recognized explicitly in the preamble to the Agreement. It also ignores the flexibility of the GATS, in that members retain full freedom to choose not only the sectors and modes of supply for which they want to make market-access commitments, but also to determine the content of those commitments and the scope of retained restrictions (Larsen, Martin, and Morris 2002, 863).

Other scholars go one step further in asserting that concerns over regulatory capacity implications are based on misunderstandings (Johnston 2002; Chanda 2003, Saner and Fasel 2003). Most of the time, these authors argue that countries are free to decide whether or not they want to make commitments. Therefore, if the GATS limits countries' regulatory capacity in certain areas and sectors it is because they have accepted it voluntarily and because they believe that the adopted commitments will benefit them.

> It is certainly true that, as with any other legally bound undertaking in the WTO (or any other international treaty), the GATS can affect the regulatory conduct of member countries. Yet countries accept such disciplines because they deem them necessary to reaping the full benefits from international co-operation in a rules-based system. The GATS affords WTO members considerable flexibility in this regard. For only those sectors, sub-sectors and modes of supply where a WTO member agrees to schedule liberalization commitments and where exceptions from the most-favored-nation treatment obligation have not been taken, what that country ultimately accepts to do under GATS is to not make its regulatory regime more restrictive in future (subject to trade concessions or retaliatory measures of commercially equivalent effect if a country decides, as it always can, to renege on its commitment) (Sauvé 2002a, 16).

GATS and Development

Development concerns have also been at the forefront of the GATS education debate. The fact that education is perceived as a strategic resource for development for Third World countries has added fuel to the controversy over the relationship between trade agreements and education.

a)   *The Unequal Exchange in Education*

Some critics warn that the GATS will exacerbate global trade inequalities in the education field. The world's centers of production and distribution of knowledge, as well as the main transnational education corporations, are all based in the rich countries. Consequently, in a context of expanded and liberalized trade in education on a global scale, Southern countries will become increasingly passive receptors of education trade flows (Rodríguez Gómez 2003; Rodríguez Gómez 2004; Schugurensky and Davidson-Harden 2003):

> Open markets, at least in higher education, reinforce the inequalities that already exist. If educational borders are completely open, the strongest and wealthiest education providers will have unrestricted access. Countries and institutions that cannot compete will find it difficult to flourish. This means that developing countries and smaller industrialized nations will be at a considerable disadvantage. Local academic institutions will find it difficult to compete with providers that choose to set up institutions in their country. A new treaty that will have the power to force countries with quite different academic needs and resources to conform to strictures inevitably designed to serve the interests of the most powerful academic systems and corporate educational providers only breeds inequality and dependence (Altbach 2002, 5).

The comparative advantage of Northern countries in the education sector could affect Southern higher education systems in various ways. Firstly, it could jeopardize the development of domestic higher education institutions because the supply chain would be increasingly dominated by transnational providers (EI 2003). In other cases, local institutions might be taken over or acquired by transnational competitors (Aboites 2004; Rodríguez Gómez 2004). Secondly, a trend toward a Western-driven homogenization of education content, language and other codes could emerge on a global scale (Robertson et al 2002).

> Transnational initiatives share in the South-to-North dynamic. They are almost without exception dominated by the partner institution in the North—in terms of curriculum, orientation and sometimes the teaching staff. Frequently, the language of instruction is the language of the dominant partner, very often English, even if the language of instruction in the country is not English. There is often little effort to adapt offshore programs to the needs or traditions of the country in which the programs are offered (Altbach 2004a, 24).

A third potential impact is brain drain (Altbach 2002; Didou 2000; Chandrasekhar 2006; Reichert and Tauch 2003).

> Since many teachers and researchers want to move to countries with more favorable working conditions and salaries, there is real concern that the most-developed countries will benefit from this mobility of education workers. (Anandakrishnan 2004, 19)

Finally, various scholars have pointed out that the GATS could exacerbate regulatory problems in Southern countries (Naidoo 2007). This is because higher education regulatory frameworks are usually less robust or less adapted to the new global environment in these countries (García-Guadilla, 2003: 26). Therefore, Southern countries could face difficulties in seeking to control foreign education provider activities, quality standards or the duration of foreign investments. This regulatory vulnerability could lead to the proliferation of low-quality educational services, primarily affecting students from Southern countries (Pillay 2003). García-Guadilla (2003) wonders how certain developing countries will regulate the excesses of the for-profit international education market when they have been unable to control the excesses of national private providers that offer very low-quality services. Other scholars point out that if business are not as profitable as expected in developing countries, foreign providers will relocate, leave the country and renege on their commitments to local students (Bhushan, 2006).

b)   The GATS Favors Education in Development Contexts

The GATS preamble states that the Agreement seeks "to facilitate the increasing participation of developing countries in trade in services and the expansion of their service exports including, *inter alia*, through the strengthening of their domestic services capacity and its efficiency and competitiveness." This statement is reiterated in Article IV. Together with the liberalization flexibilities, these points have led some authors to conclude that the GATS is the most "development-friendly" of all the Uruguay Round treaties (Sauvé 2002, 3).

Other authors argue that the GATS could lead to improvements in the higher education systems in low-income countries for various reasons. Firstly, it will free southern countries from having to invest public funds in higher education. Consequently, they will be able to use their limited budgets for basic education (Pillay 2003; Allport 2003; Sanyal and Michaela Martin 2005). Secondly, the increase of trade in education flows in mode 3 will reduce the risk of brain drain because students will be able to study at a "foreign" university without actually having to go abroad (Larsen and Vincent-Lancrin 2002). Thirdly, southern countries will have a broader higher education offer and will attract foreign expertise to their higher education systems; consequently, they will accumulate higher-quality human capital, enabling them to meet the challenges of the knowledge economy (Barrow, Didou, and Mallea 2004; WTO 2001; OECD and WB 2007).

> Reform of public universities may be difficult to introduce or sustain without external pressures. Creating a new domestic institution, public or private, that can bring in international best practice in curricula, teaching methods, research, governance and financing is often not possible with domestic resources alone. Branch campuses or the creation of international universities in partnership with foreign universities are options that can have considerable spill-over effects (Bashir 2007, 80).

Access and Rights to Education

The third focus of the debate concerns the tension between education as a tradable private good and education as a basic human right. GATS critics maintain that the trade agreement could jeopardize the achievement of the Education For All targets (Vanlathem 2003) and could increase education inequalities (EI and PSI 1999; Duff 2006; Varoglu and Wachholz 2001). However, GATS supporters maintain that the Agreement could improve education opportunities around the world. In the following section, we address the arguments advanced by both sides.

a)   GATS Privatizes Education

Private-sector higher education providers are usually profit-oriented. Consequently, if the state does not force or encourage them, they will not attempt to achieve social objectives of their own accord. According to the critical literature, the GATS will alter the balance between private and public interests in favor of the former because it limits state regulatory capacity to promote the latter. The GATS also seeks to ensure that education supply and demand are regulated according to market criteria. This makes it difficult to treat education as a public good since a public good should have two key constitutive features: 1) non-rivalry as regards consumption (i.e. increased consumption of educational services by one individual does not reduce accessibility or opportunities for another) and 2) non-excludability (nobody can be denied access to the service) (Taylor 1995, quoted by Vlk 2006, 18).

> GATS considers government monopolies to be a barrier to service trade. Many nations have systems of higher education that are largely, if not exclusively, a governmental function. Strict adherence to the principles of full service liberalization could make abandoning governmental monopolies of higher education an imperative, leading the way to substantial privatization and withdrawal of government support from public institutions of higher education (NEA 2004, 28).

The GATS only guarantees the rights of transnational service providers (Kachur 2003; Kelsey 2003) whereas the right to education and other basic human rights are completely ignored (Devidal 2004). Fredriksson (2003) finds it ironic that if a child lacks access to education—even though education is considered a basic human right—there is nowhere for that child to seek redress.[1] However, if the education industry faces trading barriers, the GATS will provide the legal right to seek and receive compensation. Katarina Tomasevski, who was the Special Rapporteur on the Right to Education of the UN Commission on Human Rights between 1998 and 2004, also pointed out to a similar contradiction.

> While the WTO Agreements provide a legal framework for the economic aspects of the liberalization of trade, they focus on commercial objectives. The norms and standards of human rights provide the means of providing a legal framework for the social dimensions of human rights. . . . A human rights approach to trade liberalization emphasizes the role of the State, not only as negotiator of trade rules and setter of trade policy, but also as duty bearer for human rights. (HCHR 2002, 10; see also Tomasevski 2005).

The GATS could also affect public funding of education. In the worst-case scenario predicted by GATS critics, all public subsidies to education would be removed because they would be considered barriers to trade (Worth 2000). In another and more feasible scenario, international private providers and national providers would benefit from the same regime of subsidies due to National Treatment commitments. This could generate a sort of magnet effect, both for foreign providers and foreign students, thereby pressuring states to cut the level of education subsidies (Beker 2004; Knight 2007).

> Given that GATS is about securing the conditions for creating and expanding private markets in the education services area, whenever governments operate in what is—or potentially could be—a market, their actions are barriers to the creation of private markets and therefore need to be controlled. Included in the challenge to government monopolies is the notion that government-funded institutions are given unfair advantages through either direct subsidies or cross-subsidization within an institution. These subsidies would either have to be removed or applied to the private sector as a matter of equal and fair treatment (Robertson et al 2002: 488).

This scenario would also have negative effects for areas of knowledge that attract small numbers of students or that are less relevant to the economy. In a bid to circumvent certain obligations derived from GATS, some countries might introduce a demand-based funding model, replacing the supply-based model. This could mean a drain on resources for certain low-er-demand courses and programs such as philology, the humanities, etc. (Scherrer 2005).

In a parallel scenario, a state could take advantage of the increased presence of private providers to gradually reduce direct funding of higher education. In this scenario, the public supply would diminish and prices would follow market criteria (PCTW 2003). In this context, the higher education system would become increasingly dual (Devidal 2004).

Finally, other authors maintain that the GATS could undermine the implementation of affirmative action policies aimed at improving access to higher education for minorities or disadvantaged groups. For instance, the South African education minister stated publicly that he was opposed to the GATS for this very reason (Santos 2004).

b) Increased Supply and Higher Investment

This repertoire of meaning refutes the concept of GATS as a privatization device. Again, the GATS text itself becomes the main tool for denying that the Agreement forces countries to privatize or cut public expenditure on education:

> Governmental services are explicitly carved out of the agreement and there is nothing in GATS that forces a government to privatize service industries. In fact the word "privatize" does not even appear in GATS. Nor does it outlaw government or even private monopolies (WTO 2001, 35).

As with the "right to regulate" issue, some scholars react to GATS critics by refering to the flexibility of the Agreement (Sauvé 2002; Knight 2002) (WTO 2002a):

> The second reason why the GATS does not jeopardize the public funding of higher education is more fundamental: countries are free to lay down as many restrictions as they wish with regard to the liberalization of a service sector. So nothing can compel a country to finance domestic and international students and institutions in a non-discriminatory way if it does not wish and is not committed to do so (Larsen and Vincent-Lancrin, 2002: 21).

A more drastic defensive argument holds that certain education community concerns are unfounded because, basicly, public services are not within the scope of the WTO, This idea was at the center of the following WTO press release:

> The GATS explicitly excludes government services from its scope and there is no question of changing those rules. The negotiating guidelines

explicitly stress that each Member Government has the right to choose the sectors it wishes to liberalize. Government services supplied on a non-commercial basis by each of the 144 WTO Member Governments are explicitly excluded from the scope of the negotiations. This is a principle to which all Member Governments attach great importance and which none has sought to reopen," said Ambassador Jara. (. . .) The Director-General added that the liberalization of governmental segments of sectors such as health and education has never come up in the discussions between governments. Even the liberalization of the commercial segments of such sectors has received little attention in the negotiations, he said. The focus of the negotiations has been on other services sectors (WTO 2002b).

Other pro-GATS scholars, in addition to refuting the critics, maintain that the trade agreement opens opportunities for improving higher education systems around the world. The transnational higher education industry and the GATS can help to solve problems in countries with overcrowded public education or where higher education is elitist and exclusive (Czinkota 2006). Specifically, the GATS will broaden access to higher education, above all in low-income countries. This is because education liberalization under GATS will lead to a broader offer of degrees and other higher education programs at no cost to the state. The elimination of trade barriers and the previsibility guaranteed by the GATS combine to create a favorable environment for private education companies and encourage them to invest abroad (Mattoo and Rathindran 2001). Moreover, commercial presence (mode 3) can democratize access to international education because it is cheaper for poor families to send their children to foreign universities in their own country than it is to send them abroad.

> Emerging nations, together with marginalized communities who have been excluded routinely from the benefits of higher education can achieve the most rapid gains from the global liberalization of the sector. Just think of detained juveniles in Malaysia who can now enroll in distance learning by universities, sit for tests by mail and be paroled early; or Native Americans who can take classes on their reservations; or any conditions in developing countries where culture or costs have constrained higher learning (Czinkota 2006: 158).

Finally, these scholars also maintain that competition between providers will also increase as a result of increased education liberalization. Consequently, education prices will go down and education will become more accessible.

> Attracted by new sources of profit, new private providers of post-secondary education services are expected to enter the market for educational

services and step up competition. In theory, keener competition should bring down costs as resource use becomes more efficient and less successful institutions leave the market. It should also bring down the cost of post-secondary educational services for those who fund them, including governments and students. (Larsen and Vincent-Lancrin 2002, 22)

Education Quality

The transnationalization of higher education has raised new concerns over education quality and fuelled debate over new challenges with respect to quality assurance. Education quality is considered of paramount importance all over the world. Low-quality educational services can have serious implications for students' future professional careers. However, it is not so easy to define what "good-quality education" is or is not, and evaluating these aspects is usually a highly subjective undertaking. The explosion of new degrees offered by foreign providers or virtual providers on an international scale and the emerging regulatory role of the GATS in this area have introduced new variables into an already complex debate.

a)   GATS Damages Education Quality

GATS critics believe that the Agreement and the specific model of education transnationalization that it promotes jeopardize education quality for several reasons. Firstly, according to the liberal theory of trade that underpins the WTO principles, the comparative advantage theory, the most efficient providers will succeed in an international free market. This means that service providers that aim to be competitive in the global education market will be forced to rationalize their resources (Kelsey 2003). When education is governed by efficiency measures alone, quality is affected because teachers are poorly paid, technology is obsolete, laboratories and libraries are substandard, etc.

Secondly, the liberalization promoted by the GATS could undermine government efforts to control the quality of new international or virtual education providers. A significant number of countries, primarily in the developing world, do not have adequate regulatory frameworks to assess and control education quality. In general, the number of substandard education providers and the number of diploma mills has increased drastically in recent years. Above all, this has occurred in the area of virtual education, or mode 1 to use the GATS terminology (Brown 2005). The legal obligations under the GATS facilitate freedom of movement for virtual education providers.

In recent years, a range of fraudulent activities connected to the broad area of higher education appear to have grown in scale and scope across the world. Many are connected with the increasingly "borderless" nature of higher education, associated with the trends of commercialization, internationalization and new technology. There are recorded problems across the "educational supply chain," at the input stage (false visas, misuse of visas, false entry qualifications, dubious admissions practices and fabricated/substandard institutional accreditation), process stage (false/misleading institutions, plagiarism, dishonest grading) and output stage (fraudulent higher education qualifications) (Garrett 2005, 1).

The diploma mill issue has become much more complex since "accreditation mills" have also emerged under the new transnational education scenario. These accreditation mills certify or sell certifications to substandard higher education providers and thus muddy the education quality debate (Knight 2007). These certification and accreditation agencies benefit because they fall within the scope of the GATS; more specifically, they are classified under "Other educational services" (Saner and Fasel 2003).

However, the GATS does not turn a blind eye to quality assurance issues; instead, it deals directly with them, although in a way that has upset the education community. Again, the critics object to Article VI on domestic regulation. The Domestic Regulation Working Group is attempting to define which quality assurance standards and regulations could be considered "more burdensome than necessary" for international trade. This means that the rules of quality assurance systems of certain member countries could be considered barriers to trade and could become the subject of disputes within the DSB. The domestic regulation article of the GATS could also complicate member countries' efforts to introduce more ambitious and stringent education quality rules (van Ginkel and Rodrigues Dias 2006; Knight, 2006). Paradoxically, instead of setting minimum requirements of education quality, the GATS is setting maximum requirements. Consequently, the GATS is contributing to the international harmonization of quality, albeit downward.

b) GATS Favors Quality

In relation to the education quality debate, GATS defenders also invoke the liberal theory of trade. According to this theory, the liberalization of the sector and the resulting competition will benefit education quality because providers will have to invest and make other efforts to attract clients/students. These providers are aware that one way to attract students is rising education quality. Low-quality educational services will be spurned, so these providers will have fewer benefits and resources to invest and will eventually be driven out of the education market. In general, open markets and competitiveness contribute to service innovation, in addition to attracting expertise, investment and technical skills. In other words, free trade contributes to the "modernization" of the service sectors (Poblano 2004).

According to the competitive rationale, trade in educational services and the liberalization of the education sector will presumably lead to an improvement in the quality of educational provision. Since service quality is certainly a comparative advantage for educational institutions, they will have to provide quality services if they are to remain profitable. Again, the financial resources generated by international trade will give universities the means (and motivation) for enhancing the quality of their facilities, libraries, recruitment and student management—and subsequently the means and motivation for enhancing the quality of their educational services. (Larsen and Lancrin 2002, 24).

Functions and Conception of Higher Education

The GATS education debate also has a philosophical and normative dimension and faces questions such as: How will trade in education and, specifically, the liberalization of education under the GATS alter the conception, functions and priorities of the education sector? Are these changes positive or negative and why?

a)   GATS Undermines the Traditional Functions of Education

The GATS conceives education as a tradable good and never refers to it as a social right (van Ginkel and M. A. Rodrigues Dias 2006). This has generated strong reactions among education representatives, many of whom believe that "the very fact that the education sector is now included in the discussions on trade liberalization is in itself alarming" (IE and PSI 1999, 13). The GATS represents a break with the traditional "common sense" understanding of education by treating it as a simple commodity. Consequently, various traditional functions of education could be undermined. The first of these relates to promoting democratic values and an active citizenry.

> There are underlying tensions between the widely recognized aims of public education and the principles of the GATS. Instead of seeing universal access to quality public education as a crucial investment in the social and economic health of any democracy, the GATS treats education as just another service sector potentially available for commercial exploitation. (Grieshaber-Otto and Sanger 2002, 76–77).

Other traditional functions that could be undermined by the GATS relate to economic development and nation building.

> Through GATS, education becomes a goal rather than a means in the process of capital accumulation. Although the goals and the means of the economic functions of education are not necessarily mutually exclusive, those aspects that may guide the expansion of education in the search of consumers may contradict those that guide education as an area of strategic investment for economic development (Robertson, Bonal, and Dale 2002, 493).

[Education traditionally contributes to] the building of national identity, the use and development of national language, a certain national policy of knowledge production and the production and reproduction of specific forms of cultural capital appropriated by the emerging new middle classes. Whatever the form of the consequence, what is important to register is that because of GATS constraints, nation-states will lose a considerable capacity to direct these outcomes in ways that they might previously have done. (Robertson, Bonal, and Dale 2002, 493)

At the higher education level, education liberalization could undermine the research functions of universities, as well as the freedom of scholars to define their own research agendas. Another traditional value that could be affected by the imposition of market rules at the university level is academic freedom. Some scholars are afraid that these traditional values and priorities could be subordinated to profit-based criteria or to the preferences of a shifting education demand.

Under pressure from the market, private for-profit institutions specializing in higher education might have to teach or give credit to false theories merely on the grounds that such instruction is in demand (. . .). An economy drive might also lead to course standardization, undermining academic freedom (and to the recruitment of less qualified teaching staff) (Larsen and Vincent-Lancrin, 2002: 26).

"Market pressure may also affect research. Some institutions might purely and simply drop research on the grounds of profitability, or restrict it to non-innovative work with less risk of failure. In fact, private for-profit universities are focusing more on teaching than research" (Ruch, 2001: 14).[2]

Finally, the GATS could also undermine the traditional dynamics of international cooperation and cultural exchange undertaken by universities, with competition and/or international relations driven by economic interests gradually coming to the fore (AUCC et al. 2001).

b) GATS Strengthens Educational Functions

GATS supporters maintain that the trade agreement can positively contribute to the social and economic functions of education. They also believe that a for-profit and trade-oriented education sector can complement the public sector in the pursuit of certain policy objectives. In particular, transnational education could be more effective than traditional public education in promoting an education model that is oriented to the international economy or in helping countries meet the standards of the knowledge economy. Indeed, certain country representatives at the WTO have actively disseminated this message. Having identified offensive interests in the education sector, these delegations have published communications on trade and education in which they highlight the positive impact of the GATS on national education systems, as well as its benign effects on public education. As shown in Box 6.1, all countries that have published these kinds of communications are enthusiastic supporters of education liberalization.

Box 6.1   Public Communications on Trade in Education by WTO Members

"[Educational services] constitute a growing, international business, supplementing the public education system and contributing to global spread of the modern "knowledge" economy. Availability of these education and training services can help to develop a more efficient workforce, leading countries to an improved competitive position in the world economy" (WTO-US, 2000).

"The reduction of barriers to trade in education does not equate to an erosion of core public education systems and standards. An international trade in education services can provide a means of supplementing and supporting national education policy objectives. For example, in New Zealand's experience it can help reduce the infrastructural commitments required of governments, and so free resources to be concentrated in other aspects of education policy" (WTO-NZ, 2001).

"Australia views the liberalization of trade in education services primarily as a means of providing individuals in all countries with access to a wide range of educational options (. . .) facilitating access to education and training courses that in qualitative and quantitative terms are not otherwise available in the country of origin; and providing a competitive stimulus to institutions with flow-on benefits to all students. Australia also sees the liberalization of trade in education services as the most effective way of encouraging the internationalization of education and enhancing flows of students between countries" (WTO-Australia, 2001).

"Recently, it has become extremely important for each country to improve the quality of education and research, responding flexibly to the rapidly changing needs of the society. Japan recognizes that, in order to pursue these policy objectives, it is effective to promote a certain level of liberalization, while taking various governmental policy measures. From this viewpoint, Japan encourages each Member in the course of the forthcoming request and offer negotiations to promote liberalization in the education services sector through better market access, further assurance of national treatment and deregulation of related domestic regulations" (WTO-Japan, 2002).

"Both types of education services [public and private] play an important role in Switzerland's further development as a prime centre for teaching and learning. In addition to these direct benefits, a dynamic education sector supports the economy at large through more intensive research activity. Thanks to the presence of international and foreign educational institutions, the attractiveness of the country as a prime location for multinational companies and international governmental and non-governmental organizations is further enhanced" (WTO-Switzerland, 2005).

Source: WTO on-line document database (http://www.wto.org/english/docs_e/ddf_e/ddf_e.htm)

Working Conditions for Teachers

The impact of trade agreements on teachers' working conditions has not been a central issue in the GATS education debate. However, the related literature contains both pro- and anti-GATS views in this regard.

a) *GATS Jeopardizes Labor and Working Conditions*

The main concern in relation to labor and working conditions is that the GATS does not touch on labor standards. The international labor movement has led a long and intensive, but unsuccessful, struggle to include labor standards in the WTO trade regime (O'Brien et al 2000). Due to this and other reasons, GATS critics think that the WTO only protects the rights of transnational service providers, not those of workers.

Moreover, the liberalization of services promoted by the GATS favors the decentralization of labor relations, the weakening of trade union power and the "flexibilization" of labor conditions (Nunn 2001). The cross-border supply of education (i.e. distance education) favored by the GATS involves even greater exploitation of human resources:

> Phoenix University in the USA is a private profit-making enterprise offering courses in virtual mode. One hour of cyber-education costs the student US$237 whereas one hour of conventional education at the Arizona State University, in the same State, costs US$ 486, i.e. more than double the amount. Why this difference? It is due primarily to salary costs, which are US$247 an hour at Arizona State University compared with US$46 at Phoenix University. No doubt this provides food for thought for all those higher-education managers engaged in the cost-containment rat race (. . .) The development of employment in the education sector—particularly in higher education—may also be significantly affected by the (inevitable?) spread of cross-border education services. With the multiplication of individual employment contracts, which this trend entails, job insecurity is undoubtedly a risk we must guard against (EI and PSI 1999, 12, 22–23).

In developing countries, there is the additional risk that transnational providers from rich countries will import their own staff. In that case, foreign investment would not result in increased jobs for local teachers (Robertson, Bonal and Dale 2002).

Other rights that could be undermined in this scenario include academic freedom and the ability of scholars to use the knowledge and materials they produce (Knight, 2002). For instance, teachers of distance courses are normally required to transfer to their corporate employer the future rights to use the material they have produced:

There are some worries related particularly to online providers where academics (and indeed teachers at secondary and primary level) provide content as part of a one-off fixed-term contract. Material then replicated by that academic in another capacity may well be subject to copyright restrictions from the online supplier (Nunn 2001, 17).

b)   GATS Can Benefit Teachers

In response to GATS critics, Larsen and Vincent-Lancrin (2002) maintain that liberalization could attract investment to the education sector. Consequently, institutions would have more resources to increase teachers' salaries:

> "While making educational institutions financially more independent (and thus more independent vis-à-vis their public supervisory bodies), this commercial income may enable national universities to provide their students and staff with better library and technological facilities, and in many cases to pay their staff more" (p. 23).

Pro-GATS scholars do acknowledge that education liberalization could lead to the loss of local jobs, but only if the country's education sector is not competitive enough. In other cases, liberalization could mean the creation of new jobs for local teachers (Mattoo and Rathindran 2001).

6.3   PROGNOSTIC DIMENSION: FROM ALTERNATIVES TO CONTINUITY

The prognostic dimension of the GATS education debate deals with alternatives and solutions to the problems diagnosed. In this case, there are three sides to the debate (instead of two): the first pushes for far-reaching alternatives to the GATS, the second proposes reforms and the third suggests maintaining the status quo.

a)   Alternatives

A number of education stakeholders believe that education should be excluded from the GATS. This view has been expressed in numerous statements issued by international civil society organizations and other stakeholders, such as "Stop the GATS attack" or "Take education out of GATS" (Verger and Bonal 2009). Advocates maintain that education issues such as internationalization, recognition of qualifications, quality standards, etc. should not be addressed in a trade forum. Instead, they should be dealt with in international forums with more expertise and legitimacy, such as UNESCO or UNICEF (Knight 2007; Saner and Fasel

2003; Barblan 2002; Oosterlinck 2002; AUCC et al 2001; Rodrigues Dias 2002a).

GATS defenders argue that the Agreement is necessary to attract education investment to poorer countries. However, critics maintain that international aid or foreign debt relief—not trade—should be the main external mechanism for increasing the available resources for education systems in the South. In other words, international cooperation should be given priority over trade and foreign investment in the education field because the latter are profit-oriented and not necessarily interested in promoting development.

> And we need to challenge the idea that the private sector can do much better in the provision of essential services than the public sector or NGOs. There is a strong push to argue—and I have heard it from the head of the International Finance Corporation and others—that the only way to get adequate resourcing and quality for education into developing countries is to let the private sector do it—or in some kind of partnership with government. This is a very self-serving argument. On the question of resourcing it is clear that even with a fairly small increase in Official Development Assistance (ODA) it would be possible to get everyone into school—the problem has been firstly getting commitments to lift the percentage of ODA for basic education and secondly in lifting the overall level of ODA (. . .). We argue that ODA should be increased to meet these global social spending goals and that it is the best possible use of ODA. We do not accept that the only way to get kids into school is to let the private sector invest in education (Jobbs 2002, 3).

b) Reformist Proposals

A second set of proposals has also been raised by GATS critics. They do not recommend taking education out of the GATS. Instead, they call for certain adjustments to prevent the GATS from undermining education quality or the idea of education as a social right. To this end, the GATS should be subordinated to state education regulations and international education conventions; furthermore, it should not interfere with public education systems (Bergan 2002).

> Trade in educational services has been going on for a long time (. . .) Given the fact that several countries, including my own home country Norway, have already inscribed 'no limitations' on marked access to tertiary education under GATS, my argument is that GATS must respect the international conventions in [the] educational sector, such as the sLisbon Recognition Convention (Nyborg 2002).

In a similar line, a widely distributed public statement about GATS signed by higher education associations proposed that: a) trade in education should not be allowed to undermine the efforts of developing countries to develop their own higher education systems; b) national education authorities should retain the ability to regulate domestic education systems (AUCC et al 2001).

It should be acknowledged that a number of reformist proposals have a procedural focus, i. e. a focus on the way the agreement is negotiated. For instance, one such proposal calls for the more active incorporation of the education community within the GATS negotiations, including more extensive consultation with education stakeholders by trade negotiators (Barblan 2002; Oosterlinck 2002; COL/UNESCO 2006). Other observers argue that the WTO should create a formal consulting body in which teachers unions would be represented (similar to the trade union advisory committee to the OECD) (Sánchez 2005). A second proposal aims to balance WTO members' negotiating power and resources by providing delegations from poorer countries with additional resources so that they can participate in the negotiations under conditions comparable to those of rich countries (Rodrigues Dias 2002a). Finally, others call for a moratorium on the trade in services negotiations and recommends that the negotiations not be taken up again until the effects of the GATS in the education field have been evaluated.

To sum up, the reformist proposals attempt to reconcile trade interests with the concerns and preferences of the international education community. This idea was clearly reflected In the OECD Forum on Trade in Services, attended by both trade and education representatives:

> As with many new trends, discussion about international trade in educational services has tended initially to be about whether it is important and whether it is desirable, before moving on to a more constructive dialogue about how it can be made to work more effectively. At this forum, while there was considerable debate about potential risks associated with such trade, there was also a general acceptance that it is bound to be a growing feature of the educational scene, and a desire to explore ways in which it can be developed as a positive force. This will be a complex task involving many actors— including not just governments and academic institutions but also private and professional bodies of many kinds. Yet there is also much work to be done in different sectors in terms of defining standards internationally and translating these into criteria for accrediting institutions, recognizing quality and awarding qualifications (Hirsch 2002: 12).

c)   Status Quo

According to GATS advocates, education liberalization under the agreement should continue; no central aspects of the current situation should be changed. Again, the countries with offensive interests in trade in services are the main proponents of continuity (see Box 6.1).

However, some GATS advocates consider that "education reflexivity" should be introduced into the negotiation process. In other words, education liberalization commitments within the GATS should be undertaken by countries taking into account the requirements and interests of national education systems:

> Countries must take into account the full range of national policy interests and goals in education policy before deciding whether or not to make GATS commitments." (Larsen, Momii, and Vincent-Lancrin 2004, 14).

> Successful strategic assessments of *threats and opportunities* of education services and possible opening of trade in education services to foreign providers require (1) the formulation of adequate strategies focusing on the future development of the respective national education sector, (2) the identification of possible export opportunities of national education services providers and their chances for market access in other countries, (3) the corresponding assessment of how to prepare their domestic market for foreign competition, (4) the clarification of how a country wants to define the role of government—as a provider or regulator of education services? (Saner and Fasel: 295).

6.4 THE POLITICS OF THE GATS AND EDUCATION DEBATE

Table 6.1 summarizes the issues at stake, as well as the main meaning repertoires within the GATS and education debate.

Within the framework of the debate, two lines of argument can be clearly distinguished. One is very critical of the agreement, while the other is clearly supportive. The lines of argument concerning the impact of GATS on education are normally in conflict. Moreover, critics of one of the axes of the debate almost always adopt critical positions in relation to the other axis. Something similar happens with the GATS advocates.

Normally, GATS supporters focus on trying to refute the opposing side's arguments. When the lines of argument and the publication dates of the related literature are analyzed, it emerges that GATS critics initiate the debate and the defenders respond. Furthermore, without the input of these critics, most pro-GATS arguments would have never crystallized publicly. Indeed, most would have no *raison d'être* at all. This was reflected in the OECD Forum on Trade in Services; in the minutes of this event it is stated that "advocates of GATS spent much of this forum talking about what it would not do in the education field" (Hirsch 2002: 9). However, GATS

Table 6.1 The GATS and Education Debate

	INTERPRETATIONS	
ISSUES	GATS critics (The GATS. . .)	GATS supporters (The GATS. . .)
a. States' right to regulate	a.1. . . . restricts the policy space of countries and their capacity to regulate education	a.2. . . . respects the regulation capacity of the States
b. Impact on developing countries	b.1. . . . promotes an unequal exchange between north and south in educational services; prevents southern countries from developing national higher education systems	b.2. . . . favors the development of the education systems in southern countries
c. Education equity	c.1. . . . privatizes education funding and blocks access	c.2. . . . creates larger offer and investment in education
d. Education quality	d.1. . . . undermines education quality	d.2. . . . favors education quality through competition
e. Education's traditional functions	e.1. . . . alters education's traditional functions (social cohesion, nation building, etc.); education becomes an end in itself	e.2. . . . strengthens and complements the traditional functions of education
f. Teachers' working conditions	f.1. . . . undermines working conditions and weakens teachers unions	f.2. . . . improves labor conditions and creates new jobs in the education field
g. Recommendations	g.1. Complete withdrawal (education out of GATS) g.2. Reform (education in GATS, but subordinated to education policies and priorities)	g.3. Continuity (in-depth liberalization commitments are positive for education)

Source: Author

supporters not only refute the critics; as we have seen, they also theorize about potential positive effects of trade liberalization for education.

Both types of discourse are mainly based on hypotheses concerning the potential impact of the GATS on education systems, whether positive or negative. Statements based on empirical evidence are rare. On occasion, arguments are based on analogies with the liberalization experience in other sectors or with the education liberalization experience under regional trade agreements (see, for instance, Aboites 2004 and Rodríguez Gómez 2004 with respect to NAFTA and the Mexican higher education system).

Most of the issues at stake are addressed from a causal or theoretical perspective. Nevertheless, the debate is clearly grounded in principle and political beliefs about what education should or should not be for and how educational services should or should not be organized and distributed. Obviously, this second kind of ideas is more difficult to refute. Most GATS critics problematize the commodification of education under the trade agreement. More significantly, they problematize the fact itself that education is being negotiated within a trade agreement. In addition to addressing such concerns, GATS critics also denounce how the WTO is reducing education to the level of a commodity that is sold and bought on an international scale. They also try to mobilize people and organizations against the GATS and, as a result, their discourse is built around slogans such as "education is not a commodity" or "take GATS out of education."

Language Barriers and Rhetoric Strategies

Most of the time, the participants of the debate are not neutral observers; in fact, they are personally committed to their positions. As Vlk (2006) observes, the GATS debate is very "emotional." This emotionality is, to some extent, a consequence of the fact that the academic community rejects the application of trade terminology and codes to education issues. Moreover, the trade language makes it difficult for education stakeholders to participate in the debate or to address certain nuances and technical details. In fact, as Vlk implies, this could be one of the sources of emotionality since "what is not entirely understood, might be perceived as potentially dangerous" (Vlk 2006: 145). Most members of the education community are not thoroughly conversant with trade provisions or technical jargon. For this reason, trade experts often delegitimize them, normally accusing them of "lack of understanding" of the GATS. In texts such as "GATS: Facts and Fiction," issued by the WTO, or in Sauvé (2002)—who is a trade expert from the OECD—GATS supporters try to legitimize their positions by saying that GATS opponents do not properly understand the issues at stake:

> The Agreement's critics allege that the GATS is nothing less than a tool of privatization, globalization, "commodification" and other assorted ills. Such statements belie significant *misunderstandings* about the GATS and its modus operandi. Whether by deliberate commission or innocent omission, GATS detractors often present false, inflammatory and misleading characterizations of the purpose, rules and policy consequences of the GATS. A more reasoned assessment of the Agreement shows that it is nowhere nearly as powerful as its critics suggest (Sauvé 2002, 12).

It should be acknowledged that, in occasions, some education stakeholders indulge in hyperbole and exaggeration when arguing against the GATS. Catastrophism is a very common mobilizing tactic for social movements because it generates a sense of urgency and triggers collective action;

however, it is easily challenged by skeptics or other interested parties. For instance, the catastrophist approach can be clearly perceived in the following quotation:

> [Because of GATS] the education policies, the content of the programs and the validity of the certificates will not be fixed by governments, but by supra-national entities controlled by big corporations (. . .). Under the GATS scope, the state will not be able to define what and how to teach because any state intervention, such as the funding of public universities, will be perceived as a trade barrier" (Sánchez 2005, 35).

However, it should be recognized that there is a thin line between the direct effects of GATS and the effects of education trade liberalization promoted by the GATS. Analysts from the education field usually mix these two dimensions. For this reason, GATS supporters feel that some criticisms are exaggerated in attributing so many negative effects to the Agreement.

For their part, GATS supporters often resort to fallacious rhetorical strategies. The most common false argument is to state that the GATS will have no negative effects for education because of the Agreement's flexibility. The voluntary decision to adopt liberalization commitments in the areas of Market Access and National Treatment does not mean that there are no other implications associated with ratifying the Agreement (such as most favored nation or domestic regulation obligations). Moreover, flexibility in certain areas of the GATS negotiations does not offset the potential impact of education liberalization. Indeed, this "flexibility" argument is more than a fallacy; it works as a kind of rhetorical shortcut that posits that "GATS is not problematic because countries are free to subscribe to commitments within the negotiations." What, however, are the implications once liberalization commitments have been subscribed to? This issue is often glossed over in pro-GATS texts.

On some occasions, the rhetorical tricks used by GATS supporters are especially evident, such as when former WTO Director-General Mike Moore said that education is not under discussion or when Alejandro Jara, former president of the Services Council, said that public services do not fall within the scope of the Agreement (see above quotations in this chapter).

Trade vs. Education Semiotic and Institutional Orders

When the transmitters within the GATS education debate are analyzed, the first noteworthy result is that all GATS critics come from the education field (education experts, university associations, teacher unions, UNESCO staff, etc.), while the GATS supporters come from the trade field (WTO staff, trade negotiators, OECD trade division staff, scholars and other trade experts). Figure 6.1 presents the main categories of stakeholders in the debate, as well as the most quoted works within each category. This figure

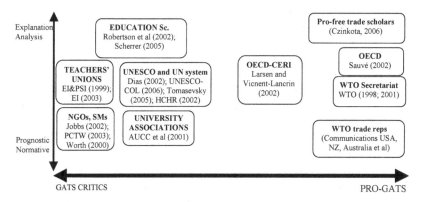

Figure 6.1 Stakeholders and positions in the GATS education debate.
Source: Author

also indicates whether a given discourse is more normative (i.e. emphasizing what should be done) or explanatory (i.e. causal beliefs or theories about the GATS/education relationship).

Figure 6.1 reasserts the idea that the GATS education debate is polarized. It also shows very clearly that the two opposing semiotic orders identified in this chapter are directly linked to two very different social and institutional orders, in Fairclough (2003) terms. The first semiotic order is linked to the education sector and principally frames and disseminates the critical interpretations concerning GATS and its negative impact on education. The second order is embedded in the commercial sector and frames the arguments concerning the positive effects of the Agreement.

Usually, the education and commercial sectors are mutually independent. Their representatives are not normally in contact with each other and the topics they deal with, as well as their spheres of influence, are very different. However, the GATS has prompted these stakeholders to interact, even though they approach to the same topic from very different rationales and disciplines. Beyond the lack of shared language/jargon (Bassett 2006), the trade field and the education field are governed, in cognitive terms, by very different meaning frames, principles and rationales. The prevailing frames in each field act as internal logical structures and systems of meaning production that clearly condition the stakeholders' semiotic activity (interpretation, explanation, recommendation, etc.). For this reason, they construct and organize very different meaning repertoires with respect to the GATS and education debate. And, for this very same reason, in occasions, they do not necessarily understand each other.

The anti-GATS discourse is clearly framed by a political commitment to education's traditional functions and, in most cases, by the idea of education as a public good and a human right. In the education field, the principles and values concerning the purpose of education (for instance, its contribution to critical citizenship or economic development) and how education should be delivered (normally, through a strong state control) act as filters for reaching a common understanding over the GATS/education relationship. Moreover, education sector representatives' discourse on GATS issues is also shaped by the perception that trade representatives and rationales are "colonizing" the education sector. These factors largely explain why education stakeholders focus on the negative effects of the GATS and are deeply critical with the agreement.

For its part, the trade field is governed by a very different set of principles, prejudices and notions. The trade sector's semiotic order consists of applying the concepts and premises of the liberal theory of trade. Free-trade theory is applied to develop an understanding of the effects of education liberalization within the GATS and it is applied to the education sector in the same way it would be applied to very different topics such as agriculture, textiles or mining. Therefore, they obviate the particularities of the education sector. The following quotation clearly reflects this line of thought by GATS advocates.

> The application of GATS rules to international ventures of higher education proposes an environment covered and protected by international rules and reduces the risk for investors. In consequence, there can be more investment, which leads to more competition, which gives a boost to productivity. In addition, rate of return expectations can be lowered, which makes it far easier to build international education capacity (Czinkota 2006: 150).

6.5 CONCLUSIONS

The GATS and education debate was initiated by the international education community and has raised global public awareness as some trade representatives have been pressured to respond to arguments put forwarded by education stakeholders. However, this does not necessarily mean that the GATS and education debate has had a tangible political impact in terms of education liberalization outcomes.

On the one hand, this debate could be a source of fresh ideas for trade representatives. It should be noted that ideas have a greater chance of becoming influential when policy-makers are facing new and complex political issues that are generating uncertainty (Finnemore and Sikkink 2001; Richardson 2005), such as the GATS. The causal beliefs and principled beliefs that have shaped the debate could thus serve as road maps for policy-makers, as Goldstein and Kehoane (1993) found. Due to the technical complexity of GATS and the uncertainties it generates in the education sector, policy-makers and trade negotiators should proactively look for new ideas to clarify their positions within the negotiations.

On the other hand, the existing sides are diametrically opposed on each issue treated in the GATS education debate. Our analysis identifies two distant epistemic groups which are embedded in two divorced semiotic orders: one highlights the negative effects of GATS and opposes its interference in the education sector, while the other clearly supports the Agreement. As Walsh (2000) states, causal beliefs are more influential when the international scientific community reaches a clear consensus on the core beliefs affecting a policy issue. In other words, if there is no clear agreement between the experts over a certain policy issue, ideas may well lose their explanatory power and, consequently, their political influence. Currently, the market of ideas for policy-making on GATS and education is far-reaching, confusing and contradictory. And, as we have seen in this chapter, it seems unlikely that the parts in dispute will reach a consensus in the near future.

7 For or Against Education Liberalization
The International Struggle

The previous chapter examined the GATS education debate. Most of the agents involved in this debate are not directly involved in the negotiation process. However, some of them aim to influence the process and the outcomes of the negotiations, including large international organizations such as UNESCO, Education International, the OECD and international associations of public universities. This chapter will address the political strategies pursued by these and other GATS stakeholders. To that end, public statements by these stakeholders will be analyzed and their efforts to influence the negotiations will be examined.

These stakeholders vary widely in terms of resources and objectives. Some are state-based international organizations such as UNESCO or UNCTAD, while others are civil society organizations or non-state actors such as teachers unions. However, all of them share two main constituencies. First, all are international actors that are organized at a planetary scale. Second, they seek to influence the GATS and education negotiations from outside the WTO subsystem since none of them have decision-making authority within the WTO.

7.1 UNESCO: MAKING ITS VOICE HEARD

UNESCO is the UN's lead agency in the area of education. It was created in 1945 and currently has 192 member states. The government representatives at UNESCO may pertain to the Ministry of Foreign Affairs of the country in question, but they always have direct links with their respective national education ministries (Heyneman 2003).

To understand UNESCO's position on GATS, we must first acknowledge that UNESCO views education as a social and human right that should be available to all. In general, UNESCO's conception of education is more humanist and less instrumental than the predominant view in other organizations such as the World Bank and the OECD. UNESCO's view on higher education was set out at the World Conference on Higher Education (Paris, 1998). The main output of this conference was the *World Declaration on*

Higher Education for the Twenty-First Century: Vision and Action, which states that:

> The mission of higher education is to contribute to the sustainable development and improvement of society as a whole by: educating highly qualified graduates able to meet the needs of all sectors of human activity; advancing, creating and disseminating knowledge through research; interpreting, preserving, and promoting cultures in the context of cultural pluralism and diversity; providing opportunities for higher learning throughout life; contributing to the development and improvement of education at all levels; and protecting and enhancing civil society by training young people in the values which form the basis of democratic citizenship and by providing critical and detached perspectives in the discussion of strategic choices facing societies.[1]

The Paris Declaration also established that international solidarity and cooperation should be the main values governing international relations between universities and other higher education institutions around the world (Maldonado 2005). Usually, UNESCO refers to the Paris Declaration when questioning the role of the GATS in the higher education field. In a number of public debates, UNESCO has clearly differentiated its model of education internationalization from that promoted by the WTO. For instance, during the Trade in Services Forum promoted by the OECD, the UNESCO representative said that "the GATS promotes the trade liberalization of higher education for purposes of economic profit whereas UNESCO promotes a non-profit internationalization concerned with full respect for cultural diversity and with the right to education for all".[2] In general, UNESCO is concerned with the WTO/GATS because the trade agreement could affect negatively issues such as education access, education quality (in particular, quality assurance measures) and linguistic and cultural diversity (Interview UNESCO staff 01, 2006). Although it is not always clearly and publicly stated, UNESCO is critical of the interference caused by free trade agreements, such as the GATS, in the education field.

However, UNESCO's criticisms of the WTO/GATS must also be considered from a historical perspective. It could be argued that UNESCO is particularly critical of the GATS because it represents a new element in the multilateral education framework that calls into question UNESCO's role and authority in the global system. When it was created in the 1950s, UNESCO was the principal agent for education development at the international level and, in particular, the main education standard-bearer for Third World countries. However, political conflicts within the organization, largely due to the international context during the Cold War, undermined UNESCO's international standing, as well as its budget (Mundy 1999). In parallel, other international organizations that did not initially have an education mandate, such as the World Bank and the OECD, have successfully intervened in the education field. The World Bank is currently the leading agent on education and development issues. As a result of the loans it grants and the related loan conditions, it has become the most influential external actor in the educational policies of Southern countries. For its part, the OECD has become the main education policy forum and think tank for rich countries (Jakobi and Martens 2007). The World Bank and the OECD are thus competing with UNESCO and limiting its scope of influence in both the developing and the developed world. Even other UN agencies, such as UNICEF, have stopped coordinating some of their education initiatives with UNESCO and now implement them directly (Mundy 1999).

UNESCO, however, has preserved its main sphere of influence in the higher education field. More specifically, it has led a number of important initiatives involving higher education internationalization, such as international cooperation programs, e-learning initiatives and the introduction of new technologies for information and communication, etc. However, in the mid-1990s, the WTO was created and UNESCO was forced to deal with a new global competitor in the area of higher education. UNESCO's new rival is unique in that it has neither a clear education mandate nor an explicit education view, but, paradoxically, it exerts much greater influence in the education field due to the binding international agreements it promotes and its more sophisticated dispute settlement system. This history of ongoing international rivalry, together with an antagonistic view of education, explains UNESCO's criticisms of the decision to introduce education within the GATS.

UNESCO's Role in the GATS Negotiations

Within the framework of UNESCO, member countries can agree to create three types of international legal instruments: conventions, declarations and recommendations. Only conventions are binding because they acquire the status of organic domestic law once they are ratified by national parliaments. However, UNESCO's conventions in the higher education field are rare. Indeed, existing conventions on higher education are regional in scope and exclusively focused on recognition of qualifications. Most likely, a UNESCO convention that explicitly rejected GATS or the international free-trade-in-higher-education model would be rejected because some influential UNESCO members actively support the trade model and play an active role promoting it within the GATS. Therefore, UNESCO members would be unable to reach a consensus on this matter. One existing UNESCO convention that directly contradicts the principles and logic of the WTO agreements is the Convention on the Protection and Promotion of the Diversity of Cultural Expressions (UNESCO 2005b; Chan-Tibergien 2006).[3] However, this convention does not explicitly deal with education issues. Therefore, legal initiatives do not appear to be a feasible way for UNESCO to counter-balance the influence of GATS.

Dialogue with the WTO could be another way of addressing UNESCO's concerns over the GATS, although this poses a number of problems. The main difficulty is that UNESCO does not have observer or member status in any of the WTO organs. Maybe, it could be argued that UNESCO is not an official WTO member/observer because it does not deal directly with trade policies. Even so, a number of other non-trade-related international agencies have observer status in the WTO Council on Trade in Services (e.g. the International Telecommunications Union, the International Civil Aviation Organization, the World Health Organization and the World Tourism Organization). An alternative explanation may be that education and culture are not key sectors in the GATS negotiations as opposed to telecommunications, tourism and banking services where more trade flows are involved. However, the most plausible explanation for UNESCO's exclusion is that the organization—as happened to the education community in general—did not get involved in the trade in services debate during the Uruguay Round.[4] Since UNESCO is not a WTO member, it has greater difficulty influencing the GATS outcomes. However, UNESCO has tried to exert its influence by spearheading certain initiatives from the sidelines of the WTO participatory subsystem.

Interestingly, UNESCO has tried to engage in dialogue with WTO representatives, but in marked occasions the latter has rejected these invitations. In the Quality Assurance Forum organized by UNESCO in 2001, one of the speakers stated that "one serious, and somewhat ironic, shortcoming of the Forum, which was clearly not the fault of the UNESCO organizers, was the failure of the WTO to participate in it apparently due to lack of funds. Since the essential issue at stake was that of trading standards, this was particularly unfortunate" (Brock 2002, 9).

Rather than direct dialogue with the WTO or legal initiatives, UNESCO's main course of action in relation to GATS has consisted of promoting public debate between education stakeholders and providing technical assistance to UNESCO members. This is consistent with UNESCO's core function within the global system of education governance. The organization defines itself as a "laboratory of ideas" and a "center of information and knowledge exchange."[5] In particular, UNESCO's main GATS-related initiatives have been embedded in broader initiatives on education quality assurance, as well as in dissemination initiatives to openly promote discussion of GATS and education issues. These initiatives, which are detailed in the following sections, have a low political profile because they have been led by the UNESCO staff. For their part, UNESCO's member countries have played a mostly passive role over the issue and none of them have attempted to place the GATS issue on UNESCO's political agenda.

a) *GATS and the Quality of Transnational Education*

The principal UNESCO initiative on quality education is the Global Forum on International Quality Assurance, Accreditation and the Recognition of

Qualifications in Higher Education. This forum is defined as a permanent platform for dialogue on issues such as quality assurance, accreditation and recognition of qualifications. To justify its existence, the forum cites the introduction of extraneous elements such as the GATS in the higher education sector.[6] Three large-scale meetings were organized within the framework of the forum; the first was held in 2002. On that occasion, most of the participants criticized the GATS and, more specifically, decried the fact that a trade organization was dealing with issues that fall within UNESCO's jurisdiction (Bergan 2002; Uvalic-Trumbic 2002).

UNESCO makes a significant effort to contribute to the strengthening of its members' education quality assurance systems by providing technical assistance. Technical assistance on quality education aspects is also justified by the challenges associated with education liberalization under trade agreements (UNESCO 2005a; Didou 2004). For that reason, UNESCO has promoted an international instrument that could help to regulate the quality of transnational education providers: the "Guidelines on Quality Provision in Cross-Border Higher Education," which have also been promoted by the OECD. Major education stakeholders, such as universities, students, teachers unions and quality assurance agencies, have also participated in this initiative. The aim of the guidelines is to propose policy measures and to synthesize best practices that help countries evaluate education quality, as well as to protect students against substandard education services (UNESCO 2005a). The guidelines are not binding; their function is to raise awareness and to empower education stakeholders in the fight against low-quality transnational education. Again, concern over GATS is not explicit in the guidelines, although UNESCO's *leitmotiv* in promoting them is to respond to the free trade model promoted by the GATS and to counteract its potential negative effects (Interview UNESCO 01, Paris, 2006).

b)   Dissemination

UNESCO has disseminated ideas about GATS and education in numerous publications. The *UNESCO Courier* has published numerous articles that were critical of GATS and education commercialization (see, for instance, the February and November 2000 issues).[7] On its website, UNESCO provides forums for discussion and publishes critiques of the GATS written by other authors and organizations, although it does not publicly endorse their point of view (UNESCO 2004). In 2006, UNESCO published Jane Knight's book on GATS and education with the aim of raising awareness and informing education policy-makers from developing countries about the importance of the trade negotiations. This book calls on developing countries to set up effective regulatory frameworks to meet the challenges stemming from the GATS (COL/UNESCO 2006).

UNESCO has also promoted the GATS debate between education stakeholders by organizing a series of seminars and conferences. In particular, it has organized regional events with the Association of African Universities and the Council for Higher Education Accreditation (Accra, April 2004), with the Korean Educational Development Institute and the Korean Council for University Education (Seoul, April 2005) and with the Centro de Estudios sobre la Universidad, the Universidad Nacional Autónoma de México and the Consejo Latino-Americano de Ciencias Sociales (Mexico DF, June 2005). UNESCO also hosted a major seminar on GATS and education organized by Education International (Paris, April 2005).

Interestingly, the former director of UNESCO's Higher Education Division, Marco Antonio Rodrigues Dias, has become one of the most eloquent critics in the GATS and education debate. Rodrigues Dias, who led the 1998 Higher Education Conference, gives speeches around the world and has written numerous articles on the topic—see (Rodrigues Dias 2002a; Rodrigues Dias 2002b; Rodrigues Dias 2002c; Rodrigues Dias 2003). One of his most politically influential appearances was at the third Ibero-American Summit of Public University Chancellors (Porto Alegre, April 2002), where he gave a speech entitled "Higher education: public good or commercial service regulated by the WTO?". In the context of that event, Rodrigues Dias's remarks motivated key university stakeholders to sign the Porto Alegre Letter, which has become a politically relevant instrument in certain countries. During the Summit, Rodrigues Dias stated:

> If higher education is regulated by the WTO like any other commercial service, we should ask ourselves: What will be the role of national governments? If this proposal is accepted, any state that does not fulfill the commitments it signed with the WTO will be forced to pay compensation to education entrepreneurs and businesses whose interests are deemed to be harmed, and they will be subject to reprisals by education exporter countries, especially in the area of distance education.[8]

Finally, as regards recommendations, UNESCO's proposals on GATS and education do not seek any specific breakthroughs. The organization is not seeking to take education out of GATS and accepts that the education liberalization process under the Agreement is inevitable (COL/UNESCO 2006: 12). UNESCO's main aim is to introduce an "education perspective" within the trade liberalization process and to ensure that "education and trade can work together and not only trade issues are respected" (Interview UNESCO 01, Paris, 2006). Within the education liberalization process under the GATS, UNESCO is thus seeking to offset the insensitivity of the WTO to education and social issues and to ensure that the emerging global education market adheres to minimum education quality and access standards.

7.2   OECD: DEFENDING MEMBERS' INTERESTS

The OECD is an international organization whose members primarily consist of developed countries committed to "the promotion of democracy and the market economy."[9] The OECD's main objective is to help its member countries compare and share their policy experiences, find solutions to common problems, identify best practices and coordinate certain policies.[10]

The OECD has dealt with education policies since its creation, but has only been a key education stakeholder since the 1990s (Jakobi and Martens 2007). The creation of the Center for Education Research and Innovation (CERI) in 1986 was an important milestone for the OECD in this regard. The OECD's approach to education consists of attempting to adapt member countries' education policies to economic change and growth in a context of an ongoing fiscal crisis (Jakobi and Kerstin Martens 2007). The OECD's higher education recommendations do not call for direct privatization; instead, they refer to funding diversification, university autonomy and competition (Maldonado 2005). The OECD maintains that the relationship between the state and higher education should be redefined (e.g. the state should not provide university services directly) and that market mechanisms should be introduced into the higher education system (Kwiek 2001).

In relation to trade policies, the OECD is clearly commited to the expansion of world trade at the multilateral level (Bassett 2006). The organization has traditionally played an entrepreneurial role on trade aspects and has been very successful in placing new issues on the international trade agenda (Metzger 2000). For instance, the OECD was very active in promoting the international discussion on trade in services in the 1970s and 1980s (Drake and Nicolaidis 1992). In this sense, the OECD could be considered one of the intellectual manufacturers of GATS. Clearly, this "rich countries club", as called by Greig et al (2007), frames new issues in accordance with the economic interests of its members (Interview GATS expert, Amsterdam, 2007). And, as we explain in the following lines, the way OECD frames the GATS and education debate is not an exception to this rule.

Since early 2000, the OECD has dealt with trade in education issues. In fact, one of the two sub-sections of the organization's tertiary education section is entitled "Trade in Education Services."[11] The OECD has focused on trade in education because the education ministries of certain member countries requested information on this topic from the OECD Secretariat. The request was made in 2001, when the GATS and education debate was just beginning and there was great uncertainty over the potential impact of GATS on education. In particular, the education ministries asked the Secretariat to provide a status report on trade in education and to establish links between the various parties (Johnston 2002). This mandate translated into in two lines of action: the Forums on Trade in Education Services and numerous publications.

a)   Forums on Trade in Education Services

The CERI-OECD organized forums on trade in education services in Washington (2002), Oslo (2003) and Sidney (2004). These three events aimed to analyze trade in education trends and to foster debate between the four key stakeholders: universities, the private sector, governments and students (Larsen, Martin, and Morris 2002). In co-organizing these events, the OECD hoped to build bridges and foster mutual understanding between the education and trade sectors, which, as observed in Chapter 6, are at odds on the GATS issue.

The first forum generated the greatest expectation and drew the most participants, with 250 stakeholder representatives in attendance. It was co-organized by the World Bank, the US Department of Education, the US Department of Commerce, the National Committee for International Trade in Education and the Center for Quality Assurance in International Education. It should be noted that the two latter organizations are pro-education liberalization lobbies from the US with strong links to the US Trade Representative and the US Department of Commerce (Saner and Fasel 2003). Surprisingly, UNESCO was not one of the event organizers. The forum featured a series of passionate debates, with GATS critics predominating (Vlk 2006). However, reporting on the event (that would be widely distributed through the OECD website and other channels) was biased toward the pro-liberalization positions. For instance, an individual reporting on one of the central debates on GATS and higher education concluded that "it should be emphasized that [opposition to GATS] was the extreme position: a number of people speaking from a higher education perspective at the forum believed that the enhancement of international trade in educational services could be of great benefit" (Hirsch 2002, 12).

b) Dissemination via Publications

The OECD has published extensively on trade in education issues. Its statistical briefings, papers, reports and conference presentations usually stress that the organization's member countries are highly competitive on trade in education services and implicitly encourage them to take advantage of this within the framework of trade negotiations (OECD 2002; 2004). However, it also maintains that the regulatory envirnoment promoted by GATS may be also of benefit to developing countries' higher education systems:

> Cross-border education is indeed one way of increasing domestic access to post-secondary education, which ultimately contributes to growth and development. While student and scholar mobility facilitates the building of international networks, which are essential to access up-to-date knowledge, partnerships of local and foreign universities in programme and institution mobility induce spillovers and can help improve the quality of local provision. Finally, commercial provision of cross-border post-secondary education can allow the building of capacity more quickly than with domestic or development assistance resources only, and grants receiving countries more negotiating power to dictate their conditions (OECD 2004, 15).

The OECD publications, more directly or indirectly, defend the role of the GATS in the education field and attempt to refute the arguments of the critics (see a clear example in Sauvé, 2002). Other documents, usually issued by the CERI, are more slightly balanced and also mention potential risks, together with the potential benefits of the GATS (see for instance Larsen and Vincent-Lancrin 2002). In other occasions, it can be percieved that the OECD publications try to play down the importance of the trade agreement for education in an attempt to smother the GATS debate.[12] In one word, if UNESCO frames the GATS and education debate in terms of "dangers and threats", the OECD does so in a more positive manner, in terms of "opportunities and challenges" (OECD 2004).

The OECD is a member of the WTO General Council and other sectoral councils, but is not a member of the Trade in Services Council. As with UNESCO, the OECD seeks to influence the GATS education negotiations from the sidelines of the participatory subsystem. It does so by disseminating data showing the clear comparative advantage of OECD country members in trade in education, along with favorable opinions on GATS in a bid to offset GATS concerns in the education field and to bridge the gap between the trade and education sectors. Finally, the scope of influence of both organizations seems to be quite balanced. On the one hand, OECD's sectoral scope is broader than UNESCO's because trade and education ministries participate actively in the OECD organs. On the other, the UNESCO's territorial scope is broader than OECD's because the members of the former include developing countries. However, rich countries frequently avail themselves of OECD's expertise and believe that UNESCO is mainly focused on developing contexts.

7.3   TEACHERS' UNIONS: EDUCATION OUT OF THE GATS

Education International (EI) is the world's largest international federation of teachers unions and defines itself as the "the global voice of education workers."[13] It is made up of 394 teacher unions from 171 countries, representing nearly 30 million education workers. Headquartered in Brussels, it also has regional offices in most regions. The staff of EI began working on trade issues in the early 1990s within the framework of broader coalitions with organizations such as Public Services International (PSI), Union Network International and the International Confederation of Free Trade Unions (ICFTU). Initially, their campaign was focused on the labor standards issue; however, they become aware that education was also directly affected by the WTO disciplines later on.

In parallel, a number of affiliated Canadian teachers unions also began working on trade and education issues. In Canada, the labor movement and other civil society organizations strongly campaigned against free trade agreements being negotiated with the US, including the Canada-US

Free Trade Agreement (1989) and the North American Free Trade Agreement (1994), which also included Mexico. By the time GATS was created in 1995, the Canadian teachers unions had acquired significant expertise on trade issues. In 1999, with the first round of GATS negotiations on the horizon, the Canadian Association of University Teachers (CAUT) initiated discussions with the Canadian Department of Trade to raise their concerns over the topic. To strengthen their position and refine their arguments, CAUT, together with other Canadian unions, commissioned an independent trade consultant to provide a legal opinion on the impacts of GATS on education. This report served to enhance their expert knowledge and effectively strengthened their opposition to the GATS.[14] Interestingly, the legal opinion also raised concerns among Canadian provincial governments (which have constitutional jurisdiction over education). Consequently, the Canadian federal government announced that it would make no commitments on educational services under the GATS (Interview EI 02, Brussels, 2006).

Also in 1999, in the run-up to the WTO Ministerial Conference in Seattle, EI's annual higher education conference was held in Budapest. The Canadian unions included a critical resolution on the GATS in the conference agenda. The staff of EI's higher education division supported the resolution, which was eventually approved by the EI membership. The resolution became the first political step in the campaign against the GATS and the issue acquired official status in EI's political agenda.

Meaning Frames

EI's interpretation of the implications of the GATS is not only based on causal beliefs. As is usually the case with social movements, principled beliefs and values are as relevant as theories in framing and interpreting the issues they deal with (Keck and Sikkink 1998). EI's principled beliefs on education issues include the defense of public education, education equality and state ownership. EI's explanatory frames focus on the implications of GATS for public education and are articulated through various impact dimensions. The main GATS-related concerns expressed in EI's numerous publications include public spending cuts and privatization of education; loss of education quality; loss of cultural diversity; reductions in academic freedom; and increased brain drain (Fouilhoux 2005; EI 2003). On behalf of its membership, EI has frequently highlighted and emphasized the potentially detrimental effects of the GATS on labor issues (EI and PSI 1999).

EI's analysis also highlights the potential impact of domestic regulation negotiations within the GATS. The education community usually focuses its analysis of GATS on the liberalization negotiations and ignores (or is ignorant of) these "other negotiations" (Verger and Robertson 2008). However, EI has been very active in raising the profile of the domestic regulation negotiations because it maintains that their output will be particularly intrusive and detrimental to the capacity of states to regulate education (EI, 2006).

As regards recommendations, EI proposes that education should be removed from the scope of the Agreement. The resolution on GATS approved at EI's 2004 World Conference states that the Conference "mandates the Executive Board to continue and broaden EI's work on GATS by campaigning for appropriate exclusions for education and research from GATS, and from regional and bilateral free trade agreements." However, EI's response to the GATS is not exclusively reactive. Its proposals also have a proactive dimension and, consequently, some alternatives to GATS have been articulated. The most specific proposal is aimed at creating an international legal instrument that would regulate cross-border education. The proposed instrument would not be based on the rationale of trade and competition, as the GATS is, but rather on cooperation and horizontal cultural exchange. Specifically, the instrument proposed should have the following objectives:

a) Recognize that higher education is a human right and a public good; b) Respect cultural and linguistic diversity; c) Balance the goal of protecting indigenous and national higher education systems with the need to encourage international cooperation and exchange; d) Advance and defend the employment and academic rights of higher education teaching personnel, staff and students; e) Defend and promote freedom of speech and thought, and in particular academic freedom and professional rights; f) Ensure the integrity and quality of higher education; g) Promote equality within and between countries; provide full equality for equality seeking groups; and, protect the rights of indigenous peoples; h) Establish global institutions that are open and transparent, and that recognize the priority of human, labor and environmental rights over commercial rights; and i) Preserve the ability of national governments to regulate higher education in the public interest, and to maintain and expand publicly-provided higher education independent of market pressures and free trade disciplines (EI 2004, 3).

Action Repertoires Within a Multi-Scalar Strategy

As part of its campaign against GATS, EI's main action repertoire at the global level has consisted of advocacy and lobbying. It has participated in most of the forums arranged by the WTO that offer opportunities for advocacy and dialogue. It has attended all of the WTO Ministerial Conferences since Singapore, in addition to several WTO public symposiums, and has interviewed a large number of services negotiators and trade representatives at the WTO headquarters, usually during the service negotiation clusters. Indeed, most of the services trade negotiators interviewed in Geneva had had some type of contact with EI staff. EI's activities were primarily aimed at raising awareness about the perils of liberalization commitments under the GATS and at generating widespread opposition to the inclusion of education (or, at least, new education liberalization commitments) within the Agreement. However, participating in these types of activities has also enabled EI to improve its understanding and knowledge of the GATS. It has also contributed to the production of first-hand data aimed at monitoring the liberalization and domestic regulation negotiations within the GATS and at increasing accountability through the dissemination of information. Perhaps the most important tool used by EI to disseminate information on the negotiation process is the newsletter entitled *TradEducation News*. This publication, which has 12 issues to date, is distributed to member unions in various languages and is also publicly available through EI's website.[15]

Initially, EI focused its struggle against the GATS at the international level, as reflected in the fact that the WTO Ministerial Conferences were the prime forums for EI's efforts. Nevertheless, over time, EI has grasped the strategic importance of undertaking advocacy and lobby initiatives at the national level. Therefore, improved understanding of the decision-making process within the GATS negotiations has produced a strategic shift. This way, EI has adopted a two-track strategy and has also brought the anti-GATS campaign to the national level. As part of this shift, EI has decided to work increasingly "to inform member organizations about GATS and to support member organizations in their work with issues related to trade in education, development of educational markets and privatization—lobbying governments not to open up education services to GATS" (Fredriksson 2004, 434).

The active participation and empowerment of national unions has thus become a key element in EI's anti-GATS strategy. This strategic shift has also altered the union's recommendations and motivation frames. Motivation frames are used by social movements to rally people and organizations around their campaigns and struggles. At the motivational level, EI's strategy has meant that national member unions have become the main targets of its communicative action. The member national unions are increasingly seen as key political players that must be activated and motivated if the anti-GATS campaign is to be successful. In this regard, the 2004 World Conference mandated EI to "raise the awareness of EI members of the relevance, impact and importance of international trade agreements to the work of national organizations representing education workers."

As a consequence, national unions have become a focus of the campaign's recommendations. As regards proposals, EI advises its member unions to lobby governments against establishing liberalization commitments and to raise public awareness of the risks of GATS for public education.

In pursuit of this strategy, EI has organized a variety of training and debate initiatives mainly geared toward its members. The following are the most significant:

- EI World Conferences: These tri-annual gatherings are EI's principal decision-making and political forums. At the 2004 and 2007 conferences, the GATS figured prominently. Workshops on the topic were organized and resolutions criticizing the GATS were approved. Similar activities were undertaken at the annual conferences of EI's Higher Education Division.
- Taskforces on GATS: In conjunction with its member unions, EI has organized taskforces to conduct research on the implications of GATS for certain education sectors and to draft position papers. Thus far, two taskforces have been organized, one focused on higher education and the other on vocational education.
- International Seminar (Paris, 2005). EI organized an international seminar on GATS and education for its members at UNESCO's headquarters. The objective was to inform member unions about the dangers of the GATS for public education and to draw up a common action plan.

Finally, to facilitate its training and advocacy work at the national level, EI has developed the *GATS Information Kit,*[16] which contains key information and data on the structure of the GATS, together with commentary on its implications for education and the current status of the countries' negotiations and liberalization commitments. EI has also produced letters and statements that can be used as is or with some adaptations by member unions seeking to organize lobbying activities addressed to their trade and/ or education ministries.

The Campaign at the Global Level

Despite having prioritized the national level as the main battleground of the political struggle against GATS, EI continues to undertake international initiatives. It has pursued its advocacy activities and has reinforced and expanded its international alliances against the GATS. It has continued to work on the GATS issue within broader unions confederations, such as PSI or ICFTU, and has networked with other international education stakeholders such as UNESCO and international students' unions. This networking strategy was also developed at the 2004 World Conference, where it was decided that EI would network with other campaigns undertaken by NGOs concerned about the GATS (Fredriksson 2004).

As regards international networking, EI recently participated in a UNESCO initiative aimed at creating quality assurance guidelines in cross-border higher education with a view to protecting students and education workers amid increasing internationalization of education (see section on UNESCO in this chapter). The guidelines by no means set out all of the demands and ambitions of the international instrument proposed by EI to regulate cross-border education, although they are viewed as a first step toward achieving similar objectives.

7.4   ASSOCIATIONS OF PUBLIC UNIVERSITIES

University associations and, in particular, associations of public universities, have participated very actively in the global debate on GATS and education. One of the key participants has been the International Association of Universities (IAU), which represents universities from all over the world and is headquartered in the UNESCO complex in Paris. In addition, numerous regional associations have been very active in the anti-GATS campaign. The main course action repertoire of these organizations has been to disseminate public statements and declarations that criticize the education liberalization process promoted by the GATS. Through these activities, they are pursuing a double objective: to denounce the trade agreement's interference in the education sector and to make the higher education community aware of this problem. The most relevant statements are as follows:

a)   Joint Declaration on Higher Education and the GATS (2001):

This was the first statement from the university sector that specifically dealt with the GATS issue. It was signed by the rich countries' main university associations[17] and is frequently cited in debates on GATS. The declaration reads as follows:

> "Our member institutions are committed to reducing obstacles to international trade in higher education using conventions and agreements *outside of a trade policy regime*. This commitment includes, but is not limited to improving communications, expanding information exchanges and developing agreements concerning higher education institutions, programs, degrees or qualifications and quality review practices" (AUCC et al 2001, 1).

b)   Porto Alegre Letter (2002)

This document was signed during the third Ibero-American Summit of Public University Chancellors (Porto Alegre, April 2002). For most of the university chancellors who attended, it was the first time they had heard about the GATS. The letter was proposed and written by Marco Antonio Rodrigues Dias, the former director of UNESCO's Higher Education Division. The signatory universities expressed their "deep concern over the policies promoted by the WTO that favor international trade in education and that treat education as an ordinary commodity." Additionally, the document warns of the "disastrous consequences of these agreements" and urges governments "not to make any education commitments within the framework of the GATS."[18] This letter was broadly circulated within the Latin American higher education community and triggered debate within specific regional associations such as the Asociación de Universidades

Grupo Montevideo and the Unión de Universidades de América Latina (Didou 2006).

c)   Accra Declaration (2004) and Other Regional Declarations

The Accra Declaration was signed by the Association of African Universities (AAU) within the framework of the seminar entitled "The Implications of WTO/GATS for Higher Education in Africa" (April 2004, Accra, Ghana), which the AAU co-organized with UNESCO and the South African Council on Higher Education. The declaration criticizes the GATS mainly from the point of view of development. The signatories expressed their concern with "the ambiguities, silences and lack of clarity in the GATS provisions, the lack of transparency in GATS deliberations and the insufficient knowledge and understanding of the full implications of GATS for higher education, especially in developing country contexts" (AAU 2004, 3). The Accra Declaration is the first and best known of a series of regional declarations promoted by UNESCO and higher education organizations.[19] All of these declarations emphasize that the concept of education as a business commodity should be subordinated to the concept of education as a right, and that cooperation should be prioritized over commercial exchange.

d)   Sharing Quality Higher Education Across Borders (2005)

This statement was drafted at the IAU International Conference held in Alexandria in November 2005 and was signed by various regional and national university associations.[20] The statement directly challenges the education internationalization regime promoted under the Agreement:

> Some governments seek to manage cross-border higher education through multilateral and regional trade regimes designed to facilitate the flow of private goods and services. There are three main limitations to this approach. First, trade frameworks are not designed to deal with the academic, research or broader social and cultural purposes of cross-border higher education. Second, trade policy and national education policy may conflict with each other and jeopardize higher education's capacity to carry out its social and cultural mission. Third, applying trade rules to complex national higher education systems designed to serve the public interest may have unintended consequences that can be harmful to this mission (IAU 2005, 3).

These university statements normally contain demands and recommendations to the effect that governments should not make education liberalization commitments, that they should adopt a cautious approach (because of the unknown effects of GATS) and/or that the negotiation process should be more democratic, participatory and transparent. Most universities that sign these statements maintain that the internationalization of higher education should be based on non-trade principles such as cooperation and cultural exchange. However, their position is not anti-free trade and they usually clarify that they are only challenging the fact that free-trade rules are affecting the education sector (AUCC 2001; Caplan 2003; Oosterlinck 2002).

Despite the foregoing, no university associations have led an ongoing political campaign, as Education International has done, nor have they participated in WTO events, such as the Ministerial Conferences, nor have they tried to influence the GATS participatory subsystem. Instead, they claim to have raised awareness among universities and national university associations about GATS-related issues, in addition to urging universities to lobby governments to make the GATS negotiations more accountable. For instance, the IAU maintains that it should not lobby against GATS at the WTO level, but should instead empower its members to pressure their governments at the state level (Interview IAU 01, Paris, 2006). The European University Association (EUA) has also promoted a number of initiatives aimed at shifting the GATS debate to the national level (EUA 2001, 5).

It could be argued that, in light of these anti-GATS initiatives, public universities are clearly committed to the struggle against neoliberal globalization. For this reason, Boaventura de Sousa Santos observes that:

> Universities have a long tradition of international networking based on common scientific and intellectual interests. This kind of globalization goes on today, and, as it refuses itself to be based on profit considerations and on rules of international trade, is becoming a counter-hegemonic globalization (Dale and Robertson 2004, 155).

However, a kind of double standard is apparent in the public universities' approach to the GATS debate. On the one hand, they sign anti-GATS statements and denounce the "commodification of education", but, on the other hand, public universities from developed countries are the key agents of education commercialization and their rationale is becoming increasingly similar to that of profit-oriented transnational corporations. Van der Wende captures this contradiction very clearly:

> It is therefore encouraging to see that certain actors, notably the higher education institutions by their representative bodies, are choosing to be slightly more open and to engage in the discussions on GATS (the risk of being left completely aside has been realized). Obviously, they are hindered by the schizophrenic nature of their sector. Although in these discussions, they like to emphasize their public role and function, most of their member institutions are at the same time very active in the marketplace. Especially across the borders, public institutions tend to behave like private entities accompanied very often with (quasi) corporate strategies (Wende 2003, 202).

Public universities from Northern countries were very active and critical participants in the GATS debate at the beginning of the Doha Round. However, the topic mostly disappeared from their agendas after a few years. According to Vlk (2006), this was because some Northern countries' associations, such as the EUA, realized that they could benefit from the global trade rules promoted by the GATS. Consequently, they have chosen to deal with this issue in a more constructive way and have tempered their initial opposition.

After becoming aware of this double standard, the IAU (together with the AUCC, ACE and CHEA) released the document entitled *Sharing Quality Higher Education across Borders: A Checklist for Good Practice* for the benefit of their members. The objective was to encourage member universities to adopt more responsible internationalization practices. Above and beyond making "easy" criticisms of the GATS, the IAU considers that universities should critically reflect on the effects of their own transnational practices. As the document states: "The 2006 Checklist is designed as a tool to help institutions ensure that the principles promoted by the Statement [Sharing Quality Higher Education Across Borders, 2004] were being respected."[21]

7.5   WORLD BANK, UNCTAD AND OTHER GLOBAL ACTORS

a)   World Bank: Placing 'Trade in Education' on the Agenda?

The World Bank's influence on southern countries' education policies is enormous. This influence is mainly reflected in loan conditions (Bonal 2002), although it is increasingly exercised through dissemination activities aimed at persuading policy-makers to adopt certain policies (Tarabini and Verger 2007).

As regards higher education, the World Bank's conditions and recommendations to southern governments are mainly oriented toward the promotion of privatized funding and supply. This is because the World Bank bases its policy recommendations on rates of return calculations and considers that public investment in education is more efficient in social and economic terms when concentrated at the lower education levels (WB 1994; Heyneman, 2003).

As regards trade policies, the World Bank's commitment to free trade is well known. Trade liberalization is one of the key measures included in the structural adjustment programs (SAPs) that were imposed on southern countries in the eighties and nineties. Currently, free trade is also promoted by more recent core development instruments of the Bank such as the Poverty Reduction Strategy Papers (PRSPs) (CIDSE/Caritas 2004). Moreover, the World Bank often states that the WTO negotiations and outcomes should be as far-reaching as possible. When negotiations occur during a critical period, the World Bank urges the trade negotiators to look for solutions and to foster understanding between the parties (Jawara and Kwa 2004).

But is the World Bank specifically dealing with the issue of the GATS and trade in education? Actually, the issue is not central in the Bank's agenda yet. A recent working paper published by the organization recognizes that "systematic analysis of the international trade in higher education has not been undertaken within the World Bank, despite its growing importance for developing countries" (Bashir 2007, 9). In fact, the topic has been only tangentially treated in the organization's official reports. In "Constructing Knowledge Societies: New Challenges for Tertiary Education," the World Bank express its commitment to a sort of embedded liberalism that balances education liberalization with the legitimate right of states to regulate education quality or preserve national culture. It believes that these objectives can be reached without "erecting rigid entry barriers" (WB 2002, 126). Despite this apparently balanced message, the World Bank recommends opening up markets to education service imports (WB 2002) and is convinced that cross-border education can contribute to improving access to higher education, attracting expertise and expanding the education offer in poor countries (OECD and WB 2007).

World Bank representatives were also present at the OECD Forum on Trade in Services. In that occasion, they supported the benefits of education liberalization, stating that universities and governments should adapt to the new global education market (Holm-Nielsen 2002)[22] and that in the context of the knowledge economy, developing countries should take advantage of global knowledge through trade (Patrinos 2002). Interestingly, the French Community of Belgium's Ministry of Childrens' Affairs addressed the role of the World Bank's representatives at that forum:

> With similar cynicism, a representative of the World Bank, also at the Washington Conference but off the record, said that if the less advanced countries want to achieve the EFA goals, they should privatize their whole system of education and to take commitments for it in the GATS (Vanlathem 2003).

The World Bank is a member of the main WTO organs, including the Services Council. However, as interviews with the trade negotiators demonstrate, the World Bank is not especially active in trade forums dealing with education liberalization issues. As with the other international organizations analyzed, the World Bank deals more actively with such issues outside the participatory subsystem (i.e. by disseminating ideas in public reports and forums). However, the World Bank, together with the IMF, has indirectly dealt with these issues by influencing the less developed countries' negotiation positions within the GATS. As previously noted, the SAPs, and more recently the PRSPs, push for trade liberalization in southern countries. In some cases, it is specified that services must also be liberalized and that this liberalization must be consolidated within the framework of the GATS. Consequently, the bargaining capacity of certain less developed countries within the WTO service negotiations has been drastically reduced (Interview UNCTAD 01).

b)   UNCTAD: from "New World Order" to "Embedded Liberalism"

The United Nations Conference on Trade and Development (UNCTAD) was created in 1964 to promote the participation of southern countries in world trade. The organization provides technical assistance, research services, policy analysis and statistical data to its members. It also serves as a forum for intergovernmental deliberation on trade issues, although countries do not negotiate trade agreements within it. The UNCTAD defines itself as an "authoritative knowledge-based institution whose work aims to help shape current policy debates and thinking on development".[23]

UNCTAD was created by the G77 (a coalition of developing countries in the UN system) as an alternative forum to the GATT. At the time, several southern countries were not GATT members and those that were felt excluded from the decision-making processes (Koenig-Archibugi 2002) (Kessie 1999). UNCTAD challenged the theories that conceived trade liberalization as a path to development (Henderson 1998) and promoted the idea of a new world order based on principles other than free trade. Today, the rivalry between UNCTAD and the WTO remains, although this is probably due more to corporative than to ideological factors (Lavelle 2005). Currently, UNCTAD accepts the core principles of free-trade doctrine and does not view free trade as representing an imposition on poor countries by rich countries (Henderson 1998). However, in contrast with the WTO's disembedded liberalism, UNCTAD promotes embedded liberalism and believes that liberalization measures must be accompanied by pro-development public policies (Peet 2003).

UNCTAD and the WTO work together because they share facilities such as the International Trade Centre, a technical agency that supports the private sector on trade issues.[24] Moreover, the WTO's country representatives are the same people as UNCTAD's country representatives. This is because both organizations are headquartered in Geneva and both deal with trade issues. So, the trade representaitves interviewed gave a valuous comparative view on both organizations. In short, developing countries' representatives normally perceive UNCTAD as an interesting forum for debate in which they can express ideas and concerns about the WTO negotiations and other trade matters more freely than within the WTO itself. However, on their part, rich countries' representatives do not take UNCTAD particularly seriously and, as happens with UNESCO, they think that it is a forum that results more useful for developing countries than for them.

UNCTAD does not specialize in education, nor does it conduct research on education liberalization. Instead, it deals with service liberalization in general. In recent reports, UNCTAD is very critical of the impact of service liberalization. There, it warns that service exports will not increase for developing countries and that GATS has damaged southern service providers. It also states that trade liberalization has occasionally led to increases in the prices of basic services and that GATS measures that could benefit developing countries, such as the Special and Differential Treatment, have not yet been implemented (UNCTAD 2005). Finally, it recognizes that trade liberalization is especially sensitive for public services and explains that the liberalization of public services has been positive in some countries and negative in others.

Despite this, UNCTAD has not called for a moratorium of the GATS negotiations or something similar. Rather, it advises its members that services should be liberalized slowly and gradually and should be accompanied by effective national policies and, if possible, by a national services plan (UNCTAD 2005). UNCTAD recommends a cautious approach to service liberalization under the GATS because countries' regulatory capacity could be affected (Abugattas 2006). As regards public services such as education, UNCTAD recommends the adoption of policy measures aimed at ensuring that liberalization does not affect access or undermine the achievement of the Millennium Development Goals (UNCTAD 2005).

In other words, UNCTAD's recommendations do not deal specifically with education, but rather with services in general. The organization calls for trade liberalization of services, but from a perspective of caution. The outcomes it seeks are thus located somewhere between liberalization and non-liberalization depending on whether the conditions for liberalization have been achieved at the national level. However, as with the World Bank, UNCTAD's scope of influence is primarily LDCs (Lavelle 2005). This is because developed countries do not view UNCTAD as a key conceptual reference; developing countries find UNCTAD's analysis on trade and development useful, although they define their positions and priorities autonomously.

c) Students, Quality Assurance Agencies and Other Stakeholders

Other international education stakeholders have participated in the international debate on GATS, although they have maintained a lower profile in the political aspects of the negotiations. Surprisingly, the INQAAHE—the most extensive network of education quality assurance agencies—has said very little on the topic. On behalf of students' unions, the European Students International Bureau (ESIB) has been quite active in disseminating anti-GATS information at the European level,[25] although it too has kept a low political profile. On their part, international corporate lobbies, such as the European Services Forum or the Coalition of Services Industries, have not shown much interest in the liberalization of education markets, although they have actively lobbied for the liberalization of services in general. However, the education industry, students' unions and quality assurance agencies have played a more important role at the national than at the international level. In fact, a number of these stakeholders will appear in the two national case studies presented in Chapter 9.

Interestingly, albeit is not well known by the education community, a number of local governments have been very active anti-GATS campaigners and have targeted international networks.[26] Indeed, the political campaign they have developed has been much more intense and international than that of most other education stakeholders. Through their campaigns, progressive local and regional governments (mainly from northern countries) have rejected GATS because it encroaches on public services that they provide and affects the welfare of their citizens (Verger 2008). The main line of action is for local governments, which are not formally able to participate in the negotiations, to declare themselves and their territory "GATS-free zones". In this way, local governments can publicly engage in civil disobedience with respect to their GATS obligations. The campaign has been especially successful in countries such as France, where the national government has even taken "rebel" local governments to court for anti-constitutional activities.[27]

7.6   CONCLUSIONS

This chapter has examined which international actors have (or have not) participated in the GATS negotiations and how they have tried to influence the outcomes of the negotiations.

Most of the stakeholders analyzed exert influence by participating in the battle of ideas concerning GATS and education, i.e. by developing and disseminating arguments in favor of or against the GATS. Moreover, these actors have a preconceived notion of how the negotiations should unfold. Some of them have attempted to halt education liberalization (e.g. EI and several university associations), while others seek to promote "cautious liberalization" (e.g. UNESCO, UNCTAD). Other actors such as the OECD have adopted a more liberal, although on occassion, ambiguous position. The World Bank, for its part, is not so involved in the GATS and education debate as other organizations, but its few public declarations point to the potential benefits of higher education liberalization in developing contexts. Table 7.1 summarizes the positions and strategies of these and other actors in the global struggle for and against education liberalization.

Table 7.1. Global Actors' Positions on GATS and Education

ACTOR	ACTION REPERTOIRES	MEANING REPERTOIRES	PROPOSALS	LEVEL
OECD	Brokers between the education and commercials worlds. Dissemination of ideas between their members	Respects policy space. Favors offer and investment in higher education. Favors development, although it could also favors an unequal exchange	Explore challenges and opportunities of trade in education	[+] Pro-liberalization
World Bank	Tangential recommendations in reports and working papers	GATS favors higher education access in developing countries	Liberalization continuity	
UNCTAD	Advice and dissemination of ideas between their members	Could restrict access to public services and favors unequal exchange. Restricts *policy space*	Caution when establishing commitments	
UNESCO	Advice and dissemination of ideas between their members	Could undermine education quality and restrict access to education. Favors an unequal exchange and does not respect cultural diversity	Caution when establishing commitments. Consider other variables (quality, access, cultural diversity)	
Universities (IAU)	Dissemination of ideas between their members. Raise the awareness of their members to make them act at national level	Restricts *policy space*. Favors unequal exchange in education. Undermines education quality. Alters traditional functions of education	Education liberalization moratorium. Broader participation of universities within the negotiations	
Education International	Advocacy / lobbying to WTO country representatives. Raise the awareness of their members to make them act at national level	Restricts *policy space*. Favors unequal exchange in education. Privatizes education funding and provision, and restricts access. Damages labor conditions. Alters traditional functions of education	Education excluded from GATS. Education liberalization moratorium. Organization of national campaigns to stop the GATS advance. Adoption of an alternative higher education instrument	[-] Pro-liberalization

This chapter has not said so much about the actual influence of these international organizations and associations within the WTO participatory and representative subsystems. The following chapters, specifically chapters 9 and 10, will provide more in-deep data and analysis about this particular issue.

8 Negotiating Education in the WTO
Key Ideas and Actors

The WTO negotiations are led by representatives of the WTO member countries representatives and facilitated by the WTO staff. These two groups comprise what we call the participatory subsystem. The country representatives are at the core of the GATS negotiations matrix since only they are authorized to make political decisions. They interact continuously with trade negotiators from other countries, as well as with members of the WTO Secretariat, with international civil society organizations and with their own national representative subsystems. So, to enhance our understanding of the education liberalization process under the GATS, the country representatives' views and beliefs must be examined in-depth. Precisely, this is one of the main objectives of this chapter. Specifically, the chapter explores the views of the trade negotiators and the WTO staff on the GATS and education issue and examines how these stakeholders interact and exchange ideas with other representative subsystems, mainly civil society organizations.

The content of the chapter is based on document analysis and on interviews conducted at the WTO headquarters with trade negotiators and WTO staff. The data collected will be used to verify similarities and differences in the views on GATS and education within the participatory subsystem. The data will also be used to determine whether the "battle of ideas" explored in previous chapters has penetrated and been reproduced within this subsystem. Finally, an assessment will be provided of how and to what extent these ideas contribute to shaping countries' positions in the education sector negotiations.

8.1 WTO SECRETARIAT: THE LIBERALIZATION ADVOCATES

In Chapter 4, we showed how the WTO system of rules drives the negotiations toward a certain outcome. The WTO rules, procedures, principles and norms all favor liberalization and discriminate against other positions, such as protectionism. The Secretariat is a key advocate and guardian of the WTO's principles and core ideas. Its strategies and initiatives aim to promote the economic benefits of trade liberalization among the WTO members and beyond. Although the WTO staff do not have decision-making powers, they attempt to persuade country delegations that liberalization is desirable. In this regard, education may not be an exception. One trade negotiator offered this assessment:

> I really get the impression that the Secretariat has an ideological bias. I am increasingly convinced that it favors liberalization. You feel it when you listen to them talking about gambling [the gambling services case], domestic regulation, etc. They make sweeping interpretations, very intrusive interpretations in some cases, because they are convinced that free trade is desirable. . . That's fine, but there are other things that must be taken into account at the same time (Interview Trade Negotiator 02, Geneva, 2006).

The WTO Secretariat promotes trade liberalization through a variety of mechanisms, ranging from technical assistance to dissemination of publications. Publications by the Secretariat, particularly those issued by the Information and Media Relations Division, defend free trade in highly persuasive style. According to these publications, free trade benefits everyone: employers and workers, citizens and consumers, rich countries and poor countries alike (WTO 2008). In these documents, comparative advantage theory and market-based solutions are "articles of faith" (Bøås and McNeill 2003). The Trade in Services Division performs a similar function with respect to services liberalization (Adlung 2005; WTO 2001).

The WTO literature on education liberalization is not extensive. In fact, the Secretariat has only published two documents on the topic. The first was distributed at the Council for Trade in Services in 1998 with the aim of providing member countries with information in advance of the education sector negotiations (Interview WTO staff 01, Geneva, 2006). This document highlights the economic and trade potential of education. It also states that the shift of education from a public good to a commodity, despite the attendant risks, is inevitable and ultimately beneficial. Liberalization is presented as the most effective way of broadening the education offer without straining public finances. The document has been considered as biased due to the description of education trends it makes and to the strong causal connections it ascribes to the benefits of trade and other market mechanisms.

> In the United Kingdom in the 1980s, a movement away from public financing and toward greater market responsiveness, coupled with an increasing openness to alternative financing mechanisms, has led universities in new directions, balancing academic quality with business management. Similarly in the Netherlands, some institutions have seen

the need to attract new funding and behave in a more entrepreneurial fashion by providing their services to businesses, e.g. contracting to perform applied research for small and medium enterprises (WTO 1998, 5).

Political bias is also evident in the document's data sources, which the country delegations are encouraged to consult for further information on education internationalization. All of the sources, except UNESCO, are organizations that support education liberalization.[1] The Secretariat document on education was also published in a book edited by the Secretariat entitled *Guide to the GATS. An Overview of Issues for Further Liberalization of Trade in Services* that was geared toward preparing policy-makers and trade negotiators for the GATS 2000 negotiations.

Interestingly, this document was assailed by some Southern countries for its bias and for strengthening the hand of the countries most interested in services liberalization. These Southern countries asked the Secretariat to stop publishing such documents because of fears that they would influence the negotiation process. This may explain why the Secretariat's second document on GATS and education did not appear until 2005. Written from a third-person perspective, this more recent document featured a very different—i.e. more impartial—style. It ostensibly reflected the positions of the member countries, not of the Secretariat. Moreover, it was presented as a compilation of countries' opinions on GATS and education, supposedly providing a more nuanced picture and a more objective point of view than the first document. However, the data presentation method is still partial because pro-liberalization positions are clearly emphasized and critical views are downplayed. Box 8.1 contains three salient quotations from the document. The first one emphasizes the Agreement's benefits for education. The second delegitimizes various critical opinions from members, citing lack of understanding of GATS issues. The third asserts that GATS critics are marginal figures within the WTO membership. As will be seen in the following section, it is true that the number of critical positions on GATS and education openly exposed by WTO countries representatives is very small. However, it should be noted that the Secretariat's writing style, despite a veneer of impartiality, actually leads the reader toward a positive view of the GATS and its implications for education and encourages the WTO members to adopt liberalization commitments.

Relations with Civil Society

The Secretariat normally avoids interacting with civil society organizations that are highly critical of free trade (see Chapter 4). The ideas that

---

Box 8.1   WTO Secretariat and Trade in Education

#1 "Domestic institutions may be given a competitive stimulus with flow-on benefits to students. One delegation noted that increased trade might support national policy objectives, especially in countries that had limited resources for expanding certain aspects of their own education sectors. Also, some countries encouraged their students, including through subsidization and other support, to study abroad in order to gain the skills and experiences needed in their own home country (. . .) Some delegations underlined that their countries' commitments on education services had not raised any problems over the last ten years, showing that a strong public sector could live in perfect coexistence with private providers."

#2 "A number of delegations acknowledged the political sensitivity of the sector due to its public good element and the high degree of government involvement. Some explained they could not envisage undertaking commitments or more commitments in the sector, while others indicated that sensitivities varied from subsector to subsector (adult and other education services being less sensitive). *They were rooted mostly in misunderstandings of the GATS and should not prevent Members from undertaking commitments in view of the benefits involved.*"

#3 "One delegation said that it was the duty of the government to guarantee effective access of all segments of the population to education. It should not be used for commercial purposes in order to avoid the risk that parts of the population without financial means would be deprived. In many cases, privatization had led to dismissals of teachers and reduced access to education. *All other Members* that commented on education services agreed that the existence of private providers did not amount to the displacement of, but would complement public education services. One negotiating proposal explicitly stated that commitments would be sought only from countries that permit private education".

Source: (WTO 2005b)

---

are critical with GATS because of the Agreement's implications for education and other public services, are not welcomed by the WTO staff either. On occasion, these ideas are strongly contested by the Secretariat. The document *GATS: Facts and Fiction*, written by the WTO Services Division in response to criticisms by civil society organizations, is a clear example of this.

Nor has the Secretariat interacted very often with civil society organizations dealing with education issues. Indeed, when civil society actors try to lobby or meet with the Secretariat staff, they are usually told that the WTO is a member-driven organization and are advised to meet with the country representatives instead. This is what happened to Education International when its representatives met with the Services Division staff to voice concerns over the Agreement's implications for education (Interview WTO staff 01, Geneva, 2006).

8.2 COUNTRY DELEGATIONS: PROTECTIONISTS, LIBERALIZERS AND MERCANTILISTS

For our purposes, analyzing the various country delegations is much more complex than analyzing the Secretariat. As we have seen, the latter has adopted a clear position on GATS and education issues and plays a well-defined role in the negotiation process. In contrast, the country delegations are much more diverse, in several key ways. First, as seen in Chapter 4, their freedom in deciding whether to liberalize education under the GATS is highly variable. Normally, delegations from Less Developed Countries (LDCs) are much more autonomous because they receive a less clear-cut mandate from their national subsystem. Moreover, human resources and expertise vary widely depending on the economic development of countries (Interviews South Centre 01, UNCTAD 02, ICTSD 01, Geneva, 2006).

However, the following section focuses on two other variables that relate more directly to the GATS/education debate: the first concerns the country delegations' attitudes toward and relations with civil society organizations involved in education issues. The second, and most relevant part of the analysis, concerns views and positions on education liberalization within the GATS context. As will be seen, the country delegations are very different in these regards.

Relations with Civil Society Organizations on Education Issues

Two very different attitudes toward civil society organizations may be distinguished among the trade negotiators in the WTO context. These reflect country delegations' openness to civil society organizations and their demands. On the one hand, some negotiators are highly critical of NGOs and trade unions and/or refer to them with disdain. They delegitimize their participation in the GATS debate by saying that civil society representatives do not understand the GATS properly. These delegations are especially critical of the teachers unions, accusing them of opposing GATS because they are resistant to or afraid of any change (Interviews trade negotiators 07, 10, 12 and 14, Geneva, 2006).

> Teachers' unions? Yes, they talk about GATS, but they have not discussed the topic very deeply, they are confused, they are afraid. . . They are afraid that education could be privatized. But in our country there has been private education for the last 50 years. Whenever the government does something to make education more efficient, they think that education is going to be privatized. . . (Interview Trade negotiator 07, Geneva, 2006).

On the other hand, some negotiators sympathize with the demands made by NGOs and unions and even encourage them to campaign against the GATS. This is often the case with country delegations that have defensive interests in the services negotiations; these countries consider that civil society anti-GATS campaigns are strategically useful in legitimizing or strengthening their positions in the services negotiations. Thus, for these countries, NGOs can become a useful ally. On occasion, they may even exchange information or cooperate on an ad hoc basis (Interviews trade negotiators 01 and 11, Geneva, 2006).

Interestingly, most country representatives believe that civil society organizations are influential in the WTO negotiations, particularly as regards the positions adopted by the less developed countries. One country representative expressed his disappointment in these terms: "Civil society organizations are part of the problem [why GATS negotiations are not advancing more smoothly] because they put pressure on the developing countries to make the wrong decisions" (Interview Trade negotiator 12, Geneva, 2006).

On Education Liberalization: Ideas and Positions

In line with the Secretariat's second education document (WTO 2005b), our interviews indicate that WTO member countries tend to emphasize the opportunities of education liberalization while minimizing the attendant risks. Most of the negotiators interviewed take the view that education liberalization within the GATS will be positive. However, positive views on the GATS do not always mean that countries will be willing to make education liberalization commitments during the negotiations. In fact, the trade negotiators do not usually analyze the pros and cons of education liberalization in-depth and do not speak from an education perspective. A clear indication of this is that they do not seem to be aware of the wide-ranging debate on GATS and education and never refer to education sources in their analysis. Instead, they analyze education liberalization using the meaning frames they would use to analyze any other "commodity", as seen in Chapter 6. Nor do they refer to or take into account the numerous statements, forums and other spaces developed by education stakeholders to address these issues.

Albeit these common patterns, the negotiators' positions on GATS and education are by no means homogeneous. Rather, different country positions are identified. For our purposes, these positions may be categorized as protectionists, liberalizers and mercantilists. It should be acknowledged that these positions are not necessarily cast in stone: a given country may change its position during the negotiations or adopt an intermediate position. These categories can be considered, in sociological terms, ideal types that may facilitate our understanding of how the GATS negotiations function and what the outcomes in the education sector may be. Broadly speaking, the protectionists refuse to make liberalization commitments for political, economic and/or technical reasons. The liberalizers are willing to liberalize education under the GATS because of the potential benefits. The mercantilists are willing to liberalize education if this will open up foreign markets in which their country has offensive interests.

The following section examines the main features and the factors underpinning these positions. We go beyond the positions themselves, which are relatively straightforward, and explore the views (i.e. based on principles and causal beliefs) and the interpretative repertoires that support each position. The various categories are defined inductively and are primarily based on our interviews with trade negotiators and country representatives at the WTO.

Protectionists

Three different meaning repertoires within the protectionist group have been identified: "against the commodification of education", "cautiousness" and "defensive interests."

a) Against the Commodification of Education

This subcategory consists of countries that reject the establishment of commitments in the educational sector for ethical or moral reasons, regardless of cost-benefit analysis or theoretical considerations. Ethical and moral reasons are associated with what Goldstein and Keohane (1993) refer to as "principled beliefs", i.e. normative ideas used to distinguish right from wrong and fair from unfair. Some countries' decisions in the GATS education negotiations are grounded on these considerations and, as a consequence, on sets of values or an explicit ideal of education shared by multiple social stakeholders. Most often, the underlying argument is that education is a social right and a public asset that should be provided by the state. Seen from this perspective, GATS and the commodification of education threaten to undermine education's public function. Consequently, these countries draw a red-line over education and trade negotiators know that they cannot offer this sector during the negotiations.

> Education is one of the most sensitive sectors, of course. In general, we have very open services sectors, telecommunications, audio-visual, etc. But education and health are two key areas for addressing the social problems that we want to face in our country. That is why we refuse to give up any sovereignty whatsoever in these two areas (Interview Trade negotiator 11, Geneva, 2006).

Interestingly, some trade representatives of countries included in the category "against the commodification of education" do not subscribe totally to their country's official position. Their personal opinions are somewhat different from the positions they formally represent (Interviews Trade negotiators 01 and 03, Geneva, 2006). As mentioned at the beginning of this section, trade negotiators are usually quite skeptical with respect to critical analyses of GATS and education. So, in the context of this category, some negotiators emphasize that their countries have adopted protectionist or defensive positions for political reasons (i.e. due to the sensitivity of the education sector), but not because they wish to defend "real" interests or avoid "real" dangers.

In general terms, the "anti-commodification" position seems contingent on national politics, since is usually adopted by countries with social democratic or left-wing governments. In some cases, civil society from these countries has lobbied against the establishment of education commitments or has called for education to be withdrawn from the GATS negotiations altogether (Verger and Bonal 2008).

b) Cautiousness

The countries in this category are also opposed to making education commitments, but for different reasons. Instead of adopting a critical position for identity-related reasons or out of allegiance to certain values, they reject the GATS due to textual ambiguities and related uncertainties. It should be reminded that the WTO trade in services agreement is still incomplete and some parts have yet to be finalized.

The main ambiguities concern: the definition of the services included in the Agreement, the future content of domestic regulation rules and rules, and the services classifications. As regards the definition of services, Article I states that the Agreement applies to all services in all sectors except for "services provided in the exercise of governmental authority," which are defined as being "supplied neither on a commercial basis, nor in competition with one or more service suppliers." Public services are not explicitly excluded; however, public universities may provide commercial services in competition with private providers in most countries. Due to this unclear distinction between public and private categories, countries that do not wish to liberalize a sector that overlaps with the public sector would refuse to make commitments.

> Technically, we have many doubts about the differentiation between public and private. The types of arrangements for public education and private education are totally different from country to country, as are the subsidy regimes and the direct provision of services. . . There are hundreds of potential arrangements. So it's difficult in the negotiations to avoid confusion and to take out the things you really want to take out (Interview Trade negotiator 02, Geneva, 2006).

Another area yet to be finalized in the Agreement is domestic regulation (Article VI). At this point, it is not known which national regulations will be considered "more burdensome than necessary" by the WTO (i.e. rules that are actually acting as barriers to trade and that, consequently, should be modified or removed). In the education sector, the new domestic regulation disciplines could affect quality assurance policies or the measures for the validation of foreign credentials. For this reason, some countries express that, before committing services liberalization, they would like to have in-depth knowledge of Domestic Regulation final disciplines. Their position is straightforward: before committing a sector or sub-sector, these countries want to know exactly what their obligations will be.

A similar phenomenon has been observed with the classification of services. Indeed, it is still unclear which subsectors will be included in the service categories during the negotiations. In some cases, the WTO Dispute Settlement Body has ruled that a service sector is liberalized in a given country even though the country considers that the sector was not specifically included in its list of commitments. As seen previously, this is what happened with online gambling services in the US—a case that continues to resonate in the minds and the calculations of many negotiators.

There are also gray areas relating to the scope and specific meaning of the GATS rules. This has led to the creation of a WTO working group in this area. Nonetheless, unlike the domestic regulation working group, it is unlikely that the GATS rules group's task will be completed in the current round. The GATS rules cover three broad areas: subsidies (Article XV), government procurement (Article XIII) and emergency safeguard mechanisms (Article X) (see Chapter 2 for an explanation of each of these areas).

In addition, the evaluation mandate envisaged in Article XIX has not been carried out. Under this mandate, some WTO resources would be devoted to evaluating the results of the liberalization of trade in services in order to determine, among other things, to what extent they help or hinder developing countries. Since these evaluations have not been carried out, there is greater uncertainty for some countries.

These fears and concerns are based on causal beliefs, i.e. on theories and views concerning cause-and-effect relationships that guide actors toward certain objectives (Goldstein and Keohane, 1993). Within this framework, negotiators' technical knowledge of the Agreement's provisions, together with the theories they construct in this regard, are key mediating variables in analyzing the position of countries in the negotiation of services. This knowledge is often theoretical in nature and does not directly relate to the world of education. If such views are predominant, country delegations may decide not to take part in the negotiations at all in order to avoid making commitments that could have unforeseen consequences and would be difficult to reverse. However, it should be noted that once these transitory issues have been resolved, these countries might be willing to adopt education liberalization commitments.

c) Defensive Interests

The discourse on defensive interests is more implicit than explicit. In fact, defensive arguments appear only tangentially in the interviews and apparently no countries have placed them at the centre of their GATS and education negotiation strategy. The discourse on defensive interests does not focus on the GATS provisions, but rather on the potential liberalization's impact on national education systems. This discourse may reflect national regulatory shortcomings in the area of education, as well as those of the national education industry. As with the "against education commodification" repertoire, education is viewed as a sensitive sector. In this case, however, moral principles are not invoked; instead, the rationale is that national education systems might be harmed if trade liberalization commitments are adopted. It is feasible that governments that subscribe to an economically nationalistic political program take this view. As they seek to define their positions, pressure from the domestic private education sector may acquire particular relevance. Indeed, in an attempt to avoid international competition, private university associations in several countries have successfully lobbied trade ministers not to make liberalization commitments. This position may be based on the theoretical and potential effects of competition, although it may also be based on the experiences of other countries whose education sectors were adversely affected after higher education was liberalized. One of the most notorious cases was the acquisition of the Universidad del Valle (Mexico's second largest private university) by Sylvan Learning Systems (an American education consortium), made possible by Mexico's ratification of the North American Free Trade Agreement (Rodríguez Gómez 2004).

Moreover, many Southern countries have not developed adequate regulatory frameworks for higher education. Making liberalization commitments could undermine efforts in this regard and complicate the creation of evaluation systems of the quality of cross-border education providers in the future. Like the advocates of cautiousness, some of the countries that are closer to the defensive interests model are not necessarily opposed to the introduction of education within the GATS. They might even embrace liberalization if certain criteria are met, such as a more solid regulatory framework or a more competitive education industry at the national level.

Liberalizers

The liberalizers category consists of two main constituencies: countries with offensive interests in education markets and fervent free trade advocates.

a) Offensive Interests

In the context of WTO negotiations, coutries with common interests or concerns are usually organized under coalitions. In the Doha Round, none of the existing coalitions has defensive interests in services—or, specifically, in education services- as its *raison d'etre*. (Narlikar and Woods 2003). However, countries with offensive interests in education have organized themselves: led by New Zealand, they have constituted the known as the Friends Group of Education. Friends groups are country groups with shared interests in advancing liberalization in certain service sectors. They exchange information and share strategic advice on gaining access to new markets within the GATS negotiations. Their members are usually developed countries since they have a greater comparative advantage with respect to trade in services. Thus far, the main initiative of the Friends Group of Education has been to coordinate a plurilateral demand on education services during the Doha Round. This demand, issued in early 2006, is focused on the higher education and "Other education services" subsectors.

Offensive interests in education are also evident in the "Communications on Education" issued by education exporters such as Australia, the US and New Zealand (see Box 6.1). These communications encourage WTO member countries to liberalize education and attempt to address concerns with respect to the potential impacts of the GATS on education systems.

> Australia currently enjoys the benefits of having a relatively open education and training regime. This openness is reflected in the significant number of commitments that Australia has entered in its current GATS schedule for the following educational services: secondary education, higher education and other education services. Australia believes that all Members should, in the context of the current round, consider entering commitments on education services similar to those already entered by Australia. This particularly applies to those Members who have previously failed to enter any commitments in relation to education services (WTO-Australia 2001, 3).

Countries with offensive interests in education have usually set the example for other countries and have already liberalized higher education under the GATS. The US is the most remarkable exception, which is why Mundy and Iga (2003) refer to the "hegemonic exceptionalism" of the US in the GATS education context. However, during the Doha Round, US's services offer includes higher education liberalization commitments for the first time.[2]

b)   Fervent Free Trade Advocates

Most of the countries in this category have already liberalized education within the framework of the GATS. They maintain that fears of educational liberalization are unfounded and argue that liberalization will benefit the education sector in a variety of ways. The most frequently cited benefits are increased competition in the education sector, increased foreign investment, improved human resources, enhanced expertise and a wider education offer. Accordingly, fervent free traders take the view that the net effect of liberalization will be to improve the quality of national education. In addition, they consider that fears relating to the gray areas of the GATS are misplaced.

> There is a clear consensus on the fact that the education system in my country is bad, and we have to find a way to improve it. This means bringing in teachers from abroad [. . .]. The GATS could increase our competitiveness, which is essential (Interview Trade negotiator 04, Geneva, 2006).

In the pro-free trade discourse, the predominant rationale is that education is an economic sector and that, as such, it must be liberalized to maximize efficiencies and wealth generation. Although these views are based on certain causal beliefs, the underlying argument is grounded on principles that are essentially ideological in nature. More specifically, these countries are strongly committed to free trade and embrace a neoliberal ideology. They also maintain that free trade is the optimal economic system and that trade liberalization is desirable across the board, not just in education.

The countries that engage in free trade discourse are usually consistent in their actions; they either liberalized their education services during the Uruguay Round or plan to do so during the Doha Round. Their governments may be characterized as neoliberal and are firmly committed to free trade. However, as is often the case with discourse analysis, it is difficult to determine whether interviewees are truly committed to certain principles or are simply "toeing the party line." It should be noted that WTO members are expected to support free trade; when asked about ideological issues by a foreign researcher, some may elect to provide "politically correct" or "acceptable" answers. It is plausible to assume that, during the Uruguay Round, some countries liberalized education as a quid pro quo and have subsequently modified or ellaborated their discourse to justify that decision. In other words, some countries that now defend free trade in education may have opened up their markets in a bid to use education as a bargaining chip tool. In the next section, this idea is developed.

Mercantilists

This category comprises a single interpretative repertoire: "education as bargaining chip." As will be observed, this is the most utilitarian approach to education negotiations within the GATS.

a) Education as Bargaining Chip

For countries in this category, the decision to liberalize education is not based on ethics, uncertainties concerning with the gray areas of GATS or vacillations between the perceived opportunities and dangers of liberalization. Instead, it is based on external factors. Outstandingly, the level of liberalization ambition achieved by the Doha Round in various sectors would be one of these external factors. This category normally includes developing countries that have no offensive interests in education whatsoever (or in services in general) but that might liberalize their education sector in exchange for greater liberalization by other countries in the areas of agriculture or textiles. Education is thus treated as a bargaining chip and theoretical or ideological considerations about education are not central to explaining the negotiating position of these countries. In such cases, education is wholly subservient to interests in other sectors of the economy. Instead of applying free trade theory or other rationales, these negotiators are simply working to protect the interests of their countries' main exporters.

> Education? No, we don't have any commitments at the WTO level. Nor have we received any demands on education. We will only commit on education if we get something in return (. . .). In the end, we present a unique list. We take stock and education is just one element (Interview Trade negotiator 07, Geneva, 2006).

> We always use services as a bargaining chip; we will make concessions if we get something back. That is our basic logic for negotiating services. The premise that 'liberalization is good' doesn't wash with us. We don't believe in that doctrine. In fact, it gets on my nerves. Here nobody really believes it, not even their preachers believe it [referring here to the WTO staff] (Interview Trade negotiator 01, Geneva, 2006).

Apparently, the mercantilist position is only held by a minority of the countries we interviewed (in fact, it represents only one in six positions identified). However, it should be noted that other positions may fall within the scope of mercantilism. As we said, the positions of mercantilism, liberalism and protectionism are presented as ideal types. In practice, countries often adopt mixed and ambiguous positions. For instance, apparently protectionist positions (characterized by cautiousness and defensive interests) may include some mercantilist aspects. If certain technical problems (e.g. ambiguities with respect to some parts of the Agreement or loopholes in national education regulations) are resolved, cautious and defensive countries may be willing to make education liberalization commitments in return for market access. A similar effect could occur with countries that adopt liberalizing positions: having offensive interests or believing in the benefits of free trade does not mean that they will open up their education markets to trade unless they receive something in return.

Various scholars have already explained the relevance of mercantilism in the current international system of trade. For instance, Robert Putnam (1999) has argued that, beyond promoting free-trade, international trade negotiators are pressured to primarily satisfy "national interests" and promote them in light of offers made by negotiators from other countries. On his part, Paul Krugman captures the dominant rationale within trade forums such as the WTO with this clear-eyed assessment:

> Anyone who has tried to make sense of international trade negotiations eventually realizes that they can only be understood by realizing that they are a game scored according to mercantilist rules, in which an increase in exports—no matter how expensive to produce in terms of other opportunities foregone—is a victory, and an increase in imports—no matter how many resources it releases for other uses—is a defeat (Krugman 1997, 114).

In fact, one of the trade negotiators interviewed expressed disappointment with this prevailing rationale:

> In the WTO context, there are a lot of things that are irrational. The basic premise of the system is that free trade is good, that Smith and Ricardo were right. That is the essence. However, the negotiation process is inverted. First, we talk about liberalizing the economy as a 'concession', as a cost, when actually it is a benefit. There, it is like a game. A lot of countries, above all the developing countries, do not understand the basic premise of free trade and the rules of the game . . . [In the negotiations] there is a deeply wrong ideology, because there is too much academic literature in one sense. The recent history demonstrates that the free trade premise is right, that it works. . . If we organize an open discussion, it is clear which argument is going to win. However, it doesn't happen (Interview Trade negotiator 12, Geneva, 2006).

In one word, mercantilist ideology works as a master frame in the WTO context. Interestingly, mercantilism amounts to an informal set of rules that casts a shadow over the ostensibly pro-free trade WTO rules, as well as over its protectionist opponents. Within the framework of the WTO's "all unique" negotiation procedure (see Chapter 4), this means that education can be treated as yet another bargaining chip.

8.3   CONCLUSIONS

The Secretariat is the most pro-liberalization actor within the WTO participatory subsystem. The WTO staff is ideologically monolithic and fervently pro-free trade. Indeed, the WTO has consistently disseminated the benefits of opening up education markets to international trade. However, this is not the case for the WTO country delegations, which hold a variety of positions. Member countries may adopt a pro-liberalization or protectionist position depending on the issue at hand and, more specifically, depending on whether "national interests" are enhanced or undermined by liberalizing a given sector. Contrary to WTO principles, the negotiators' central rationale is not free trade, but mercantilism. Mercantilism may not be the sole rationale in the GATS education negotiations, but it is predominant.

Table 8.1 summarizes the negotiators' positions and meaning repertoires as regards the education sector. Each position is characterized according to the underlying rationale, the underlying conception of education (as applicable) and the way in which these ideas could influence the final outcomes of the negotiations. The table also shows how the three positions overlap; in this regard, they are not so rigid after all.

Table 8.1   Ideas for the Negotiation of Education in the GATS Context

Repertoires	a.1. Education is not a commodity	a.2. Caution	a.3. Defensive interests	c.1. Bargaining chip	b.1. Offensive interests	b.2. Free trade believers
Type of ideas	Moral principles ('Education is not a commodity.')	Causal beliefs (ambiguities of GATS)	Causal beliefs (dangers of liberalization for national education)	Instrumental, not ideational	Causal beliefs (comparative advantage)	Ideology (opportunities derived from education liberalization)
Conception of education	Public asset provided by the State	Irrelevant	Supplied by national providers	Irrelevant: a 'bargaining chip'.	Source of national income	Scarce asset - commodity
Result expected (Yes/No education liberalization commitments)	No. Education liberalization non-negotiable	No or Yes. Necessary condition: that the grey areas of GATS are cleared up	No or Yes. Necessary condition: possess an adequate regulatory framework or a competitive domestic industry	Yes or No: Liberalization commitments in function of results in other areas	Yes: Liberalization to give example	Yes: Liberalization to improve education
Position		'Protectionist'			'Liberal'	
			'Mercantilist'			

Source: Author

Beyond the Development Factor

Analyzing the discourse and ideas of trade negotiators enables us to provide a more comprehensive explanation of the GATS negotiations than one based solely on economic development. Based on the qualitative analysis in this chapter, economic development overlaps with other factors, including countries' ideas on the GATS/education relationship and, more importantly, on how education should be strategically negotiated under the GATS. These ideational factors complement the economic development variable and enable us to provide a more sophisticated explanation of why countries decide to liberalize education under the GATS.

Economic development has proved itself to be a very significant variable for understanding education liberalization commitments in the Uruguay Round (see Chapter 5). Indeed, it is still valid for understanding the positions of some countries in the Doha Round. For instance, a strong correlation still exists between the level of economic development and defensive or offensive positions. However, it appears that the north-south education liberalization gap will diminish after Doha. A number of developing countries, which avoided liberalizing education during the Uruguay Round, have already offered education liberalization during the current round. Moreover, as this chapter has shown, another group of developing countries may be willing to liberalize (higher) education if certain GATS ambiguities are resolved. And, an even larger group will do so if education can be used as a profitable bargaining tool and if ambitious liberalization quotas are offered in exchange in sectors such as agriculture during the Doha Round.

9 National Case Studies
Argentina and Chile

In previous chapters, the GATS and education negotiations and debates were analyzed at the global level. In this chapter, we focus on the national level with a view to providing a more complete and pluri-scalar picture of the negotiations. It should be noted that a number of important variables, such as the negotiating positions of the countries, are defined at the national level. Therefore, interactions, procedures and institutional arrangements at this level should be key elements in understanding the global outcomes of GATS.

To appreciate the full complexity of the negotiations at the national level, two country case studies were realized. During the first stage of the research, the behavior and results for all the WTO member countries were analyzed statistically (Chapter 5). However, a number of intermediate variables that play a key role in understanding national negotiations were not examined during that stage, e.g. the role of non-state actors, the importance of advocacy and lobbying, the impact of national politics, the higher education system, etc. Case study methodology has permitted to incorporate these and other variables in the research framework.

Specifically, two case studies have been carried out, one in Argentina and the other one in Chile. Both studies are presented in this chapter. Each case is divided in two main sections. Firstly, higher education policies and national politics are contextualized. Secondly, the GATS and education negotiations procedures and events are explained using the technique of process tracing and by reviewing the role of key stakeholders. At the end of the chapter, a comparison of both countries is provided.

9.1 ARGENTINEAN HIGHER EDUCATION: FROM CÓRDOBA TO DOHA?

Historical Context

Argentina's higher education system is still marked by a far-reaching program of reforms undertaken in 1918. This initiative was known as the Reform of Córdoba because it stemmed from student demonstrations at Córdoba

University. As a result of this reform, the political autonomy of universities was guaranteed and measures to extend and facilitate access to higher education were implemented. This democratization process was enhanced during President Juan Domingo Perón's first term in office (1946–1955), when free access to university was guaranteed. As a result, enrolment soared across the country (Fernández Lamarra 2003). The military government that overthrew Perón's (1955–1988) regime subsequently authorized the creation of private universities, which led to a proliferation of Catholic-run institutions. However, private universities were legally prohibited from receiving public funding. To this day, private universities cannot receive state subsidies (for ordinary operations) in Argentina (Sánchez Martínez 2002).

The following military dictatorship (1976–1983) ended free university access and brought in tuition fees. However, this government was more concerned with politically controlling the universities than with radically privatizing them. In fact, a number of private universities were nationalized to make political control easier. After democracy was restored in 1983, one of the new government's first steps was to abolish tuition fees.

The neoliberal government of Carlos S. Menem (1989–1999) adopted the *Ley de Educación Superior* (LES) [Higher Education Act] in 1995. The LES deregulated the universities and promoted competition and self-financing. However, it also led to new forms of state control via public funding formulas and the creation of a quality assurance system (Mollis 1997). In a reference to this law's dual function, Schugurensky (1997) characterized the Menem administration as "market interventionist."

The LES was contested by the university community and the government was forced to withdraw some of the initial privatization measures, such as the introduction of tuition fees. The law was also criticized for having been drafted by the Ministry of Economy under the structural adjustment program imposed by the World Bank and the IMF. Indeed, a sector of the Ministry of Education staff opposed a number of the market-oriented measures in the LES (Schugurensky 1997).

In the 1990s, the number of private universities in Argentina increased drastically. Between 1990 and 1995, 23 new private institutions were created—the same number that had been created during the previous 30 years (from 1960 to 1990). However, the establishment in 1995 of the Argentina's university evaluation and accreditation agency (Comisión Nacional de Evaluación y Acreditación Universitaria, CONEAU), ended the radical privatization trend, and opening a private university became much more difficult. Between 1996 and 2003, CONEAU received 72 applications, of which only nine were accepted (Villanueva 2003).

Breaking with Neoliberalism

Following the major economic crisis in 2001, neoliberalism was widely discredited in Argentina. Most analysts, journalists and the public opinion of the country attributed to Menem's radical liberalization policies the cause of this appalling period in the country's history (Seoane 2002). The Kirschner administrations (Néstor Krischner: 2003–2007; Cristina Fernández Kirschner: 2007-present) have attempted to move away from neoliberal discourse and, to some extent, to abandon certain neoliberal policies promoted in the 1990s; a rhetoric and, to some extent, a program of economic nationalism has been adopted instead. Members of the Kirschner administrations are also highly critical—and occasionally belligerent—in the context of neoliberal international organizations (Öniş 2007). Moreover, the government's foreign affairs agenda has been focused on south-south regionalism through initiatives such as Mercosur (Southern Common Market), rather than on the neoliberal globalization policies promoted by organizations such as the WTO. As regards education, the government has also tried to distance itself from the policies of the 1990s. To that end, the generalist *Ley de Educación Nacional* (LEN) [National Education Act]) was adopted in 2006 and revoked the menemist Federal Education Act. A proposal to repeal the LES is being studied and will be probably passed in 2009.

Setting aside the ambiguities of the past, the LEN clearly states that education funding at all levels is the direct responsibility of the state, which must "ensure the free provision of state services at all levels and modalities" (LEN, Art. 11).

Trade in Higher Education in Argentina

Argentina's higher education sector is not extensively internationalized. Only one foreign institution—Bologna University—is operating under mode 3 (commercial presence).[1] Foreign universities in Argentina are regulated by Decree 276 (March 1999). Under this edict, foreign and local universities are subject to the same regulations (Fernández Lamarra 2003). A number of foreign universities, including Lynn University, have submitted applications that were rejected by CONEAU (Interview CONEAU 01, Buenos Aires, 2006). The number of private institutions in Argentina is so small because public universities are well established and tuition is free. In addition, private universities have difficulty competing because they cannot receive public funding. However, twinning and joint degree programs involving domestic and foreign institutions (usually American or Spanish universities) are much more common. In this case, the barriers are low because only one of the universities, usually the Argentine, must be accredited (Fernández Lamarra 2003). On the other hand, Argentina is not an exporter under mode 3, and none of the country's domestic universities have foreign branches (Theiler 2005).

Under mode 2, Argentina's trade balance is negative. There were only 3,261 foreign students in Argentina (2,682 coming from countries in the region) in 2004. Only some international students pay tuition fees and each public university is allowed to decide whether its foreign students should pay tuition (Hermo and Pittelli 2008). In contrast, 8,485 Argentines are studying abroad, including 3,644 in the US, 838 in France and 802 in Spain; they do not normally study in other Latin American countries (UNESCO 2006). Students can have their foreign credentials validated (as established by LES, Art. 29) and some foreign programs have been approved under international agreements (Marquis 2002).[2]

Growing numbers of Argentinean citizens are enrolling in educational services distance education courses (mode 1), although the exact numbers have not been determined. The main distance education providers are Universidad Nacional de Educación a Distancia, Universidad Politécnica de Madrid, Universidad del Pacífico Oeste, Universidad Abierta Iberoamericana, New York University, Harvard University and Universidad de Salamanca (Villanueva 2003). Argentina has only one totally e-learning university, although most traditional universities offer some distance education courses. However, Argentina's distance education providers do not export services and their students are mostly local (Theiler 2005). Validation of degrees and qualifications obtained at foreign distance education institutions is difficult because the recognition mechanisms have not been finalized (Interview Ministry of Education 01, Buenos Aires, 2006).

Education in Trade Agreements

As noted in the introduction, Argentina is very reluctant to make liberalization commitments in education under the WTO/GATS. However, it has opened up its education sector within Mercosur; these commitments involve higher education, primarily modes 2 and 3. Argentina explicitly excluded mode 1 because it is still an underregulated subsector (see established commitments in Appendix 2).

Making liberalization commitments under Mercosur is very different than under the GATS: the GATS is a global trade agreement that benefits the rich countries' main service exporters and does not have an education mandate; it simply views education as a marketable commodity. In contrast, Mercosur is more than just a free trade agreement: it is also a political integration process between various South American countries. Although there are inequalities between Mercosur members, Argentina is highly ranked within the organization. Moreover, Mercosur has an education agenda. In the context of what is called "Mercosur Educativo", education ministries of member countries deal with sensitive issues such as accreditation, quality assurance and student/staff mobility.

Mercosur's members are currently negotiating a trade agreement with the EU that would cover educational services, but these negotiations are currently at an impasse. So far, Argentina has not made any education offers during the negotiations.[3] This process is also accompanied by a higher education component, specifically, the EU and Mercosur have launched an initiative to establish common evaluation and accreditation criteria.[4]

9.2   POLITICIZING THE NEGOTIATIONS IN ARGENTINA

At the beginning of the Uruguay Round, Argentina was highly critical of services liberalization. At the time, it led the G10 coalition, which opposed the creation of a WTO services agreement (Narlikar and Woods 2003). However, this round ended during Menem's term in office and Argentina's final list of commitments on services was highly liberalized. Six service sectors were opened up, although education was not one of them.

Since the Doha Round began, education liberalization within the GATS has been a subject of passionate debate in Argentina. As we will see, this debate has been fostered and, to some extent, exacerbated by two consultations on education led by the *Cancillería* (Argentina's trade ministry). Following the 2001 crisis, the government promoted a policy of systematic consultations with stakeholders—another way of distancing itself from the Menem administration. Indeed, the Kirschner administrations have been very active in establishing alliances with social movements and forging closer ties with them. This strategy has included the co-optation of some of their leaders, and has become a key element in achieving political stability in Argentina.

During the Menem years, trade policies were top-down and business representatives were the only government-recognized stakeholders (Guiñazú 2003).[5] Now, the country's trade representatives are mandated with systematically consulting civil society organizations and listening to their concerns. The Cancillería has also formally established a number of civil society consultation forums.[6] Consequently, opportunities for education stakeholders to influence trade policy are greater than they were in the 1990s.

First Consultation [2002]: The Public Universities Boycott

Consistent with the views of most trade negotiators around the globe, the Cancillería does not believe that the GATS will harm education. It maintains that education stakeholders are opposed to the GATS because they are "afraid of the unknown," or because they "confuse" liberalization and privatization (Interview Argentinean trade negotiator 02, Geneva, 2006). Accordingly, the country's trade negotiators have emphasized the potential benefits of education liberalization. They believe that Argentina should identify various offensive interests because many business opportunities are being lost as a result of the conservative attitude of the educational community.

P: How do you perceive the threats identified by the educational community?

R: Let's see . . . We try to be as objective as possible. We try to explain the meaning of these negotiations, and we have tried to explain them in terms of business opportunities, rather than threats. More specifically, if certain markets for developing educational services are opened, perhaps Argentina will be able to take advantage of this. For instance, we could establish a presence in China. Let us suppose that 10% of China's 1.3 billion people want to learn Spanish. We would have a major advantage (Interview Argentinean trade negotiator 03, Buenos Aires, 2006).

Before the first consultation was launched, the Cancillería wrongly believed that it could identify offensive interests in education together with the national higher education industry. The education stakeholders, however, held a radically different position.

The first consultation took place in 2002, coinciding with the start of the demand phase of the GATS negotiations. The stakeholders included the Public Universities Council (CIN), the Private University Chancellors Council (CRUP) and the Higher Education Division of the Ministry of Education (SPU). All of them declared their opposition to the establishment of liberalization commitments in education, for a variety of reasons. The private universities were opposed to the GATS for various reasons, but principally fearing competition with universities from richer countries.

We don't need concessions within the WTO framework to sell education abroad; we are already doing that. Any negotiations are going to be detrimental to Argentina because we are currently a net exporter of education. We thought that our position would be undermined and that we would become net importers [. . .]. Our message to the Cancillería was that we have nothing to win and everything to lose (Interview CRUP 01, Buenos Aires, 2006).

In contrast, the position of the public universities was more politically-oriented. Prior to the consultation, they had signed a declaration—the Porto Alegre Letter—at the Summit of Iberoamerican Public Universities Chancellors in 2002. In the letter, they stated that the GATS violates the principle of education as a public good and that it could be detrimental to the education sector (see Chapter 7). Based on the letter, Argentina's Public Universities Council (CIN) categorically rejected the idea of introducing education within the GATS. It also refused to take part in the consultation; in its letter rejecting the Cancillería's invitation, CIN stated that "the market does not have values, it has appetites. And its desires can only be satisfied with profits, which have nothing to do with education" (Fernández Lamarra 2003).

At that time, the SPU did not have extensive information on the topic. One of its members acknowledged that "when we met with the Cancillería, we realized that we didn't know what the consolidated lists were or what commitments had been adopted. We didn't know that [the Ministry of] Education hadn't proposed anything. . ." (Interview SPU 04, Buenos Aires, 2006). The SPU therefore kept a low profile and adopted a cautious position during the consultation; it subsequently decided to support Argentina's public and private universities. In solidarity, the SPU stated that it subscribed to the principle of education as a public good and was concerned that the GATS would be harmful in this regard (Interview SPU 03, Buenos Aires, 2006). Following the consultation, the SPU, in response to the "profound concern" of the Argentinean universities over the GATS (Theiler 2005, 83), began researching and working on this issue; it subsequently organized public debates and issued publications and other information on GATS and education.

Argentina presented its initial offer on services at the WTO on April 8, 2003, and it did not include educational services commitments.[7]

Second Consultation [2006]: Veto Power and the Montevideo Declaration

The second consultation was organized in 2006 within the framework of the plurilateral negotiation round of the GATS. At that time, Argentina was targeted in the plurilateral demand on education coordinated by New Zealand. The Ministry of Trade again sought to determine the education sector's views. For the purposes of this consultation, only the Ministry of Education SPU was invited. Education providers, whose defensive attitude toward the GATS was well known, were left out.

However, the SPU reiterated that liberalization commitments in education could not be established since the Ministry of Education had previously declared in a public statement (known as the Montevideo Declaration) that Argentina would not include educational services in free trade agreements. Based on that declaration, the SPU stated that a red line had been drawn with respect to the sector and that education was non-negotiable. The trade negotiator who organized the second consultation offered this account:

> The Ministry of Education replied to our consultation offer on the basis of a declaration signed by the Mercosur education ministries some years ago (. . .), emphasizing the state's role in education. The Ministry said that this should be taken into account at the WTO meetings, in the sense of not treating education as a commodity. It also urged the parties involved not to establish commitments in this area (Interview Argentinean Trade negotiator 04, Buenos Aires, 2006).

The rigid position of the SPU increased tensions between the trade and education representatives. The trade negotiator was eager to obtain a concession from the education regulator and was very insistent and persuasive in this regard. The trade negotiator eventually lost patience and told the education representative that the Trade Minister would "solve this problem with the Education Minister at the political level" (Interview SPU 04, Buenos Aires, 2006). In the end, the Ministry of Education position prevailed.

The Key Role of CTERA

Argentina's largest teachers union—the Argentine Education Workers Confederation (CTERA)—has played a key role in understanding the dynamics of the second consultation.[8] Even though CTERA is one of the country's most powerful education and socio-political stakeholders (Gajardo 2003), the Cancillería excluded it from both consultations. However, the teachers union's political maneuverings ended up determining the position that the Cancillería was obliged to defend at the WTO.

CTERA launched a national anti-GATS campaign after attending the triennial conference of Education International (EI) in 2004, at which the GATS issue figured prominently. The union subsequently decided to place the issue on its domestic agenda (Interview CTERA 02, Buenos Aires, 2006).[9] CTERA's assessment of the issue is quite similar to that of Education International. Indeed, the union essentially framed its arguments against GATS based on work of EI. However, CTERA's assessment emphasizes the threats for developing countries and for relatively "young" nations such as Argentina:

> We view education as a social right, not as a commodity. We must also take into account the fact that GATS would mean absolutely unequal competition: we would be like sardines trying to compete with sharks [...] The education markets are controlled by transnational actors that have the capacity to undermine the cultural defenses of other nations. We believe that economic domination means cultural domination. We are not cultural fundamentalists, but we believe that certain cultural and national values must be upheld if we wish to exist as a nation (Interview CTERA 01, Buenos Aires, 2006).

CTERA's anti-GATS campaign, instead of targeting Cancillería, targeted the Ministry of Education. CTERA pressured the Ministry of Education to make a clear commitment that education would not be included in trade agreements, and it responded positively to the union's demands. This commitment was set out in three public documents, only one of which was mentioned during the 2006 consultation organized by Cancillería. However, all of them were politically relevant to the GATS debate in Argentina. As shown below, these documents, which bear the hallmarks of CTERA's campaign, made the Ministry of Education to act as a veto player within the GATS negotiations.

a) Brasilia Declaration (November 2004). In this declaration, the Argentine and Brazilian education ministries, together with CTERA and

Brazil's largest teaching union, undertook not to establish liberalization commitments within the GATS. The document also states that signing such agreements would be a violation of national sovereignty.

b) Montevideo Declaration (November 2005). The provisions of this document and the signatories are similar to those of the Brasilia Declaration, although the geographical scope is wider since it was a Mercosur initiative. The Montevideo Declaration was the main outcome of a meeting between the Mercosur countries' education ministries and the education sector of the Southern Cone Trade Union Coordinating Committee, in which CTERA plays a strong leadership role:

"[The education ministries] reaffirm, within the framework of the WTO services negotiations, their view that education is a public good (. . .) and underline the importance of protecting state jurisdiction over education regulation, which would be drastically limited if our governments were to establish liberalization commitments in this sector."[10]

c) National Education Act (LEN): The LEN replaced Menem's Federal Education Act, apparently, thanks in part to an unprecedented lobbying effort by CTERA (Interview CTERA 01, Buenos Aires, 2006). CTERA also called for the inclusion of a clear statement opposing the interference of free trade agreements in the education field.[11] As a result, Article 10 of the LEN stipulates that:

"The state shall not subscribe to bilateral or multilateral free trade agreements in which education is viewed as a profit-oriented activity or in which the commodification of public education is encouraged in any way."

The LEN was publicly presented by the Minister of Education and CTERA's Secretary General at a joint event designed to illustrate the parties' excellent relations. The Minister described Article 10 as one of the most progressive aspects of the new law.[12]

On the Outcome of the Consultations

The trade negotiators from the Argentinean *Cancillería* were very disappointed with the outcome of both consultations. During the consultations, trade negotiators—not only from Argentina—seek to identify offensive interests in their home countries (so they would have "national interests" to promote at international forums) and to identify as few defensive interests as possible (because having more sectors to offer would enhance bargaining capacity when defending the national interests of export industries). In the reverse situation (i.e. if there were many sectors to protect and few to offer), the negotiators' role loses sense during international negotiations. They would therefore have fewer opportunities to open up foreign markets.

Indeed, this is what happened with the education sector in Argentina. Stakeholders did not establish offensive interests in education and strongly rejected the possibility of opening up Argentine's education sector. Furthermore, the trade negotiators were uncomfortable defending a position at the WTO that they viewed as "philosophical-conceptual" and that was based on "unfounded" concerns (Interview Argentinean Trade negotiator 03, Buenos Aires, 2006).[13]

The outcome of the first consultation was less of a disappointment to Argentina's trade negotiators than the second. In 2002, Argentina had only received one demand on education (from Korea). However, in 2006, the plurilateral demand on education was submitted to Argentina by the "big players." Therefore, education could have become a valuable bargaining chip for the country. It should be acknowledged that education was highly strategic because it was one of Argentina's five still uncommitted service sectors (Interview Argentinean Trade negotiator 01, Geneva 2006).

It is also important to note that the GATS education debate was highly politicized in Argentina; it is one of the few countries where the national legislature has debated this specific topic.[14] Moreover, during the 2003 election campaign, Menem proposed including education in the GATS in a bid to combat the economic crisis (Schugurensky and Davidson-Harden 2003).[15] This suggests that opposing the inclusion of education in the GATS was another way for Kirschner to set the neoliberal policies of the 1990s aside.

9.3   THE BORDERLESS PRIVATIZATION OF CHILEAN UNIVERSITIES

Historical Background

Prior to Pinochet's coup d'état in 1973, the funding of the Chilean higher education system was guaranteed by the state and tuition was free (Levy 1995). However, the military junta (1973–1990) introduced a number of radical changes. Pinochet's regime, which is considered the first neoliberal government in history (Harvey 2005; Santiago 2000; Marcus Taylor 2003), introduced pro-market rules in all policy areas. Higher education was no exception.

The most radical changes came with the far-reaching university reform in 1981. This initiative promoted the privatization of higher educational services (Brunner and Bricall 2000) and completely liberalized the sector, paving the way for new private universities. According to Levy (1995), the only requirement for creating a new institution was to submit a straightforward application, i.e. specifying only a small number of educational ideas; applications were usually approved automatically in case not were rejected within 90 days.

Box 9.1   Public-Private Universities in Chile

In Chile, the terms "public" and "private" are less commonly used to refer to university ownership. Instead, universities are categorized as "traditional" or "non-traditional." The country has 25 traditional universities (public and private). They receive state funding under competition formulas and are grouped within the Consejo de Rectores de Universidades Chilenas (CRUCH) (Salazar 2003). The non-traditional universities were created under the liberalization program launched in 1981, and in 2004 there were 39, all of them private (Brunner 2004).

Source: Author

In addition, public funding was reduced and the universities were forced to look for private sources. As a result, public institutions introduced tuition fees. Under another finance-oriented measure, whose objective was also political control, state-run universities were fragmented. For example, the Universidad de Chile and the Universidad de Santiago de Chile were split into 14 separate smaller institutions. Labor relations were also undermined and university professors lost their civil servant status (Torres and Schugurensky 2002).

The military junta's last organic act pertained to education. Passed in March 1990, the Education Constitutional Organic Act (LOCE) extended privatization in the sector. For the first time in the country's history, an accreditation and quality assurance system was created for higher education institutions. However, this system had many weaknesses. First, institutions were evaluated when they were already operating, not beforehand. Since the evaluation process took from 6 to 11 years, substandard educational standards could be maintained for long periods. Second, the evaluation criteria were determined by the higher education institutions themselves, not in accordance with centralized state-imposed standards. Third, once evaluated, the institutions could cut back on quality with no repercussions because follow-up measures were not provided for. As one of the most qualified experts on quality assurance issues in the country recognizes:

> [Licensing in Chile] has some weakness [. . .] . As it focuses on the fulfillment of institutional purposes, institutions quickly learned that in order to achieve autonomy, their proposals had to be kept to a bear minimum; as a result, mediocre institutions survive, become autonomous and then are free to act as they wish, sometimes offering very poor programmes. (Lemaitre 2005a, 28)

Democracy and Policy Continuity

Chile's democratic period, which began in 1990, has been characterized by continuity in several policy fields with respect to the military junta's period and by the consolidation of neoliberalism as the hegemonic policy paradigm. As regards education, none of the democratic administrations have had the necessary political support (or will) to repeal the organic law (LOCE). They have limited themselves to passing lower-ranking education laws and making minor amendments to LOCE (Bernasconi and Gamboa 2002). Some of these amendments, refer the higher education quality assurance system and, specifically, to the introduction of an initiative for the acreditations of university programmes. However, this accreditation regulatory framework is considered lax because it is undertaken on voluntary basis (except for medicine and pedagogy degrees).[16]

Neoliberal scolars argue that Chile's ultraliberal framework has dramatically increased access to higher education without requiring a corresponding increase in public spending. In fact, the level of public spending on higher education in Chile is one of the lowest of the world, accounting for only 15.3% of total education spending. Moreover, the level of enrolment in higher education institutions is also one of the highest of the world (Brunner 2008). Only the Philippines, Korea and Japan have a higher percentage of students enrolled in private institutions (Bernasconi and Gamboa 2002).

Most Chilean universities do not do research (Goic Goic 2004) and lack basic infrastructure such as up-to-date libraries. Some new universities even tell students to find the books they need at traditional universities (Interview Universidad de Chile 01, Santiago, 2006). However, Chilean education policymakers do not even stop to consider the possibility of establishing higher quality standards. Steeped in neoliberal dogma, they strongly believe that market forces will solve most quality assurance problems because students will not willingly choose low-quality services; consequently, any low-quality institutions will eventually disappear without the state having to intervene. They are also convinced that institutions will apply for accreditation because it is the best way of enhancing their appeal among education consumers.[17] Chilean policymakers also believe that the state's principal role should be to inform citizens about existing institutions and to foster choice (Armanet 2003). To that end, the government, for instance, provides information on students' subsequent professional careers depending on the degree and the university they have attended (Brunner 2006).

Internationalization of Higher Education

In Chile, the internationalization of higher education is much more advanced than in Argentina. In Chile, 7.5% of all students are enrolled in 10 foreign-owned institutions (mode 3). The most popular are Spain's Universidad SEK and the US-based Sylvan Learning Systems, which owns the Universidad de las Américas and the Universidad Nacional Andrés Bello (González 2003). Non-traditional universities also organize twinning programs with

European universities. Most of the times, linking one's name to an European institution is a very effective way for Chilean universities to attract local students (Interview CNAP 02, Santiago, 2006).

Chile can be perceived as an attractive market for foreign providers because they benefit from the same slack accreditation rules as national providers do. As Lemaitre (2005a) has observed, "the lack of regulation and the difficulty in obtaining information on transnational programs make it very hard to determine the actual quality of a given program" (24–25).

Chile is a discreet exporter under mode 3. Only two Chilean universities have foreign branches, both located in Ecuador. The country is much more successful under mode 2. Chile's higher education system attracts numerous students (5,211), most of whom (2,983) come from Latin America (UNESCO 2006). Due to the saturated domestic market, most Chilean universities have created business units to attract foreign students (Ramírez Sánchez 2005). Chile is also a major education importer and has 5,873 students abroad. The most common destinations are the US (1,612), Argentina (712), Germany (624), France (512) and Spain (427). These students have no difficulty having their degrees validated once they return to Chile. Three main procedures are available to them: the first is through the Universidad de Chile; the second is set out in automatic certification agreements entered into by Chile with various regional countries (Lemaitre 2005b); and the third is provided for in Act 19.074 (passed in 1991), which was designed to facilitate the return of political exiles who had fled the dictatorship.

Mode 1 data are also scarce in Chile. However, many Chileans are currently enrolled in distance learning institutions such as the Universidad Nacional de Educación a Distancia, the Universitat Oberta de Catalunya, Quebec's Télé-université, the Open University of Israel and the virtual university of the Tecnológico de Monterey. In contrast to Argentina, distance-education degrees can be validated in Chile under procedures similar to those for in-class programs (Lemaitre 2005a).

Chilean University Services and Trade Agreements

As we have seen, Chile's regulatory framework is very open to trade in education. Under the 2006 National System of Quality Assurance in Higher Education Act, the country also opened its doors to foreign quality assurance agencies. Moreover, pro-trade regulations have been reinforced via various trade agreements. Of all the Latin American countries, Chile and Mexico have signed the most free trade agreements (FTAs) (Sáez 2005). Since the 1990s, Chile has signed FTAs (usually bilateral) with numerous countries, including the world's most powerful trading nations. Educational services are provided for in most of these FTAs, including those with Canada, the US and New Zealand (see Appendix 3 for the complete list). Consequently, even though Chile has yet to make any education commitments under the GATS, the country's education system is almost completely liberalized on a global scale.

Paradoxically, Chile has not signed degree recognition agreements with the northern countries with which it has entered into FTAs. This may be because rich countries usually impose limits on professional mobility from developing countries because this is such a sensitive issue at the national level.

9.4   THE TECHNIFIED DISCUSSION IN CHILE

The Chilean Consensus on Free Trade

WTO members are supposed to believe in the benefits of free trade and to consider it the best system for organizing international trade. However, powerful member countries, such as the US and the EU, actively espouse free trade doctrine, but have difficulty putting theory into practice. In contrast, Chile is a confessed free trade believer and a radical practitioner: beginning in the 1980s, it has removed trade barriers unilaterally and voluntarily. Chile put free trade into practice without entering into binding trade agreements or requesting any form of compensation. As the military junta opened up the country to trade, it laid the foundations for an export-oriented economy. The social costs of trade liberalization in Chile were high but neglected by the Junta and any attempts to protest or mobilize against the structural changes met with violent repression (Garretón 1989).

In the post-Pinochet era, Chile's trade policy is still faithful to free trade (Angell 2002). Various democratic administrations have not seen any need to redefine this model, for several reasons. Firstly, the main social costs were absorbed during the dictatorship. Secondly, after the fall of the Berlin wall in 1989, the free trade model gained international legitimacy and was intensively exported to—or imposed on—developing countries. Thus, a combination of external and internal factors therefore created a broad consensus among Chile's political parties on the benefits of free trade.

Chile's international trading patterns are still those of an underdeveloped country, with exports focused on raw materials and agricultural products. However, the country's current trade policy aims to promote exports of more sophisticated products, most notably services (Interview Chilean Trade negotiator 04, Santiago, 2006). To carry out this shift, the government enlisted the country's service industries and helped them to organize a lobby group known as the Chilean Export Services Coalition.[18] This coalition is the main interlocutor for Chilean trade negotiators seeking to define the country's strategy and demands in the context of the service negotiations, both within the GATS and at the bilateral level (Interview Chilean Trade negotiators 03 and 04, Santiago, 2006).

From Cautiousness to Liberalization

During the Uruguay Round, Chile made no education commitments in the service negotiations. At that time, "services" were a new and uncharted territory for the country's negotiators, and Chile only committed three out of 12 service sectors. This decision revealed a degree of caution, although, as seen in the following quotation, it was also designed to increase the country's future bargaining power.

> At that time, we were so ignorant about services that we just did what the other countries did. If the developed countries weren't going to commit on education and health, neither were we. Anything else would have been naive. Our starting point was the offers made by the developed countries. From then on, we started to take things out. We did so out of bias, not for any fundamental reason. We also wanted to leave negotiating room for the future [. . .] In that moment, we were very cautious (Interview Chilean Trade negotiator 04, Santiago, 2006).

So far during the Doha Round, Chile has not introduced education in its services offer list. In general, the current offer is not particularly ambitious; according to the Chilean negotiators themselves, "the initial offer is very bad" (Interview Chilean Trade negotiator 03, Santiago, 2006). However, they concede that the offer could become more ambitious depending on the course of the negotiations; consequently, education could be committed. Indeed, Chile's negotiators have *carte blanche* from Santiago to introduce educational services. As the country's ambassador to the WTO said after reviewing a restricted document from the Ministry of Foreign Affairs, "If we wanted to put the entire education sector on the table we could do so. Yes, we could. I don't know if we're going to, but it could be done" (Interview Chilean Trade negotiator 01, Geneva, 2006).

Chile's initial cautiousness has clearly and drastically changed during the Doha Round. This shift is reflected not only at the WTO, but also in numerous FTAs that Chile has signed or is currently negotiating. As one negotiator said, "Chile has done everything it can at the bilateral level" (Interview Chilean Trade negotiator 03, Santiago, 2006), meaning that it has committed itself to liberalizing virtually all sectors of the economy under bilateral trade agreements.

Currently, the "bargaining chip" approach to the education negotiations is accompanied by the strong belief that trade liberalization will significantly improve Chile's education system.

> [In education] we receive various interesting offers from other countries, both in relation to the teaching profession and to curriculum-related aspects. This also offers our students the possibility of receiving

foreign university services without having to leave the country" (Interview Chilean Trade negotiator 02, Geneva, 2006).[19]

Defining Preferences

The negotiation process at the national level in Chile has been very different to that in Argentina. In Chile, education stakeholders have not been systematically consulted and the process of defining preferences has been much more centralized within the Ministry of Foreign Affairs and, specifically, with the division of this ministry in charge of trade negotiations, called Dirección General de Relaciones Comerciales Internacionales (DIRECON). Nor did the multilateral demand on education in 2006 did not lead to consultations at the national level. As one negotiator recognized:

> Negotiations with the Ministry of Education on this matter, i.e. about including the education sector in our offer, are virtually non-existent. This has not been a priority sector for us, in contrast with other sectors [. . .] This issue is not widely discussed in Chile. To tell you the truth, people don't really know what we're doing in *our* agreements about education. The issue is barely acknowledged (Interview Chilean Trade negotiator 03, Santiago, 2006).

There are various possible reasons why consultations to education stakeholders in Chile on GATS issues are not so transcendental. Firstly, the country's education sector was initially opened up by the Pinochet regime. Education commitments would therefore mean "consolidation", but not significant regulatory changes. Secondly, education has already been committed in various FTAs involving most of the developed countries; therefore liberalization commitments within the GATS would not mean a drastic change. This last point leads to an interesting question: was Chile's educational community consulted during the free trade negotiations?

In the context of Chile's FTAs, the education stakeholders that were consulted were mainly the quality assurance agencies, particularly in the case of the agreements with Europe and the US. Unlike in Argentina, the purpose of this consultation was not to seek permission for education liberalization, but rather to refine certain technical aspects of the process. These agencies were not consulted in the context of other free trade negotiations because once the negotiators knew which technical issues had to be taken into account, no further consultation was necessary. However, other observers maintain that the real reason for the consultation was EU and US concerns over the value and quality of Chilean degrees (Interview CNAP 02, Santiago, 2006). That would explain why the country's education quality assurance agency was the key actor to be consulted. Whatever the reason, the consultation process was clearly not intended to make the negotiation process more participatory or inclusive.

The Chilean Ministry of Education's Higher Education Division (HED) was also invited to attend some meetings in the FTAs negotiations context, although it was not extensively involved in the process. The HED was satisfied with the fact that the representative of the quality assurance agency attended the meetings; it did not explore the GATS issue in depth because it was busy dealing with "national issues" (Interview HED 01, Paris, 2006). According to this person, who has the head of the Higher Education Division of the Ministry of Education when the Doha Round started, "we didn't debate a lot and all of us agreed on the direction we should pursue. I mean, there was full agreement . . .".

The consultation process in Chile was therefore very different than in Argentina. In Chile, education stakeholders were not consulted on the feasibility of committing education; they were simply asked about the technical adjustments that would be required. The discussions never touched on political considerations. In the words of one Chilean negotiator:

> There was no debate. We had some contact with the universities and with the Higher Education Division of the Ministry of Education. Nobody was worried because there was nothing, no commercial commitments, that could be a threat . . . (Interview Chilean Trade negotiator 04, Santiago, 2006).

For the purposes of this research, the data provided by the Ministry of Trade was compared with the opinion and views coming from the Chilean education stakeholders. The stakeholder interviews confirm that the GATS has led to virtually no conflict or debate in the country's education sector. What is more, the ideas and preferences of the Ministry of Trade and those of the education stakeholders are remarkably similar.

Positions of Higher Education Stakeholders

In Chile, the educational community has been debating trade and internationalization of higher education since the 1990s, most notably at annual seminars organized by the HED and the quality assurance agencies. At these seminars, higher education representatives meet with officials from trade-related institutions such as the World Bank, the Inter-American Development Bank (IADB), the Economic Commission for Latin American and the Caribbean (ECLAC), NAFTA and DIRECON and maintain open lines of communication with them.

In general, the discourse on trade issues of higher education regulators and policymakers is highly pragmatic. They take the view that education has already been introduced in trade agreements and that this trend is unstoppable; instead of organizing "pointless" debates about whether education is (or is not) a commodity, they hold that it is best to think more positively and to debate on how education should be adapted to the new situation—see also (Lemaitre 2003; Bitar 2004). In this respect, the former HED representative offered the following observation: "I think that offering unconstructive criticism is the worst thing we can do. When issues are not discussed on a timely basis, reality ends up being imposed and then we have to regulate to correct the distortions" (Armanet 2004, 125).

Education authorities in Chile prefer to view trade in education in terms of opportunities and challenges, rather than threats and concerns. Opportunities are seen in the areas of professional mobility, policy learning from developed countries systems and education quality improvement.[20]

> This openness means that our universities have stopped seeing themselves in terms of a small enclosed space; they now understand that they must compete in a globalized world. Consequently, they have to measure themselves according to global parameters and make sure that their quality is up to standard (Interview HED 01, Paris, 2006).

Oddly the Chilean Ministry of Education also signed the Montevideo Declaration within the framework of Mercosur. However, this document did not have the same political repercussions in Chile as it did in Argentina. Indeed, none of the Chilean Ministry of Education representatives interviewed even referred to it. This shows that the local recontextualization of global events is mediated by national politics, ideational frameworks and domestic institutional settings.

For their part universities have been described as the "great unseen" during the trade negotiations in Chile (Aravena and Pey 2003). However, it is unlikely that their participation would have altered the outcome of the negotiations because the Chilean university establishment is so amenable to pro-free trade ideas. As research on the topic has shown, the prevailing goal of the internationalization policies of Chilean universities is to contribute to "Chile's participation in the global economy" (González 2003, 11)—see also (Ramírez Sánchez 2005). According to some university representatives, Chilean universities should actively support and promote their country's trade policies:

> Under the FTAs, we should be preparing future professionals to meet new challenges [. . .] The universities have a key role to play when a FTA is signed. Their personnel must be prepared; they must have the technical skills. Moreover, we must study the cultures of the people we are trading with. If we are going to export to Vietnam or Japan, we must know how they think, what they like, etc. How do they prefer fruit freshly picked or riper? Do they like wine dry or sweet? (Interview Universidad de Chile 01, Santiago, 2006).

More importantly, Chilean universities are proactive on trade issues. CRUCH, the association of traditional universities, has an international affairs committee that, among other things, aims to promote the exportation of its members' educational services—see also (Lavanchy 2003). Another groundbreaking initiative clearly illustrates local universities' pro-trade bias: the University Services Export Committee (CESU). CESU was created in 1998 by the DIRECON and Prochile (a governmental division to promote Chilean exportations) and includes traditional and non-traditional universities. Among its core objectives, it seeks "to strengthen Chile's image as an exporter of university services, to contribute to the establishment of Chilean universities abroad, (. . .) to develop awareness, to facilitate activities in the area of university services exports and, in general, to support the internationalization of Chilean universities" (González 2003, 11–12). Chilean universities were not initially eager to embrace CESU. Over time, however, they have adapted very well to the new trade situations. As the Prochile services sector product manager said in a universities-corporations meeting:

> The first time we called on the universities to become part of the export sector was in 1997 at an ECLAC seminar. There was a level of mistrust. They were favorably disposed to the idea but were concerned that the proposal could radically alter the universities' essential function. Now, five years later, I am pleased to note that the academic community has embraced the imperative of linking our universities with the external world. The idea is to sell the city and sell the region. . . (Tramer 2002, 91–92).

Two Chilean universities signed anti-GATS documents—the Porto Alegre Letter (2002) and the San Salvador Letter (2003)—during the Iberoamerican Summits of Public University Chancellors.[21] However, as with the Montevideo Declaration, these statements had no political impact in Chile.

A Critical Minority

Chile's trade policy is skewed in favor of business interests. Since the country's economy is export-oriented, trade negotiators make a point of consulting exporters when defining the country's preferences. However, they do not consult so often with civil society organizations such as NGOs and trade unions (Aravena and Pey 2003).

Chilean teacher unions—most remarkably the Colegio de Profesores (CDP), the country's largest—have been very critical about the inclusion of education in the GATS and other trade agreements.[22] The CDP is a member of Education International and, together with CTERA, it has participated in various anti-GATS events organized by EI.

The CDP has kept its members up to date and has tried to encourage debate on the impact of trade agreements on education. A key communications tool has been the union's journal *Docencia* (see issue numbers 19, 23 and 24 in particular). However, the CDP has not been successful in its lobbying efforts and has not been granted access to decision-making forums.[23] The union's members are disappointed that they have never been consulted on trade issues (Interview CDP 01, Santiago, 2006). The trade negotiators themselves recognize that the teachers unions are not particularly influential in Chile:

> Are you asking whether the teaching unions play an important role in commercial matters? No, they don't have any influence. If we don't commit on education within the GATS, it's a strategic/tactical decision. It's not out of some deep concern for civil society (Interview Chilean Trade negotiator 01, Geneva, 2006)[24]

Furthermore, the trade negotiators constantly delegitimize the trade unions' demands and concerns with respect to education and trade agreements. The negotiators feel that the unions focus on "phantom problems" and do not have an adequate grasp of trade issues. They also accuse the unions of being afraid to compete with foreign teachers:

> The unions make a lot of noise, but instead of protecting education they just want to protect their jobs. They want to prevent teachers coming from other countries from working in Chile (Interview Chilean Trade negotiator 01, Geneva, 2006).

9.5   COMPARATIVE ANALYSIS

Argentina and Chile take very different approaches to negotiating education within the framework of the GATS and other free trade agreements. In trade forums, Chile has adopted a pro-liberalization stance, while Argentina has drawn a red line on education, meaning that education is non-negotiable, at least during the Doha Round. These markedly different positions stem from domestic politics and from the way the negotiation process has developed in each country.

As the empirical data show, the negotiation process has been substantively different in Argentina and Chile. Table 9.1 summarizes both processes and the various decisions, events and actors involved. The first column presents information on key events in the global participatory subsystem, corresponding to events at the national level in the following columns. The table shows that Chile is more open to trade (especially at the bilateral level), while Argentina has adopted a more participatory negotiation approach. The first column of Table 9.1, between brackets, also presents key international events that are external to the participatory subsystem and the national representative subsystem.

Table 9.1 GATS and Education Negotiation Process in Argentina and Chile

DATES AND GENERAL EVENTS	ARGENTINA	CHILE
1986-1994: Uruguay Round	Argentina does not establish liberalization commitments in education	Chile does not commit education 1996: Education commitments in FTA with Canada
2000: Services negotiations start 2001: Services are incorporated to the Doha Round		
2002: First Doha Round services demands [Porto Alegre Declaration signed by Latin American public universities]	Korea makes a demand on education to Argentina Trade Ministry consults education stakeholders. All of them are opposed to make an offer in education	Education commitments in FTAs with El Salvador and Costa Rica
2003: First Doha Round services offers	First services offer is published. It does not include education	First services offer is published. It does not include education Education commitments in FTAs with Korea and USA
2004: Countries carry on with the negotiations [EI World Congress: EI strengthen the anti-GATS campaign]	Brasilia Declaration is signed	
2005: WTO Ministerial Conference in Hong Kong: Plurilateral demands are allowed [Montevideo Declaration is signed]	Montevideo Declaration is signed Argentina does not present revised offer in services	Revised offer: does not include education Education commitments in FTA with N. Zealand, Singapore, Brunei
2006: Plurilateral negotiations start - New Zealand coordinates a plurilateral demand on higher education and other education services	Argentina receives plurilateral demand on education coordinated by N. Zealand The HE Division is consulted. They respond appealing to the Montevideo Declaration New Education Act establishes that Argentina will not commit education in trade agreements	Chile receives plurilateral demand on education coordinated by N. Zealand Chile will commit education depending on the evolution of the Doha Round

Source: Author

The data contained in this first column enable us to observe how global and regional events have affected the negotiation process in each country. As expected, the negotiations rhythm at the global level is in step with negotiations at the national level. This is more evident in Argentina, where education demands by other countries correlate with consultations at the national level. In terms of influences that are external to the WTO subsystem, the empirical data indicate that several international events and actors have also affected the positions of education stakeholders. This is the case with Argentina's public universities, which adopted an anti-GATS position after attending the Summit of Iberoamerican Public University Chancellors in 2002 and signing the Porto Alegre Letter. This is also the case with Argentina's main teacher unions, which placed the GATS issue on their political agenda after attending the EI World Conference in July 2004. Finally, the Montevideo Declaration, signed in the context of the Mercosur, was the tool used by the Argentinean Ministry of Education to veto any possibility of committing education liberalization within the Doha Round.

Negotiation Procedures and the Role of Education Stakeholders

The procedures for the GATS education negotiations at the national level are much more open for education stakeholders in Argentina. Procedural differences are both quantitative (because more education stakeholders were consulted in Argentina) and qualitative (because these stakeholders played a more influential role within the consultation process in Argentina). In the 1990s, both countries had similar ideas on trade policies, as well as similar procedures and styles to deal with trade policy. However, in the wake of the economic crisis in 2001 and massive social protests, Argentina's Ministry of Trade and other government agencies were mandated to be more responsive to the demands of civil society. And, more importantly, when the crisis subsided, mainstream political groups became skeptical about the benefits of free trade and economic liberalization. In contrast, trade issues in Chile are more technical and less politicized, and free trade still enjoys hegemonic status. The trade liberalization policies introduced by Pinochet after a lengthy period of economic nationalism have been maintained during the democratic period that began in 1990 (Agosin 1999). Today, economic liberalization still guides political decisions in most sectors (Angell 2002). As one of the trade negotiators stated:

> Chile is much closer to the free trade model: open economy, predominant private sector, no state intervention, or as little as possible. Regulations must be as pro-market as possible . . . These ideas are deeply rooted and have generated a strong consensus (. . .) There is consistency in the statements of various public or private institutions; they all speak the same language. A few years ago, some public institutions took a different approach than that adopted by the Treasury or the Central Bank. But today there is consistency between all institutions (. . .) We speak the same language (Interview Chilean Trade negotiator 04, Santiago, 2006).

In Chile, the free trade consensus also extends to the educational community. As seen in Table 9.2, which summarizes key stakeholders' positions and preferences on GATS and education issues, Chile's education stakeholders are much more pro-liberalization than their Argentinean counterparts. In Chile, there is a significant correlation between the opinions of the trade representatives and the education representatives; education stakeholders

Table 9.2   The Stakeholders Approach to GATS and Education in Argentina and Chile

ACTOR	COUNTRY	POSITION / PREFERENCES	INTERPRETATIVE REPERTOIRES
Trade Ministry	Argentina	PRO-GATS: · Education as a bargaining chip	· GATS Respects the regulation capacity of the states · Increases the exportation opportunities for the country
	Chile	PRO-GATS: · Education as a bargaining chip · Free Trade can benefit education	· GATS Respects the regulation capacity of the States · Increases the exportation opportunities for the country · Creates more offer and investment in education and favors education quality
Education Ministry	Argentina	AGAINST GATS: · Education is not a commodity	· Alters traditional functions of education
	Chile	PRO-GATS: · Free Trade can benefit education	· Liberalization is positive if it has the capacity to assure quality
Universities	Argentina	AGAINST GATS: · Education is not a commodity (public universities) · Defensive interests (private universities)	· Alters traditional functions of education (public universities) · Unequal exchange in education (private universities)
	Chile	PRO-GATS: · Free Trade can benefit education	· Increases the export opportunities for the country and the available resources for universities
Teacher Unions	Argentina	AGAINST GATS: · Education is not a commodity	· Restricts policy space · Unequal exchange in education · Privatization of education · Alters traditional functions of education · Damages labor conditions
	Chile		
Quality Assurance Agencies	Argentina	[non defined preferences]	[non defined discourse on the topic]
	Chile	PRO-GATS: · Free Trade can benefit education	Liberalization is positive if it has the capacity to assure quality

Source: Author

do not subscribe to widely held views on the dangers of the Agreement for the international educational community. The Ministry of Education, the quality assurance agencies and the education providers generally agree that education liberalization presents opportunities and, to some extent, they participate actively in their country's trade strategy. The teachers unions are the only key stakeholder group that has opposed the GATS and the commodification of education in both countries.

Negotiators from both Argentina and Chile would be willing to open up the education sector to trade, particularly if that would result in concessions by other countries during the GATS negotiations. In both Argentina and Chile, actions by the trade ministries in this area have been driven by mercantilist considerations. For instance, as an Argentinean negotiator expressed:

> I always see the services area as a way for the developed countries to open up new markets, which is totally legitimate. [However], we are not going to improve our current services offer, which is actually a good one, without getting something in return—and something more than empty promises in agriculture (Interview Argentinean trade negotiator 03, Buenos Aires, 2006).

On the other hand, the trade negotiators are always skeptical about the Agreement's negative implications for education. In fact, they believe that liberalization will improve education quality and will provide the national education industry with access to new income streams (Interviews Argentinean negotiators 02 and 03; Chilean negotiators 01, 02 and 04, 2006).

In Chile, the trade negotiators' preferences on the education negotiations were adopted. They did not face significant opposition from actors in education, partly because they all share the same views on the benefits of trade liberalization for education. In contrast, Argentina's education stakeholders were able to modify the trade representatives' mercantilist positions and contributed significantly to the decision to draw the line on education under the GATS.

The Role of the Teachers Unions

Table 9.2 shows that the teachers unions are the only group of education stakeholders to maintain a common position in both countries. The main teachers union from Chile (CDP) and the main teachers union from Argentina (CTERA) are both very critical of GATS. The trade ministries in both countries have systematically ignored these unions during the GATS negotiations. Nevertheless, CTERA has influenced the course of the negotiations at the national level and has therefore influenced Argentina's official negotiating position at the global level. Based on responses to the contra factual question on the political influence of CTERA (i.e.

whether the outcome of the negotiations in Argentina would have been different if the union had not intervened) we can conclude that CTERA is a key element in understanding Argentina's official position in the GATS education negotiations.

Most likely, Argentina would have been critical of education liberalization in any case, seeing as public and private universities are also critical. Nevertheless, the "line in the sand" on education might not have been quite so categorical. This is due to the fact that CTERA has been the promotor of the Brasilia and Montevideo Declarations, together with Article 10 of the LEN, which states that Argentina will not make commitments on education under free trade agreements.

The Chilean teachers union, however, has not been as influential as CTERA, even though it has promoted similar initiatives, invested a similar amount of resources and adopted a similar discourse and explanatory frame over the topic. These different outcomes are less related to the unions' intrinsic capabilities or strategies and more to contextual factors. As Colin Hay (2002) has observed, the context is strategically selective. This means that certain strategies, actors and discourses are favored, while others are not, depending on the context they are located. Therefore, some outcomes are not possible for certain stakeholders and strategies at any given moment and at any place.

In this sense, CTERA benefited from the political climate in Argentina in the wake of the 2001 economic crisis. The new government is attempting to distance itself from the neoliberal policies of the 1990s because they are seen as the main cause of the crisis. In this context, the government's anti-GATS position is entirely consistent with its strategy of breaking with the past. It is also consistent with its at times theatrical stance against neoliberal international organizations.

The current government of Argentina has actively forged alliances with progressive social movements and other civil society organizations in a bid to ensure social peace after years of political instability. Making concessions to the teachers union—a key player in the socio-political arena— serves this strategy and facilitates policy-making in the education sector, which has traditionally been problematic and contentious. Evidently, this political context has opened up several windows of political opportunity for CTERA. Moreover, the union's sphere of influence has expanded since other stakeholders (such as public or private universities) have not worked against its interests. Instead, they have pressured the government in the same direction.

In Chile, the political scenario is almost the opposite. The pro-free trade consensus in the country, backed by key higher education stakeholders such as the Ministry of Education and the traditional and non-traditional universities, makes it very difficult to voice ideas that are critical of trade liberalization. These contextual factors have largely prevented CDP from achieving a level of political success commensurate with that of CTERA.

The Weight of Higher Education Regulation

Comparing the state of art of the negotiations in Argentina and Chile reveals a kind of paradox because Chile—which has more leeway to use education as a bargaining chip—cannot use it so effectively within the GATS because it has already committed itself to education liberalization under other free trade agreements with the world's largest trading nations. Therefore, the value of education offers within the GATS for Chile is relatively low due to the commitments it has already adopted in bilateral agreements. For Argentina, the value of the education sector within the GATS negotiations is potentially high, but the trade negotiators are not permitted to use it to bargain.

This comparison also reveals another apparent contradiction. This relates to the role of "education factors" and to the fact that the requirements and shortcomings of education regulation do not correspond to countries' positions with respect to trade agreements. This contradicts again the assumption that countries make commitments on education within the GATS depending on the actual needs and priorities of their education systems—see (Sauvé 2002).

Chile's higher education system has been qualified as "diverse, unstable and unpredictable" (Goic Goic 2004). Its regulatory framework is lax with respect to substandard private providers and private universities (and their students) can benefit from state funding. The GATS could therefore exacerbate the Chilean education system's regulatory shortcomings. Nevertheless, these potential dangers are not perceived as such by the Ministry of Education or other stakeholders. In other words, Chilean uncritical position of the education stakeholders with respect to GATS does not reflect the realities of the country's regulatory framework.

In contrast, Argentina's higher education sector is much more regulated; the state oversees a stringent quality assurance system and guarantees access to higher education. Although under funded, Argentina's higher education system is made up almost exclusively of national providers (only one of the country's 80 universities is foreign-owned); private universities are prohibited from receiving state funding. For these reasons, trade liberalization would be less problematic in Argentina than in Chile. However, the official position of the former categorically excludes this possibility. Argentina's position is based more on political considerations and principled beliefs than on technical reasons—or, as the Argentine trade negotiators have complained, on "philosophical" reasons.

In light of the above, Argentina is more faithful to the spirit of the Cordoba manifesto of 1918 than it is to the Doha imaginary. For its part, Chile abandoned the centralized model of education and the principle of education as a social right long ago. The military junta unilaterally and drastically liberalized higher education in the 1980s. Since the 1990s, a series of democratic governments have consolidated the liberalization efforts of the dictatorship under various free trade agreements without generating a significant conflict within the higher education community.

Conclusions

Conclusions

10 Explaining the GATS Results in Education

This book has aimed to reveal the factors that lead to the results of the GATS negotiations in the field of education. To achieve this objective, the book has dealt with some broader analytical axis that, when related to the GATS, can be formulated as follows:

- The role of ideas in the process of commercial liberalization of educational services.
- The political impact of non-state actors on the results of the GATS negotiations.
- The scalar division manifested in the GATS negotiations, and how the scalar interaction between actors, systems of rules and procedures at the national and the global levels affects the results of the negotiations in the education sector.

This conclusion chapter discusses these three issues and includes an explanation of education liberalization based on mechanisms. The chapter ends with brief reflections on methodology for researching global issues and global politics in the education field.

10.1 THE ROLE OF IDEAS AND NON-STATE ACTORS

In social sciences, there is a broad consensus on the relevance of ideational factors in explaining political processes and results. The relevance of ideas is even stronger if we consider, as constructivism does, that ideas precede and contribute to constructing the interests and preferences of different actors. However, these assumptions on the role of ideas contain certain nuances. Firstly, it should be acknowledged that the concept of ideas refers to very a broad range of issues (from abstract ideologies and world views to more concrete causal beliefs). Secondly, ideas can affect political outputs in very different ways (as road maps, coalitional glue or in a more institutionalized way). Thirdly, the level of autonomy and causality that can be attributed to ideas as explanatory factors of political outcomes is also highly variable. The research carried out on the GATS and education deals directly with these and other aspects.

The debate on the role of ideas can be also linked to that dealing with the role of non-state actors in international politics. Ideas, arguments and persuasion tend to form the main political weapons used by actors such as trade unions or NGOs, which do not have any decision-making powers in international forums such as the WTO. The research also offers some valuable empirical evidence for understanding how and when civil society organizations, both at the national and the global levels, can influence international politics.

As observed in Chapter 6, the international educational community, led by non-state actors such as Education International and global and regional university associations, has been capable of generating a passionate debate on GATS. The ideas and causal theories contained in the debate could potentially have a political influence in the negotiations. The GATS is a relatively new and complex issue, and its effects in the education sector are uncertain. Given these conditions, policy makers might be expected to turn to experts to strengthen their positions on the topic. However, it is not clear whether the 'GATS and education debate' has penetrated the WTO participatory subsystem and whether it has become a policy-making referential. Two major barriers to making this debate more politically relevant have been identified.

Firstly, the most important points of the debate have not been resolved and agreed by the broad international epistemic community in their reflection on GATS and education issues. The GATS and education debate is replete with ideas, but, very often, these ideas are completely opposing and there is clear disagreement in relation to most of the topics contemplated by the debate. Moreover, the two opposing positions (pro- education liberalization and anti-liberalization) are embedded in two very different semiotic orders, clearly linked to very distant institutional settings and orders of moral principles and priorities for education. These aspects make it difficult for existing ideas to act as roadmaps for policy makers within the WTO forum. It must be recognized that causal theories are more influential when there is a clear scientific consensus between the international scientific community (Walsh 2000), as could be the case today for issues such as climate change. However, the GATS and education currently involves very different policy choices which could be both supported and rejected by the existing theories.

A second, even more determining barrier resides in trade ministries not defining their position within the GATS and education negotiations grounded on 'education rationales'. Many scholars have assumed that the decisions and positions on the GATS and education are adopted by countries after taking into account the opportunities and risks of education liberalization under the agreement. However, having opened the black box of the negotiations, a clear need to question this assumption has emerged. As shown in chapters 8 and 9, a significant number of countries are liberalizing (or willing to liberalize) education through the GATS without considering an education rationale. Only a few are taking decisions placing education at the core of the decision-making process: those that explicitly problematize the commodification of education promoted by the GATS (these countries do not establish liberalization commitments in education) and those that consider that trade liberalization will improve the quality of their higher education systems or will contribute to generate a regional higher education hub in their country (these countries decide to establish them). However, 'educational reasons' are absent from the scope of those countries that would liberalize education on the understanding that this could be exchanged for liberalization commitments in other areas (such as agriculture or textiles) where they have offensive interests. This appears to be the dominant form of negotiating education. In fact, as trade analysts observed, treating education—as well as other sectors—as bargaining commodities is the "natural" cognitive framework for negotiating in trade forums such as the WTO (Krugman, 1997). Interestingly, this leads to an apparent paradox: in the GATS context, countries are building up an international regime on trade in education, without any shared principles on why this regime is necessary for education, and relegating the conception, functions, and objectives of education to the background.

Trade representatives are the central actors in the GATS negotiations and the position they hold in the center of the negotiation matrix empowers them. They are the brokers between the participatory subsystem and the national representative subsystem, they coordinate the procedures and calls for consultations with national stakeholders, they have better knowledge, information and expertise on the issue than other agents, etc. However, trade negotiators and trade ministries cannot always push their priorities and interests to the forefront. Neither can they negotiate education as a bargaining chip wherever this is necessary to satisfy their interests or to implement their agenda. Despite their privileged position at the core of the negotiations, they are also subjected to other forces. Educational actors such as universities or teaching unions form part of these forces; as such they are able to make the negotiation process much more accountable and, in some cases, to alter the mercantilist approaches that the trade ministries have for the education sector.

Which Ideas Matter? Lessons from the Case Studies

The national case studies undertaken in Argentina and Chile show that ideas on the GATS and education cannot be conceived in themselves as autonomous explanatory factors of GATS results. In both cases, the influence of the arguments on GATS has been strongly subordinated to the ideational, historical and institutional context of each country. In *Chile*, neoliberal ideology dominates the arguments of trading agents, but also the rationale of leading education representatives. There, negotiation preferences for education are defined based on path dependencies originating from the GATT, and on pro-free trade ideas that are embedded in an institutional context where free trade is a hegemonic idea. Therefore, the debate on the GATS and education has not served to open up new paths in Chile. Rather, the settlement of preferences has followed the known path of free trade. Trade negotiations in Chile are very much centralized in its Ministry of Trade. This partially explains the pro-free trade bias. However, most education stakeholders in the country also share the preferences of the trade representatives.

To explain this frame alignment between the trade and education representatives in Chile it should be acknowledged that a monetarist-neoliberal policy paradigm clearly prevails there.[1] The core ideas of this paradigm reflect a certain mode of regulation, a fixed accumulation regime and a system of production and exchange of commodities and services. Hence, the link between ideas and material factors is very strong and is coherently structured and institutionalized. As Colin Hay (2002) suggests, in contexts where a policy paradigm is hegemonic, the role of ideas is more subtle, certain fixed ideas become naturalized and their influence is less evident. This means that policy paradigms are to be understood as sources of inculcation of ideas, and policy actors that have been socialized within a fixed paradigm act routinely according to these ideas.

Consequently, the strength of a policy paradigm delimits the parameters of acceptable behavior and acceptable political demands. Actors that reproduce the core ideas of the paradigm, such as the universities that participate in the University Services Exports Committee in Chile are therefore rewarded. However, those with contradictory ideas are penalized or marginalized, such as the Chilean teachers union with its demands to exclude education from the free trade agreements scope. This makes it more difficult for non-conformist political actors to influence politics, even though their power capacities and material resources may be high.

The core ideas of a policy paradigm are questioned in periods of crisis (Hall 1993). This is, in fact, what happened in Argentina. During the 1990s, the neoliberal and monetarist policy paradigm was also dominant in this country, but the deep economic crisis that broke in 2001 shook the paradigm, and a process of redefining some of its core ideas began. The crisis opened new windows of opportunity and some ideas and actors that had been outsiders in the 1990s, were able to penetrate the new network of governance. Economic nationalism, third–worldism, the redistribution of wealth and the direct intervention of the state in the provision of basic services gained centrality on the Argentinean political agenda as well as in the official discourse. The opposition to introducing education into the GATS fits perfectly into this broader set of principles and the arguments against the GATS resound positively in the new dominant ideological framework. Therefore, although the Argentinean teachers union has used similar resources and discourses to its Chilean counterpart to fight against the GATS, it has been much more successful. This reinforces the idea that actors with similar cognitive and material capabilities will have more or less influence depending on the political and ideational context in which they are embedded.

It should be pointed out that in Argentina there is a clear correlation between the official government position and the critical ideas on the GATS and education spread by the teachers' union and other stakeholders. However, this does not necessarily mean that these ideas are the direct cause of the government behavior in the negotiations, or that they have acted as road maps (i.e. clear guide lines for decision-making). Rather, ideas have acted as lenses and coalitional glue that helped the Argentinean government to reaffirm its ideology and to embed its preferences on the topic in a broader political program. The Argentinean case is also a good example of how, beyond ideational factors, other tactic and relational aspects are very important to explain the success of social movements. In contexts where dialogue, exchange of ideas and arguments are not enough to influence political outputs (such as the GATS negotiations), non-state actors have to resort to measures of force if they want to succeed. This was the case of CTERA, which became influential not because it convinced trade negotiators of the best decision to take (in fact, there was no personal interaction between them), but because it made the Ministry of Education act as a veto player in the context of the negotiations.

In short, the capacity of non-state actors to influence the final decision on the GATS and educational affairs is contingent to broader ideational and institutional settings. Non-state actors and their ideas matter most when they are linked to specific material factors and institutional backgrounds because new ideas are more easily internalized if they are congruent with historically formed ideologies and with the dominant order of political discourse in a country. Moreover, tactics and the politics of alliances by social movements, involving key state actors and veto players, are necessary to ensure a governmental commitment that education will not be liberalized in the scope of the GATS.

Global Civil Society Against the GATS: EI and the University Associations

At the international level, non-state actors have been as active as state-based international organizations, such as the OECD or UNESCO, in promoting the GATS and education debate. As shown in Chapter 7, Education International and the public universities associations are the non-state actors to have promoted a more systematic campaign to introduce the GATS issue into the public domain and to advocate against the agreement due to its effects on education. These organizations have tried to achieve their objectives by means of an intense effort in the construction and dissemination of knowledge. They have created their own forums and spaces for knowledge production on the GATS and education, established strategic alliances with key international actors such as UNESCO to strengthen and legitimate their arguments, and have actively disseminated this knowledge through publications, the organization of seminars or the approval of political statements. In doing so, they have contributed to making the GATS issue more comprehensible for a non-trade specialist audience. Moreover, the 'pedagogic' role undertaken by these international organizations has provoked common and trans-border patterns of discourse with regard to GATS and its effects between teachers unions, southern countries universities and other education players with regard to the agreement and its effects.

The ideas disseminated by these agents combine causal theories and principled beliefs. This results in a differentiation between the cognitive actions of social movements and those of conventional scientific communities, whose arguments are based exclusively on causal theories. Discourses that appeal to principled beliefs are more likely to trigger political action (Keck and Sikkink 1998). Civil society discourses also trigger action because contemplate 'motivation frames', i.e. discursive repertoires that have the objective of motivating people to struggle against situations that are considered unfair (Benford and Snow 2000). As observed in Chapter 7, the meaning frames of both Education International and the international universities associations specifically encourage their members to organize debates and campaigns against the GATS at the national level.

In fact, as our case studies show, there are at least two national unions that, after being partially activated by EI, have undertaken a successful campaign against the GATS at the national level. These are CTERA from Argentina and Confederação Nacional dos Trabalhadores em Educação (CNTE) from Brazil. Both unions became aware of the importance of acting against the agreement in the 2004 EI World Conference, and since then they have embarked upon a political campaign against the GATS. One of the key stages of the campaign occurred when they lobbied the ministries of education asking that a clear commitment for education not be included in the GATS and, as a consequence, the *Brasilia Declaration* was signed.[2] Something similar happened with the Argentinean public universities which, after attending the 3rd Ibero-American Summit of Public University Chancellors, became aware of the potential implications of the GATS and denied the trade representatives the possibility of offering higher education in the first round of consultations.

Interestingly, the effects of these global campaigns in national politics can also be understood in a less direct manner. This is because by raising awareness of a certain topic and introducing it into the public domain, the power relationships and the procedures for dealing with this topic may become altered. And that is probably what happened in the GATS context. In the Uruguay Round, education was negotiated with much less consideration to educational actors and related education aspects (Vlk, 2006; Mundy and Iga 2003; Ziguras et al 2003; Frater 2008b). At that time, dozens of WTO member countries committed education liberalization in the GATS without this causing a ripple, as the interested parties in the educational community were not aware of it. Trade agents could therefore achieve their objectives by taking decisions in secret, or rather out of the scope of global and national public opinion. Yet by the end of the 1990s, in a setting of strong international protests against the WTO, criticism towards the GATS and its interference in education emerged. Consequently, more countries were pressurized to legitimize and to publicly justify their decisions to liberalize education and other sensitive sectors (such as health or cultural services). For the same reason, some countries formalized consultation processes with the stakeholders and attempted to make the negotiations process more transparent.

In short, the global campaigns against the GATS have not directly influenced the final decision of countries on the GATS, but they have opened up new political opportunities at the national level to address the demands of the education stakeholders. To some extent, this is due to the fact that, in democratic countries, once the topic has been introduced into the public arena, the political cost of liberalizing education without taking into account the voice and demands of the education stakeholders would be greater than before.

Towards a New Complex Multilateralism?

This research contributes to the debate on the validity of the thesis on new complex multilateralism, which propounds that multilateralism is moving away from an exclusively state-based structure, and that civil society organizations can currently play an increasingly important role in multilateral structures without the need for mediation by the states. The case study of the Education International campaign against the GATS, which is the only global non-governmental association to participate at the WTO level, advocating for education issues, shows that the complex multilateralism idea needs to be applied with some caution. Some elements that ratify this thesis have been identified. Firstly, we have observed that international civil society is formally recognized within the WTO participatory subsystem (see Table 4.1) and, in fact, EI has actively participated in activities of advocacy and dialogue favored by the WTO. Another indicator of the rise of a new multilateral scenario that is more sensitive to global civil society inputs is that the WTO itself has reacted directly to the criticism raised by EI and other international civil society agents over the implications of the GATS for public services—see (WTO 2001). Thirdly, the participation of EI in the design of the UNESCO/OECD 'Guidelines for quality assurance in cross-border education', which is interpreted as a response to the GATS hegemony, is another initiative that validates the idea of an emerging complex multilateralism that leapfrogs the need for state mediation within international politics.

However, several aspects that refute the complex multilateralism thesis have also been identified. In fact, it seems that there are more continuities than changes in the evolution of multilateralism for us to be able to talk about a paradigm shift in this terrain. Firstly, the participatory mechanisms agreed by the WTO are not conducive to the principal demands of EI ("education out of GATS"), partly because they are too challenging and do not resound positively within the current WTO system of rules. This would demonstrate that current multilateral institutions are not equally open to any kind of civil society organization or to any kind of discourse. Secondly, and more importantly, the more direct and fruitful political impacts of the GATS campaign have been mediated on the state scale. EI appears to have had the biggest effect on the result of the GATS negotiations when it put more energy into the activation of anti-GATS campaigns at the national level. Initially, EI brought direct advocacy work to bear on the WTO negotiators, but once it had acquired a complete picture of the geography of the decision-making process in the organization, it redefined its strategy. Thus it adopted a tactic that we describe as a 'reverse boomerang effect' (Verger and Novelli 2009) because it works in the opposite direction of the boomerang effect mentioned by Kekk and Sikking (1998). In this case, the international actor realizes that their access to the decision-making spaces are blocked at a global level, and in order to make the pressure more effective, activates other NGOs to pressurize the states at the national level (see Appendix 4).

In short, the state is still the key arena in influencing global politics. Nevertheless, to be fair to the importance of the political action on a global scale, it should be reiterated the idea that the national campaigns against the GATS would not have had the same probabilities of becoming successful if other international actors had not previously introduced the topic into the global public domain.

10.2   LOCAL VS. GLOBAL?
THROUGH A PLURI–SCALAR EXPLANATION

The statistical analysis carried out in Chapter 5 draws some general trends on the national decisions on education liberalization under the GATS. Specifically, this stage of the research showed that: a) Developing countries are more reticent with regard to liberalizing education than developed countries; b) certain extra-educational factors affect the liberalization of education in the GATS, particularly the WTO rules of access, which oblige candidate countries to apply ambitious liberalization packages; c) the characteristics of higher education systems in countries are not statistically related to the level of liberalization commitments.

The second stage of the research (mainly described in the second block of this book) introduces new micro variables (interests, rules, procedures, ideas and mechanisms activated by human agency within the politics of services negotiations) that complement the macro variables of the first stage. The results obtained allow a better understanding of why countries liberalize education in the GATS context. The new variables refer, firstly, to global factors, such as the GATS negotiations rationale, the methodology of the services liberalization negotiations, other WTO system of rules and the external influences activated by the WTO itself. Secondly, they refer to domestic factors such as the demands of the education stakeholders, the ideology of the national governments, and the consultation procedure coordinated by the ministry of trade at the country level. As developed in the following lines, all these variables can be arranged in a coherent and pluri-scalar explanation.

At the global level, it has been observed that the WTO openly promotes the trade liberalization of education. Indeed, the WTO system of rules and its policy instruments, far from being neutral, try to drive the behavior of member countries towards the application of free trade policies in education and all other service and commodity sectors. To do that, various mechanisms for influencing the decisions of member countries are activated in the context of this organization. These mechanisms (dissemination, harmonization, standardization and dissemination) and the way they operate are detailed in the following box (Box 10.1).

Box 10.1 The WTO's Mechanisms and Instruments of Influence

1. HARMONIZATION: The negotiations about National Treatment and Market Access in the sphere of services are developed as a gradual process of harmonization between the members. They are carried out with the perspective of achieving progressively higher liberalization quotas.

2. IMPOSITION: By means of the Dispute Settlement Body disciplinary measures and the WTO accession rules, certain types of behavior and decisions can be imposed on members.

3. STANDARDIZATION: GATS Rules and Domestic Regulation working groups define shared international binding standards regarding criteria for evaluating the quality of services, granting of licenses, subsidies, etc.

4. DISSEMINATION OF POLICIES: The Trade Policy Review is one of the main instruments for disseminating liberal trade policies. The Secretary of the WTO is also highly active in disseminating free trade principles by means of technical assistance or the publication of reports.

Source: Author

The WTO rules are powerful, but they are not absolute. Once the negotiation black box was opened, it was seen that actions and decisions by member countries are not guided mainly by the principles and rules of the WTO. If their action was driven by the logic of appropriateness at the WTO level, as conceptualized by March and Olsen (1998), they would act in accordance with the ideas constructed and accepted in the framework of this international organization and, consequently, would be more willing to liberalize education. If this was the case, members would be convinced that opening education to trade would improve education delivery in their countries (better offer, higher quality, etc.). But, as observed in chapter 8, only a minority sustains this liberalizing rationale and member countries respond normally to other and contradicting rationales and subsystems of norms.

Beyond simplistic and top-down relationships between the WTO and its members, the existing situation is much more complex. The research undertaken leads to a set of observations that indicate this. Firstly, the effects of the WTO on countries are not always direct and do not affect all member countries with the same intensity. For instance, it has been observed that both 'new members' and less developed countries are much more sensitive to external influences than other countries.

Secondly, several external mechanisms and rationales are activated at the global level simultaneously and in contradictory ways. For instance, the strategy adopted by most member countries of using education as a bargaining chip contradicts the policy orientation of the WTO external mechanisms. The bargaining chip strategy, which is a consequence of the predominance of the mercantilist ideology in international trade forums, has become the key rationale during the Doha Round. In fact, it seems that mercantilism has cast a shadow over the cautious rationale that was more apparent in the Uruguay Round. The predominance of the mercantilist rationale is the consequence of having most WTO member countries pushing for their own national interests (or, more precisely, for the particular interests of their national export industries) in the context of the negotiations, instead of keeping 'free-trade' on a world scale as being the core ideal to achieve.

Third, the powers and effects of the mercantilist ideology and the WTO rules are mediated by factors, institutions and conditions, mostly located at the domestic level. One of these conditions is endogenous to the WTO system and involves the level of liberalization ambition achieved by the negotiation round in question. This means that, for example, if the northern countries are not willing to remove export subsidies and other trade barriers to agriculture during the negotiations, the agriculture-exporting countries will not use education as a bargaining chip. They will choose to protect this and other sectors to gain more bargaining power in future episodes of the negotiations. The other factors identified have a more domestic scope. They are: a) the level of centralization of decision-making within the ministry of trade; b) the ideology of the country's government; c) the role played by education stakeholders in the negotiation process. The country cases analyzed show that in a context of a social-democrat and/or an economic nationalistic government, with civil society campaigning against the GATS and a low level of centralization of the final decision in the trade ministry, education will not be committed. In short, these three factors clearly favor the rejection of education commitments within the GATS and obstruct the activation or the effectiveness of the bargaining chip mechanism.

All these endogenous and exogenous factors, as well as the relationships between them, are presented in Figure 10.1. In this figure, the explanatory model of education liberalization in the GATS context is detailed. The figure shows that education trade liberalization is not something that can be explained only through top-down models and that, currently, the constitution of an international regime of trade in education is still at an unstable stage. As can be observed, the bargaining chip mechanism is placed at the core of the explanatory model because it clearly mediates between WTO rules, domestic factors and the final decision by countries of whether to liberalize education or not.

Indeed, this research on the GATS and education suggests that the global and the local scales are not necessarily related in a deterministic and top-down way (i.e. only the global affecting the local). Without a doubt the global, represented by the WTO system, imposes certain decisions on certain countries and activates the harmonization of trade and non-trade policies; the preferences shaping and the agenda negotiating settlement are also normally developed at the global level. Nevertheless, the locus of decision-making remains mainly at the national level where local agents are particularly active and strategic in pushing for their particular interests and

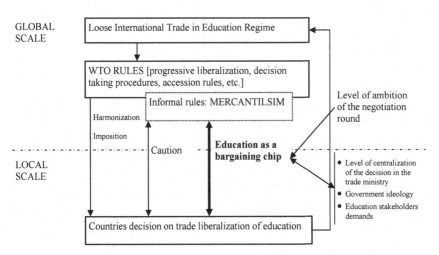

Figure 10.1   Education liberalization causal model.
Source: Author

ideas. Under certain conditions, these actors are able to successfully challenge the WTO external influences as well as the mercantilist rationale of trade representatives. As a consequence, they are able to alter the outcomes of the GATS negotiations.

10.3   METHODOLOGICAL CONCLUSIONS

The findings of this research support Dale and Robertson (2007)'s problematization of certain theoretical and methodological assumptions—still strongly present in the comparative education field—in the current globalization context. As mentioned in the introduction of this book, these assumptions are 'methodological statism', 'methodological nationalism' and 'educationism'.

In relation to 'methodological statism', the GATS negotiation procedure itself shows that the state cannot be conceived as a monolithic unit but rather as a field made up of different units that act according to different agendas and priorities that can overlap or contradict (Jessop 1990). The clash of preferences in relation to the GATS negotiations between the education ministry and the trade ministry, which has been observed very clearly in the Argentinean case study, exemplifies this idea. Another aspect that challenges 'methodological statism' is the observation that non-state actors are playing an active role, decisive on occasion, in governance activities. In the GATS negotiations context, non-state actors do not have decision-making powers, but in some countries they have had the capacity to alter government preferences and decisions on the subject.

This research also reflects the need to challenging 'educationism'. The GATS negotiations, and the GATS text itself, show how deeply non-education factors affect education transformations and processes. Consequently, the emergence of this non-conventional, but powerful element in the education field also reinforces the idea of having to apply non-traditional education theoretical frameworks in order to understand the changes that are occurring in the education field.

In relation to 'methodological nationalism', the education liberalization process promoted by the GATS is a perfect example for reflection on the relevance and the nature of the scalar division of education governance in the global age. The data obtained show that, while the nation-state continues being the key decision-maker in international forums such as the WTO/GATS, international organizations, powerful states and global civil society are capable of framing and influencing the decisions taken by the states. In fact, the multi-level explanation of education liberalization (represented in Figure 10.1) also shows that the 'global' and the 'local' do not represent a simple zero-sum relationship.

In one word, globalization is challenging the territorial, theoretical and methodological frameworks, as well as the traditional units of analysis used by education scientists and comparativists. Globalization is also modifying the field of action for those educational actors advocating public and quality higher education on a world scale. The WTO/GATS case is a perfect example for understanding these changes, which are occurring at both scientific and political levels in the field of education. Hopefully, this book has contributed to explaining how the WTO/GATS operate and how the strategic action of the education agents is important for understanding the results and implications of this trade agreement in the education field.

Appendices

Appendices

Appendix 1

Table A.1 Edu-GATS Values in Higher Education and All Education Sectors

	Edu-GATS Higher Education	*Edu-GATS All education sectors*
Australia	0,59	0,36
Austria	0	0,43
Japan	0,21	0,20
Liechtenstein	0,43	0,34
New Zealand	0,66	0,39
Norway	0,55	0,44
Switzerland	0,70	0,40
United States	0	0,23
Belgium	0,64	0,51
Denmark	0,61	0,49
France	0,55	0,45
Germany	0,62	0,49
Greece	0,58	0,48
Ireland	0,62	0,49
Italy	0,58	0,48
Luxembourg	0,64	0,51
Netherlands	0,64	0,51
Portugal	0,62	0,49
Spain	0,60	0,49
United Kingdom	0,64	0,51
DEVELOPED COUNTRIES AVERAGE	*0,52*	*0,44*
China	0,42	0,42
Taiwan	0,70	0,52
Costa Rica	0	0,11
Ghana	0	0,37
Jamaica	0,81	0,49
Jordan	0,65	0,55
Mexico	0,70	0,56
Oman	0,69	0,55
Panama	0,57	0,34
Thailand	0	0,29
Trinidad and Tobago	0,33	0,20
Turkey	0,91	0,63

(continued)

Table A.1   (continued)

	Edu-GATS Higher Education	Edu-GATS All education sectors
DEVELOPING COUNTRIES AVERAGE	**0,48**	**0,42**
Congo	0,76	0,15
Cambodja	0,73	0,44
Gambia	0	0,45
Haiti	0	0,20
Lesotho	0,89	0,89
Mali	0	0,20
Nepal	0,67	0,40
Rwanda	0	0,2
Sierra Leone	0,53	0,53
LDCs AVERAGE	**0,40**	**0,38**
Albania	0,92	0,7
Armenia	0,86	0,34
Bulgaria	0	0,30
Croatia	0,72	0,52
Czech Republic	0,38	0,68
Estonia	0,75	0,75
Georgia	0,62	0,52
Hungary	0,70	0,56
Kyrgyzstan	0,72	0,58
Latvia	0,87	0,69
Lithuania	0,77	0,61
Macedonia	0,67	0,40
Moldova	0,88	0,88
Poland	0,62	0,50
Slovakia	0,67	0,67
Slovenia	0,65	0,39
TRANSITION COUNTRIES AVERAGE	**0,67**	**0,57**

Source: Author

Appendix 2

Table A.2   Specific Liberalization Commitments of Argentina in Education in the Context of MERCOSUR (5th Round)

Mode / Education Services	Mode 1		Mode 2		Mode 3		Mode 4	
	MA	NT	MA	NT	MA	NT	MA	NT
Primary (5A)	NC	NC	NI	NI	NI	RE	NC/CH	NC/CH
Secondary (5B)	NC	NC	NI	NI	NI	RE	NC/CH	NC/CH
Higher Education (5C)	*NC/NR*	*NC/NR*	*NI*	*NI*	*NI*	*NI*	*NC/CH*	*NC/CH*
Other (5D)	NC	NC	NI	NI	NI	NI	NC/CH	NC/CH

Legend > MA: Market Access; NT: National Treatment; NI: none restrictions; NI/RE: none restrictions, except specified national regulation; NC: Non consolidated; NC/NR: No consolidated because it is non regulated; NC/RE: Non consolidate, except specified national regulation; NC/CH: Non consolidated, except horizontal commitments; RE: specified restriction.

Source: Peixoto (2007)

Appendix 3

Table A.3   Chilean Education Liberalization Commitments in FTAs

AGREEMENT (date signed)	SCOPE OF THE AGREEMENT IN THE SERVICES AREA	EDUCATION COMMITMENTS
Canada – Chile (05-12-96)	• Air services, financial services, and services provided by government authorities are excluded. • Non-state education services are included.	• Chile commits education. • Canada does not commit education.
Chile – Mexico (17-04-98)	• Air services and financial services are excluded. Non-state education services are included. • Education services are included.	• Chile and Mexico commit education.
EU – Chile (18-11-02)	• Air services, financial services, audio-visual and national maritime coastal shipping are excluded. • Education services are included.	• The EU commits education. • Chile does not.
Chile – Costa Rica (14-02-02)	• Air services, financial services, government procurement, and services provided by government authorities are excluded. • Non-state education services are included.	• Chile and Costa Rica commit education.
Chile – El Salvador (03-06-02)	• Air services, financial services, government procurement, and services provided by government authorities are excluded. • Non-state education services are included.	• Chile commits education. • El Salvador does not commit education.
EFTA – Chile (26-06-03)	• Air services are excluded. • Education is included.	• Norway, Liechtenstein and Switzerland commit education. • Chile does not.

(continued)

Table A.3   (continued)

AGREEMENT (date signed)	SCOPE OF THE AGREEMENT IN THE SERVICES AREA	EDUCATION COMMITMENTS
Korea – Chile (15-02-03)	• Air services, financial services and government procurement are excluded, as well as services provided by government authorities (they explicitly refer to public education). • Non-state education services are included.	• Chile and Korea commit education.
US– Chile (06-06-03)	• Air services, financial services and government procurement are excluded. • Education is included.	• Chile commits education. • The US does not commit education.
N. Zealand, Singapore, Brunei D. (12-06-05)	• Finance and air services are excluded. • Education is included.	• Chile does not include reserves in education services.
China – Chile (18-11-05)	• Air services, financial services, national maritime coastal shipping and government procurement are excluded. • Education is included.	• China and Chile commit education (positive list method). • Chile commits post-secondary technical and vocational education and adult education.
Panamá-Chile (26-06-06)	• Air services, financial services, and government procurement are excluded. • Education is included.	• Commitments lists have not been published yet.
Japan – Chile (04-05-07)	• Air services, financial services and maritime services are excluded. • Education is included.	Commitments lists have not been published yet.

Source: Author, data from: http://www.direcon.cl/index.php?accion=tlc_camerica#

Appendix 4

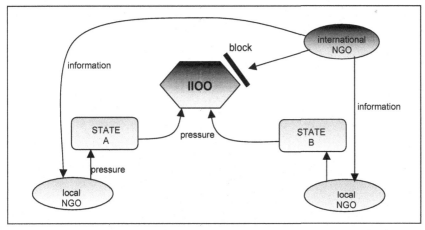

Figure A.1 Representation of the 'reverse' boomerang effect.
Source: Verger and Novelli (2009)

Notes

NOTES TO CHAPTER 1

1. Initially, it was exepected that the round, that was launched in 2001, would finish in 2005. However, it was still ongoing in the middle of 2009.
2. Some of the most relevant events for the research that I have attended to have been: Education International World Conference (Porto Alegre, July 2004), GATS and Education Seminar for unionists (EI-Latin America, Buenos Aires, October 2004), GATS and Education Seminar for unionists (EI-UNESCO, Paris, April 2005), WTO Public Symposium (Geneva, May 2005), Trade negotiators and civil society meeting organized by Public Services International (Geneva, June 2005), WTO 6th Ministerial Conference (Hong Kong, December 2005); IADB Seminar for Latin American negotiators titled *"Las Negociaciones en la OMC y los procesos de Integración en América Latina"* (Buenos Aires, September 2006).
3. Additionally, doing case studies in developing countries is more pertinent than in LDCs because, as will be shown in the following chapters, discussions on GATS and education are more causal in LDCs and external influences are more relevant than national politics in this type of countries.

NOTES TO CHAPTER 2

1. The Uruguay Round lasted four years longer than initially forecast.
2. The system for resolving differences under the GATT was inefficient because it required the consensus of all member countries for the litigation report to be approved. Conversely, under the WTO system, consensus of members was required to reject the report. Consequently, reports are always approved in the WTO system and the sanctions can be applied (Davey 2005).
3. Agricultural products were already included in the GATT, but were subject to very lax disciplines.
4. Ruggie (1982) uses this concept to talk about commercial regimes, inspired in the concepts of *embedded* and *disembedded markets* used by Polanyi in *The Great Transformation*.
5. Other governing principles of the WTO are reciprocity, non-discrimination, previsibility, multilaterality, sustainable development and special and differential treatment (SDT) for less developed countries. It has to be said that some of the abovementioned principles are contradictory. E.g. non-discrimination and SDT, or sustainable development and progressive liberalization of trade. It is not clear how this contradiction can be overcome, although it appears

that the dominant principles—or at least those that are most evidently being implemented—are more congruous with the free trade proposal.

6. See OCDE, *Report by the High Level Group on Trade and Related Problems*, Paris, 1973. Quoted in (Feketekuty 2005).

7. Source: http://www.commercialdiplomacy.org/whowe/feketekuty.htm [Last retrieved: 23/07/08].

8. Free trade is an international trade model grounded on the principle of "comparative advantage", which says that "countries prosper first by taking advantage of their assets in order to concentrate on what they can produce best, and then by trading these products for products that other countries produce best" (WTO 2005a, 13). The WTO clearly supports this theory and considers that "liberal trade policies (. . .) sharpen competition, motivate innovation and breed success. They multiply the rewards that result from producing the best products, with the best design, at the best price (WTO 2005a, 13).

9. See for example the Uruguay Round communications issued with the following code: MTN.GNS/W/48 and MTN.GNS/W34. Source: http://www.wto.org/english/docs_e/gattdocs_e.htm [Last retrieved: 08/11/08].

10. In the trade negotiators jargon, when a country has "offensive interests" in a sector means that it is pushing proactively for the international trade liberalization of the sector in question because of its competitive advantage.

11. See, for example, MTN. GNS/W/29. Source: idem.

12. The incomplete parts of the agreement are specified in the next section.

13. In this section we quote from GATS articles. The GATS can be found in annex 1B of the (GATT Secretariat 1994). See: http://www.wto.org/english/docs_e/legal_e/legal_e.htm#services [last retrieved: 14/07/08].

14. Depending on the country in question, some of the disciplines of the GATS are incorporated in state regulations through the incorporation mechanism, i.e. where the rules of the agreement automatically become part of national legislation without requiring additional legislation, or through transformation, which requires the explicit inclusion of agreement content in domestic regulations and also requires the drawing up of additional legislation (Vlk, 2006).

15. In practical terms this measure, which in principle is an attempt to combat *free rider* behaviour, has encouraged open markets to remain "provisionally open" while the closed markets remain already closed (García López 1999).

16. For example, members are not obliged to make public information that could put their security in danger, nor to adopt measures relating to the armed forces or to fissionable materials.

17. In Annex 3 of the GATS, services related to air transport, such as aircraft repair and maintenance, sale and trade in air transport services and computerised reservation system services are excluded from the scope of the agreement.

18. This is reflected for instance in an European negotiators strategy document. See: (EC 2005).

19. According to the GATS, additional commitments may also be signed up to (Article XVIII). These are different to those described in the MA and NT articles and tend to refer to certificates of aptitude, rules or questions related to licenses.

20. This is reflected, for example, in one of the first demands of the EU: (MTN. GNS/W/56).

21. See MTN.GNS/W/7, MTN.GNS/W/11, or GATT Secretariat (1994)

22. See MTN.GNS/W/19.

23. Other lists on the table were the *International Standard Industrial Classification* (ISIC), the *System of National Accounts* (SNA) and the *Balance of Payments* (BOP) of the International Monetary Fund.

24. For example, the CPC distinguishes between 600 services products, while the ISIC only recognizes 130 service activities. The latter classification considers education as a single category, while as we shall see, the CPC defines five different types of education. The pros and cons of each classification can be seen in the *Note by the Secretariat: Reference List of Sectors*, 13/04/89, code: MTN.GNS/W/50.

25. Another factor influencing this decision was the fact that many countries considered that the liberalization of this sector could compromise national security.

26. See: http://www.educationnz.org.nz/about_goals.html, consulted on 05/02/07. Public and private educational centers form part of this platform.

27. *WTO: GATS: Education Services Negotiations*, copy of restricted document, 19/10/05.

28. The *friends groups* are groupings of member countries of the WTO organized within the framework of the Chamber of Commerce for Services because they have a common interest in one of the service sectors.

29. The demand was seconded by Australia, Chinese Taipei, Malaysia and the USA. The full demand can be consulted at: http://commerce.nic.in/wto_sub/services/Plurilateral_Requests.htm [Last retrieved: 15.10.06]

30. See the barriers to the trade in educational services identified by the NCITE at: http://www.tradeineducation.org/general_info/frames.html [last retrieved: 23/03/06].

31. The particular form of RTAs can differ. The most common are economic association, free trade agreement, and custom agreement.

32. See WTO RTAs Data Base: http://rtais.wto.org/UI/PublicAllRTAList.aspx [last retrieved: 23/03/09]

33. "WTO: 2006 News Items, 10/07/06, RTAs: Lamy welcomes WTO agreement on regional trade agreement", available in: http://www.wto.org/english/news_e/news06_e/rta_july06_e.htm, [last retrieved: 06/02/07].

NOTES TO CHAPTER 3

1. According to this author "university markets are politically installed; they are not the product of a lengthy Braudelian evolution. In fact, they come not from the slow development of "exchange games"—starting out from elementary markets whose origin "is lost in the night of time" and ending up in the "generalized market society" that globally dominates today—but from the intervention of the public authorities" (Brunner, 2006).

2. The label "knowledge society" was introduced by Bell (1973) in a study of post industrialization which presented the hypothesis that knowledge would replace energy as a primary resource in the new society.

3. The main companies of this type are: Apollo Group, De Vry Inc., ITT Educational Services, Sylvan Learning Systems and Strayer Inc. Of the new providers of educational services, the *for profit* higher education centers was one of the few company sectors that was unaffected by the stock exchange crisis of 2000 (OBHE 2003). The most successful company in terms of business is Apollo Group, which has an annual income of 300 million USD and 30% annual growth (Global Alliance Limited 1997).

4. Source: www.cisco.com [last retrieved: 03/04/05].

5. Despite this, the economic results of these companies are not always satisfactory (TFP, 2002). Moreover, virtual education providers were seriously affected by the *dotcom* crisis of April 2000 (OBHE 2003).

6. Market research, such as that carried out by Proexport, has identified the educational sector as one of those with the highest potential in the international market. Source: www.proexport.com [last retrieved: 03/04/05].

7. "Competition and dynamism are two aspects where the EU has fallen behind the USA. Education must play a decisive role to attract talent to Europe and to avoid the brain drain" (EC 2003, 6).

8. Specifically, there are many transnational companies that place value on workers with multicultural and international abilities and skills, of the type that it is assumed can be acquired by studying abroad.

9. Once students have decided to study abroad, according to Larsen et al (2002), they decide on a specific destination for practical reasons such as the language (whether it is the same or similar to their language, or one that they want to learn), cultural and geographical proximity, quality of life, recommendation of other students, accessibility of registration fees and cost of living in that country, recognition of the studies, accessible housing, ability to obtain a visa, etc.

10. The term dependence refers to a situation in which the economy of different countries is conditioned by the development and expansion of another economy (Vidal Villa 1976).

11. According to Hirst and Thompson, currently "governance is a function that can be performed by a wide variety of public and private, state and non-state, national and international, institutions and practices" (1995, 422).

12. It is interesting to note that the term *constitutionalization* is used by Gill as a metaphor to indicate the legal weight of these agreements. However, the author does not express this forcefully. The national constitution of many countries is legally subordinate to the results and contents of the free trade agreements. Consequently, when a country ratifies an agreement of this kind, it may find it has to adapt the content of its national constitution to the obligations included in the agreement.

13. These are numerous Regional Conventions on the Recognition of Studies, Diplomas and Degrees in Higher Education. See: www.unesco.org/legal/index.shtml [Last retrieved: 15/03/07].

NOTES TO CHAPTER 4

1. This observation was also verified in the case of the GATT (Curzon and Curzon 1973).

2. This classification ignores the fact that, on occasion, civil society—as seen in the large-scale demonstrations against the WTO ministerial conferences—participates on the margins of the international organization system in a more disruptive and less collaborative way. This is the case for an important sector of civil society against international economic institutions such as the World Bank, the IMF and the WTO itself (Gómez 2001; Routledge 2003).

3. "Seattle protesters make me sick, says trade chief," *The Independent*, Tuesday, February 6, 2001.

4. See the DISPUTE DS285 "USA—Measures Affecting the Cross-Border Supply of Gambling and Betting Services" in http://www.wto.int/english/tratop_e/dispu_e/cases_e/ds285_e.htm.

5. However, officially, the WTO only recognizes the LDC category, which is adapted from the UN classification system. The WTO itself maintains that the "developing countries" category is controversial and ambiguous. Consequently, countries must decide of their own accord if they wish to remain in the "developing countries" group, even though this term is rejected by various WTO

organs. See: http://www.wto.org/english/thewto_e/whatis_e/tif_e/org7_e.htm [Last retrieved: 12/05/07].

6. For example, during the preparations for the Doha Ministerial Conference, two mini-ministerial conferences were held in Mexico and Singapore. These events played a key role in setting the Doha agenda. They were attended by all Quad members, but by only 3% of LDCs, 6% of low-income countries and 3% of middle-low income countries (Jawara and Kwa 2004).

NOTES TO CHAPTER 5

1. In these figures, we include the EU as a single member—that is, the member countries are not included separately.
2. See the WTO on-line document database: http://www.wto.org/wto/ddf/ep/search.html. Last retrieved: 12/07/08.
3. This request is available at http://commerce.nic.in/wto_sub/services/Plurilateral_Requests.htm [retrieved: 15/10/06].
4. These calculations do not include the four newest members of the organization: Vietnam and Tonga, which formally became WTO members in 2007, and Cape Verde and Ukraine, which joined in 2008. See: http://www.wto.org/english/thewto_e/whatis_e/tif_e/org6_e.htm [retrieved: 01/09/08].
5. In these figures, the EU is counted as a single member.
6. It should be noted that the economic development categories applied by the WTO in its services database have been used here.
7. It should be noted that this correlation is weaker in the case of the LDCs. More specifically, we have shown that 81.81% of these countries are new WTO members and that they have not made education commitments as frequently, for instance, as transition countries (most of which are also new members). This means that LDCs have enjoyed more favourable and flexible WTO accession conditions than other countries have (WTO 2005a). They are not thus subject to equally intense pressure to open up their markets.

NOTES TO CHAPTER 6

1. Quoted in Robertson and Dale (2006).
2. Quoted in Larsen and Lancrin (2002: 26).

NOTES TO CHAPTER 7

1. Summary of the Paris Declaration from AUCC et al (2001, 1).
2. Stamenka Uvalic-Trumbic in Workshop III of the OECD Forum on Trade in Services (2002) entitled Promoting Access to Post-Secondary Education: Meeting the Global Demand. Available at www.oecd.org/dataoecd/44/13/2756964.pdf [last retrieved: 12/09/08].
3. The convention establishes that culture is not a commodity and that the market cannot be the exclusive regulator of the international exchange of cultural goods because it would mean the loss of cultural diversity. Therefore, policies for the protection of cultural diversity should be allowed even if they become barriers to trade (Article 2.2).
4. The unique UNESCO Secretariat communications during the Uruguay Round dealt with Intellectual Property Rights issues. See the documents:

MTN.GNG/NG11/W/63/Add.2, MTN.GNG/NG11/W/19 and MTN.GNG/NG11/W/5/Add.2 in http://docsonline.wto.org [last retrieved: 19/11/08].

5. See "About UNESCO" in: http://portal.unesco.org/en/ev.php-URL_ID=3328&URL_DO=DO_TOPIC&URL_SECTION=201.html [last retrieved: 10/10/08].

6. "The Global Forum responds to the growing demands of the international community to have UNESCO proactive in the debates concerning borderless higher education and trade in higher education in frameworks such as the GATS as well and the related key issues of quality and recognition." Source: http://portal.unesco.org/education/es/ev.php-URL_ID=41247&URL_DO=DO_TOPIC&URL_SECTION=201.html [Las retrieved: 04/05/07].

7. Source: http://unesdoc.unesco.org/ulis/courier/index_sp.shtml [Last retrieved: 04/05/07].

8. See: "XXXIII Plenario de Rectores de la AUGM" at http://www.universia.com.ar/portada/actualidad/noticia_actualidad.jsp?noticia=3780 [Last retrieved: 12/01/06].

9. Source: www.oecd.org/ [last retrieved: 05/06/07].

10. "About OECD": http://www.oecd.org/pages/0,3417,en_36734052_36734103_1_1_1_1_1,00.html [last retrieved: 05/06/07].

11. See http://www.oecd.org/topic/0,3373,en_2649_34549_1_1_1_1_37455,00.html [last retrieved: 05/06/07].

12. For instance, in OECD (2004) it is emphasized that "student visa requirements and policies regarding quality assurance, accreditation and recognition of qualifications are, for example, much more important than the GATS" (p. 13).

13. See: www.ei-ie.org [last retrieved: 08/06/08].

14. The report is available at http://www.caut.ca/en/issues/trade/gats-opinion.asp [last retrieved: 06/06/07]. The unions also framed their analysis of GATS and education at a civil society forum known as the Trade and Investment Research Project, coordinated by the Canadian Center for Policy Alternatives.

15. See: http://www.ei-ie.org/en/publication/ [last retrieved: 25/06/08].

16. See: http://www.ei-ie.org/gats/en/documentation.php [last retrieved: 01/11/08].

17. Specifically: Association of Universities and Colleges of Canada (AUCC), American Council on Education (ACE), European University Association (EUA) and Council for Higher Education Accreditation (CHEA).

18. Source: http://www.iigov.org/cg/?p=18_03 [last retrieved: 12/01/06].

19. Others are, for instance, the "Seoul Recommendations on Future Action" and a public statement produced during the seminar entitled "Academic Mobility in Trade Environment: Issues, Risks and Opportunities" (Mexico DF, June 7–8, 2005).

20. More specifically, the ACE, ACCU, CHEA, AAU, VSNU, Conférence des Grandes Ecoles, Ecuador's Consejo Nacional de Educación Superior, Asociación Colombiana de Universidades, Sri Lanka's Committee of Vice-Chancellors and Directors, Hong Kong's Heads of Universities Committee and the European Universities Association.

21. Source: www.unesco.org/iau/internationalization/i_checklist.html [last retrieved: 12/05/07].

22. This WB representative concluded by quoting Charles Darwin: "It is not the strongest species that survive, nor the most intelligent, but the ones most responsive to change" (Holm-Nielsen 2002, 37)

23. "About UNCTAD" in http://unctad.org/Templates/Page.asp?intItemID=1530&lang=1 [last retrieved: 16/06/07].

24. See: http://www.intracen.org/menus/itc-s.htm [last retrieved: 16/06/07].

25. See for instance the "Commodification" section of ESIB at www.esib.org [last retrieved: 08/12/06]. Interestingly, ESIB's application to attend the WTO Ministerial Conferences was systematically rejected by the WTO staff, who argued that the students' organization does not deal with trade issues (Interview ESIB 01, Brussels, 2006).
26. This network has been developed at events such as the "Convention européenne des collectivités locales contre l'AGCS" (Liège, France, October 2005) and through the activities of global organizations such as ATTAC.
27. See : "L'intérêt local reconnu et triomphant de l'Etat" in: www.hors-agcs. org/agcs/article.php3?id_article=149 [last retrieved: 23/01/06]

NOTES TO CHAPTER 8

1. These sources are as follows: United States International Trade Commission (USITC); Association of International Educators (NAFSA); Institute of International Education (IIE) (Publication: Open Doors); IDP Education Australia; American Association for Higher Education (AAHE); Global Alliance for Transnational Education (GATE); Canadian Association for Distance Education (CADE); and the OECD.
2. Document TN/S/O/USA/Rev.1: p. 68, in WTO Documents on-line [last retrieved: 04/07/08].

NOTES TO CHAPTER 9

1. A number of other foreign universities have branches in Argentina, including Harvard University and New York University, although they do not recruit students in Argentina and rather bring them from the US (Fernández Lamarra 2003).
2. Ministry of Education/Higher Education Division Resolution number 252/03.
3. Schedule presented on September 27, 2004. Available at www.mre.gov.br [last retrieved: 15/09/06].
4. The project is known as ACRO (accreditation and official recognition between EU and Mercosur universities).
5. Guiñazu (2003) noted that during the FTAA negotiations in the 1990s, no civil society organizations were consulted.
6. See for instance the Civil Society Council at http://www.mrecic.gov.ar/ccsc/ [last retrieved: 12/06/07].
7. See TN/S/O/ARG in the WTO's on-line documents [last retrieved: 01/10/05].
8. CTERA is a union for primary and secondary education teachers. Higher education unions in Argentina are numerous, but none of them put the that GATS issue in their political agendas.
9. Albeit this 'external influence' was important to understand why CTERA launched the anti-GATS campaign, it should be acknowledged that the current leadership of the union also used the campaign to counteract the growth of internal opositional currents. To some extend, the fact that the Argentinean Ministry of Education responded positively to the demands of the campaign (see below) permitted to the leadership of the union to justify their controversial political support to the Krischner administration(s). In one word, to capture the rationale of the anti-GATS campaign in Argentina it is also important to understand the internal politics within CTERA.

10. Mercosur/XXIX RME/ACTA N° 2/05, November 2005. Source: www.sic. inep.gov.br [last retrieved: 26/10/06].
11. When the new law was being drafted, CTERA submitted a document to the Ministry of Education stating that "We reaffirm our opposition to any form of privatization and/or commodification of public education and to its inclusion in free trade agreements." Source: "El ministro de educación de la nación recibió a CTERA y a organizaciones sociales," Oct. 17, 2006, in http://www.ctera.org.ar/item-info.shtml?x=58980 [last retrieved: 05/07/07].
12. See *La Nación*, 17/09/06, p. 19.
13. However, Argentina's negotiators in Geneva also appreciated the fact that the country's position on the topic was so clear since this facilitated the negotiation process: "This is what we've always asked Buenos Aires to do: send us precise instructions" (Interview Argentinean Trade negotiator 02, Geneva 2006).
14. See Declaration Project 7945-D-04 at http://www.hcdn.gov.ar/ [last retrieved: 121/09/08].
15. See also *Página 12*, April 24, 2003.
16. See http://www.cnachile.cl/cnachile/ [last retrieved: 05/07/07].
17. Another reason why they accreditate their programs is that accreditation is a necessary condition for their students to be able to apply for scholarships or state supported loans.
18. See http://www.chilexportaservicios.cl/ces/ [last consulted: 05/07/07].
19. This idea was also expressed in the interviews with Chilean negotiators 01, 03 and 04.
20. See "Los TLC ponen a universidades chilenas entre la espalda y la pared," *La Segunda*, Sept. 17, 2003, pp. 42–43.
21. *Universidad Metropolitana de Ciencias de la Educación* and *Universidad del Bío-Bío*.
22. Another critical voice on education issues is the ACJR (Alliance for Fair and Responsible Trade). The CDP is a member of the ACJR and has occasionally asked it to provide legal advice as part of its campaign against trade agreements (Interview CDP 02, Santiago, 2006). The ACJR members published a book titled, which directly deals with the issue (see Frederick et al 2005).
23. There is one exception. The ACJR, the CDP and other organizations maintain that their lobbying efforts were responsible for the inclusion of a provision that states that Chile reserves the right to regulate all aspects of foreign teachers' activities (cross-border supply of services by natural persons) at all levels of formal education (ACJR 2004). See this provision in the Chile-US FTA, Appendix II, *Listas de Medidas Disconformes Futuras de Inversiones y Servicios* at http://www.direcon.cl/index.php?accion=tlc_eeuu_01_vd [last retrieved: 19/10/08].
24. A former DIRECON negotiator wrote: "Some opposition [to FTAs in Chile] emerged from labor representatives and non-governmental organizations related to the *social movement*. But this latter opposition *has never been very influential and articulated*." (Sáez 2005, 20).

NOTES TO CHAPTER 10

1. A *policy paradigm* is an ideational framework that specifies the policy goals and the kind of instruments that can be used to attain them, as well as the nature of the problems they are meant to be addressing. Policy paradigms have a solid economic base and a clear orientation to policy-making. That is why they are conceived as guidelines for policies (Hall 1993).

2. Other authors have shown that teachers unions from Canada, UK, Australia, Germany, US, Norway, the Netherlands and Sweden have also actively lobbied their governments (Fredriksson 2004; Vlk 2006). The teachers unions of these countries are members of EI and most of them have framed their discourse on the GATS in the framework of the federation (see for instance Bassett 2006). However, it should be pointed out that others, specifically the Canadian and Australian unions, instead of being 'passive takers', have been active promoters of the campaign against the GATS at the EI level.

References

AAU. 2004. Accra Declaration on GATS and the Internationalization of Higher Education in Africa. *Association of African Universities* 29/04/04, Accra, Ghana.

Aboites, H. 2004. Derecho a la educación o mercancía: La experiencia de diez años de libre comercio en la educación mexicana. *Memoria. Revista Mensual de Política y Cultura* 187.

Abugattas, L. 2005. GATS-plus and GATS-minus in US Free Trade Agreements. *TradEducation News*, 3: 3–4.

———. 2006. Domestic Regulation and the GATS: Challenges for Developing Countries. In *www.ictsd.org/dlogue/2006–02–28/celli.pdf* [last retrieved: 13/03/07].

ACJR. 2004. Educación y comercio en tiempos de globalización. www.generacion80.cl/documentos/download1.php?nombre_archivo=ponencia_acjr_foro-educacion.pdf [last retrieved: 12/06/07].

Adlung, R. 2005. Public Services and the GATS. *Working Paper ERSD (WTO)* 2005–3.

Allport, C. 2003. Building the Public Interest: GATS and Higher Education and Research. EI/GEW Forum. Berlin, April 10–12 2003.

Altay, S. 2006. Ideas, Private Actors and Regime Creation after US Hegemony: The Case of the GATS. In *BISA Conference 2006*. Cork, December 18–20 2006.

Altbach, P. G. 2004a. Higher Education Crosses Borders. *Change* March-April: 18–24.

———. 2004b. Globalization and the University: Myths and Realities in an Unequal World. *Tertiary Education and Management* 1: 3–25.

Anandakrishnan, M. 2004. Internationalization of Higher Education: Policy Concerns. In National Conference on "Internationalization of Higher Education-Issues and Concerns", NIEPA, New Delhi. August 26–27 2004.

Angell, A. 2002. La descentralización en Chile. *Instituciones y Desarrollo* 3: 131–172.

Apple, M. 1997. *Teoría Crítica y Educación*. Buenos Aires: Miño y Dávila.

Aravena, F. R., and C. Pey. 2003. La sociedad civil en el proceso de integración comercial: el caso chileno. In *El ALCA y las cumbres de las Américas: ¿una nueva relación público-privado?* Buenos Aires: Biblos.

Armanet, P. 2003. Garantía de la Educación Superior en el Contexto de la Globalización. In *VIII Seminario Internacional 2003. Cruzando fronteras: Nuevos desafíos para la educación superior.* Santiago: CSE/CNAP.

———. 2004. Movilidad Estudiantil, Académica y Profesional. Una Mirada desde el Ministerio de Educación. In *Seminario Internacional 2004. Movilidad Internacional de Profesionales: Condiciones para la Confianza Recíproca.* Santiago: CSE/CNAP.

228   *References*

Aronowitz, S. and W. De Fazio. 1997. The New Knowledge Work. In *Education, Culture, Economy and Society*. Oxford: Oxford University Press.

Arts, B. 2005. Non-State Actors in global environmental governance: New arrangements beyond the state. In *New Modes of Governance in the Global System: Exploring Publicness, Delegation and Inclusiveness*. New York: Plagrave Macmillan.

AUCC, ACE, EUA, and CHEA. 2001. Joint Declaration about HE and the GATS. Access Date. http://www.aic.lv/ace/gats/jointdec.html.

Ball, S. J. 1998. Big Policies/Small World: an introduction to international perspectives in education policy. *Comparative Education* 34, no. 2: 119–130.

Barrow, C. W., S. Didou, and J. Mallea. 2004. *Globalisation, Trade Liberalisation, and Higher Education in North America: The Emergence of a new market under NAFTA?* Dordrecht: Kluwer Academic Publishers.

Barton, J. H., J. L. Goldstein, T. E. Josling, and R. H. Steinberg. 2006. *The Evolution of the Trade Regime: Politics, Law, and Economics of the GATT and the WTO*. Princeton: Princeton University Press.

Bashir, S. 2007. Trends in international higher education: implications and options for developing countries. *Education Working Paper Series* 6: 1–98.

Bassett, R. M. 2006. The WTO and the University: Globalization, GATS, and American Higher Education.

Beker, V. 2004. El AGCS y la Educación Superior. *[manuscript]*.

Bell, D. 1973. *The coming of post-industrial society. A Venture into Social Forecasting*. New York: Basic Books.

Bello, W. 2002. Learning from Doha: A Civil Society Perspective from the South. *Global Governance* 8: 273–279.

Benford, R.D., and D. A. Snow. 2000. Framing Processes and Social Movements: An Overview and Assessment. *Annual Review of Sociology* 26: 611–639.

Bergan, S. 2002. Notes on Developments in Higher Education in Europe. In *First Global Forum on International Quality Assurance, Accreditation and the Recognition of Qualifications in Higher Education,* 107–116. UNESCO: Paris.

Berlinski, J. 2001. La liberalización del comercio de servicios en los países del Mercosur. In *El Desafío de Integrarse para Crecer: Balance y Perspectivas del Mercosur en su Primera Década*. Buenos Aires: Siglo XXI.

Bernasconi, A. and M. Gamboa. 2002. *Evolución de la Legislación sobre Educación Superior en Chile*. Caracas: IESALC-UNESCO.

Bhushan, S. 2006. *Foreign Education Providers in India: Mapping the Extent and Regulation*. London: OBHE.

Birtwistle, T. 2006. Higher education and the general [lack of] agreement on trade in services: from Doha to Hong Kong and beyond. *Education and the Law 18*, no. 4: 295–307.

Bitar, Sergio. 2004. Discurso Inaugural. In *Seminario Internacional 2004. Movilidad Internacional de Profesionales: Condiciones para la Confianza Recíproca*. Santiago: CSE/CNAP.

Blyth, M. M. 2004. Structures Do Not Come with an Instruction Sheet: Interests, Ideas, and Progress in Political Science. *Perspectives on Politics 1*, no. 4: 695–706.

Bøås, M. and D. McNeill. 2003. *Multilateral Institutions. A critical introduction*. Sterling: Pluto Press.

Bonal, X. 2002. Plus ça change. . . The World Bank Global Education Policy and the Post-Washington Consensus. *International Studies in Sociology of Education 12*, no. 1: 3–21.

Bonal, X., A. Tarabini-Castellani, and A. Verger. 2007. *Globalización y Educación: Textos Fundamentales*. Buenos Aires: Miño y Dávila.

Brock, C. 2002. First Global Forum on International Quality Assurance, Accreditation and the Recognition of Qualifications in Higher Education: A Review. In

First Global Forum on International Quality Assurance, Accreditation and the Recognition of Qualifications in Higher Education. UNESCO: Paris, 7–18.
———. 2006. Regulation and Accreditation of Higher Education: Historical and Sociological Roots. In *Higher Education in the World 2007. Accreditation For Quality Assurance: What Is At Stake?* New York: Palgrave Macmillan.
Brown, G. M. 2005. Three 'Controversial' Virtual Universities: Lessons from the Australian Experience. London: OBHE.
Brown, P., and H. Lauder. 1997. Education, Globalisation and Economic Development. In *Education, Culture, Economy and Society.* Oxford: Oxford University Press.
Brunner, J. J. 2004. La Educación Superior Chilena al comenzar el Siglo XXI. *Anales del Instituto de Chile* XXIV, no. 2: 127–138.
———. 2006. Mercados Universitarios: Ideas, Instrumentos y Seis Tesis en Conclusión. http://mt.educarchile.cl/mt/jjbrunner/archives/2006/03/mercados_univer.html [last retrieved: 12/03/08].
———. 2008. Chile's Higher Education: Mixed Markets and Institutions. *Die hochschule.* 2/2008: 53–70.
Brunner, J. J. and J. M. Bricall. 2000. *Universidad Siglo XXI. Regulación y Financiamiento.* Paris: Columbus.
Burton-Jones, A. 1999. *Knowledge Capitalism.* NY: Oxford University Press.
Carnoy, M. 1999a. Globalización y reestructuración de la educación. *Revista de Educación* 318: 145–162.
———. 1999b. *Globalization and Educational Reform: what planners need to know.* Paris: UNESCO.
Cerny, P. G. 1997. Paradoxes of the Competition State: The Dynamics of Political Globalization. *Government and Opposition* 32, no. 2: 251–274.
Chanda, R. 2003. Social Services and the GATS: Key Issues and Concerns. *World Development* 31, no. 12: 1997–2011.
Chandrasekhar, C.P. 2006. A Foreign Hand for Higher Education. *Macroscan* 28/09/06.
Chan-Tibergien, J. 2006. Cultural Diversity as Resistance to Neoliberal Globalization: the Emergence of a Global Movement and Convention. *Review of Education* 52: 89–105.
CIDSE/Caritas. 2004. *PRSP: Are the World Bank and IMF Delivering on Promises?* Brussels: CIDSE.
COL/UNESCO. 2006. *Higher Education: Crossing Borders: A Guide to the Implications of the General Agreement on Trade in Services (GATS) for Cross-Border Education.* Paris: Commonwealth of Learning / UNESCO.
Cox, R. W. 1995. Social forces, states, and world orders: beyond international relations theory (1981). In *Approaches to World Order,* 85–123. Cambridge: Cambridge University Press.
Cox, R. W. and H. K. Jacobson. 1972. *The Anatomy of Influence: Decision Making in International Organization.* New Haven: Yale University Press.
Curzon, G. and V. Curzon. 1973. GATT: Traders'Club. In *The Anatomy of Influence: Decision Making in International Organization,* 298–333. New Haven: Yale University Press.
Czinkota, M.R. 2006. Academic freedom for all in higher education: The role of the general agreement on trade in services. *Journal of World Business* 41: 149–160.
Dale, R. 1994. Applied education politics or political sociology of education?: Contrasting approaches to the study of recent education reform in England and Wales. *Researching education policy: Ethical and methodological issues:* 31–42.
———. 1999. Specifying Globalisation Effects on National Policy: focus on the Mechanisms. *Journal of Education Policy* 14, no. 1: 1–17.

――――. 2003. The Lisbon Declaration, the Reconceptualisation of Governance and the Reconfiguration of European Educational Space. In RAPPE Seminar. Institute of Education, London University, London, March 20 2003.

――――. 2005. Globalisation, knowledge economy and comparative education. *Comparative Education* 41, no. 2: 117–149.

Dale, R. and S. Robertson. 2004. Interview with Boaventura de Sousa Santos. *Globalisation, Societies and Education* 2, no. 2: 147–160.

――――. 2007. Beyond Methodological 'Isms' in Comparative Education in an Era of Globalisation. In *Handbook on Comparative Education*, 19–32. Netherlands: Springer.

Davey, W. J. 2005. The WTO Dispute Settlement System. The First Ten Years . *Journal of International Economic Law* 8, no. 1: 17–50.

Della Porta, D. and M. Diani. 1999. *Social Movements*. Oxford: Blackwell.

Devidal, P. 2004. Trading Away Human Rights? The GATS and the Right to Education: a legal perspective. *Journal of Critical Education Policy Studies* 2, no. 2.

Didou, S. 2006. Internacionalización de la educación superior y provisión transnacional de servicios educativos en América Latina: del voluntarismo a las elecciones estratégicas. In *Seminario internacional IESALC—UNESCO*. Panamá, March 16–17 2006.

Drake, W. J. and K. Nicolaidis. 1992. Ideas, Interests, and Institutionalization: "Trade in Services" and the Uruguay Round. *International Organization* 46, no. 1: 37–100.

Duff, J. 2006. Internationalisation of university education, university rankings and the transformation of Australian university education into a provate good. In *XVI ISA World Congress of Sociology*. Durban, 23–29 July 2006.

EC. 2002. Detailed work programme on the follow-up of the objectives of Education and training systems in Europe. *Official Journal of the European Communities* 45: 1–22.

――――. 2003. Invertir eficazmente en educacion y formación: un imperativo para Europa. *Comunicación de la Comisión, Bruselas, 10.01.2003*, no. COM(2002) 779 final.

――――. 2005. Non Paper on Complementary Methods for the Services Negotiations. Possible Elements. *Room Document. Council for Trade in Services—Special Session* 13/09/05.

EI. 2003. Globalization, GATS and Higher Education. *www.ei-ie.org/hiednet* [last retrieved: 10/09/04].

――――. 2004. Resolution for a New International Instrument for Higher Education. http://www.ei-ie.org/highereducation/file/(2004)%20A%20New%20International%20Instrument%20for%20Higher%20Education%20en.pdf [last retrieved: 30/11/08].

――――. 2006. Note on GATS Domestic Regulation Disciplines and Education Services. www.ei-ie.org/gats/file/(2006)%20EI%20GATS%20Information%20Kit%20-%20Note%20on%20Domestic%20Regulations%20en.pdf [last retrieved: 30/11/08].

EI, and PSI. 1999. The *WTO and the Millennium Round: What Is at Stake for Public Education? Common Concerns for Workers in Education and the Public Sector*. Brussels: Education International

EUA. 2001. *What is GATS (WTO) and what are the possible implications for Higher Education in Europe?* Geneva: European University Association.

――――. 2002. *The Bologna Process and the GATS negotiations*. Geneva: European University Association.

Evans, M. 2006. Elitism. In The State: Theories and Issues. London: Palgrave.

Fairclough, N. 2003. *Analysing Discourse*. London: Routledge.

Fehl, C. 2004. Explaining the International Criminal Court: A 'Practice Test' for Rationalist and Constructivist Approaches. *European Journal of International Relations* 10, no. 3: 357–394.

Feketekuty, G. 2005. International Trade in Services. An overview and blueprint for negotiations. *Institute for Trade and Commercial Diplomacy* www.commercialdiplomacy.org [last retrieved: 02/12/06].

Fernández Lamarra, N. 2003. *La educación superior argentina en debate: situación, problemas y perspectivas*. Buenos Aires: Eudeba.

Fidler, D.. N. Drager, C. Correa and O. Agiman. 2005. Making commitments in health services under the GATS Legal Dimensions. In *International Trade in Health Services and the GATS: Current Issues and Debates*, 141–168. Washington DC: The World Bank.

Finnemore, M. and K. Sikkink. 2001. Taking Stock: The Constructivist Research Program in International Relations and Comparative Politics. *Annual Review of Political Science* 4: 391–416.

Fligstein, N. 1993. Market as politics: A Political-Cultural Approach to Market Institutions. *American Sociological Review*, 61: 656–673.

Ford, J. 2002. A Social Theory of Trade Regime Change: GATT to WTO. *International Studies Review* 4, no. 3: 115–138.

Fouilhoux, M. 2005. Entender el AGCS: la perspectiva del movimiento sindical. In *GATS and Education Seminar*. Education International. Paris, April 4 2005.

Francois, J. and I. Wooton. 2000. Market Structure, trade Liberalisation and the GATS. *Centre for International Economic Studies. Policy Discussion Paper*, no. 3.

Frater, T. 2008a. *Jamaica's Higher Education Committment under the GATS*. Univeristy of Toronto, Adult Education and Counselling Psychology.

———. 2008b. Jamaica's policy toward GATS. *International Higher Education* 53: 13–14.

Frederick, P., C. Candia, I. Castrillo, and C. Pey. 2005 *Educación y comercio en tiempos de globalización*, Santiago: Lom Ediciones.

Fredriksson, U. 2004. Studying the Supre-National in Education: GATS, education and teacher union policies. *European Educational Research Journal 3*, no. 2: 415–441.

Gajardo, G. 2003. La educación y la participación de la sociedad civil. In *El ALCA y las cumbres de las Américas: ¿una nueva relación público-privado? Buenos Aires: Biblos.

García López, R. 1999. *La liberalización del comercio de servicios en la OMC*. Valencia: Tirant lo Blanch.

García-Guadilla, C. 2002. General Agreement of Trade in Services, Higher Education and Latin America. Paris: UNESCO.

———. 2003. Balance de la década de los '90 y reflexiones sobre las nuevas fuerzas de cambio en la educación superior. In *Las universidades en América Latina: ¿Reformadas o alteradas?* 17–37, Buenos Aires: CLACSO.

Garrett, R. 2005. Fraudulent, sub-standard, ambiguous the alternative borderless higher education. *OBHE Briefing Note* 24.

Garretón, M. A. 1989. Popular Mobilization and the Military Regime in Chile: The Complexities of the Invisible Transition. In *Power and Popular Protest: Latin American Social Movements: 259–277. Berkeley: University of California Press.

GATT Secretariat. 1991. Services Sectoral Classification List. Note by de Secretariat, Document code: MTN.GNS/W/120. Geneva: WTO.

———. 1994. Marrakesh Declaration. http://www.wto.org/english/docs_e/legal_e/legal_e.htm#services [last retrieved: 05/02/09].

Gill, S. 2003. *Power and Resistance in the New World Order*. London: Palgrave.

Gilpin, R. 1987. The *political economy of international relations*. Princeton: Princeton University Press.

van Ginkel, H. J. A., and M. A. Rodrigues Dias. 2006. Retos Institucionales y políticos de la acreditación en el ámbito internacional. In *La Educación Superior en el Mundo 2007. Acreditación para la garantía de calidad: ¿Qué está en juego?*, 37–57. Barcelona: Ediciones Mundi-Prensa.

Giugni, M. G., Doug McAdam, and Charles Tilly. 1999. *How Social Movements Matter*. Minneapolis: University of Minnesota Press.

Global Alliance Limited. 1997. *Australian Higher Education in the Era of Mass Customisation*. Tokio: Global Alliance Limited.

Goic Goic, A. 2004. Descripción y Análisis Crítico del Actual Sistema de Educación Superior en Chile. *Anales del Instituto de Chile XXIV*, no. 2: 83–125.

Goldstein, J., and R. O. Keohane. 1993. *Ideas and Foreign Policy: Beliefs, Institutions and Political Change*. New York: Cornell University Press.

Gómez, J. M. 2001. ¿Desafiando a la gobernancia neoliberal? Sociedad civil global, activismo transnacional y agencias económicas multilaterales. *Revista OSAL* 3: 172–176.

González, L. E. 2003. *Los Nuevos Proveedores Externos de Educación Superior en Chile*. Caracas: IESALC.

Gould, E. 2004. The US-Gambling Decision. A Wakeup Call for WTO Members. *CCPA Briefing Paper. Trade and Investment Series* 5, no. 4.

Green, A. 2003. Education, Globalisation and the Role of Comparative Research. *London Review of Education* 1, no. 2: 84–97.

Greig, A., D. Hulme, and M. Turner. 2007. *Challenging Global Inequality: Development Theory and Practice in the 21st Century*. New York: Palgrave Macmillan.

Grieshaber-Otto, J. and M. Sanger. 2002. *Perilous Lessons. The Impact of the WTO Services Agreement (GATS) on Canada's Public Education System*. Ottawa: Canadian Centre for Policy Alternatives.

Guiñazú, M. C. 2003. La sociedad civil en el proceso de integración comercial: el caso argentino. In *El ALCA y las cumbres de las Américas: ¿una nueva relación público-privado?* Buenos Aires: Biblos.

GUNI. 2006. *Higher Education in the World 2007. Accreditation For Quality Assurance: What Is At Stake?* Barcelona: Ediciones Mundi-Prensa.

Haas, P. M. 2002. UN Conferences and Constructivist Governance of the Environment. *Global Governance* 8: 73–91.

———. 2004. When does power listen to truth? A constructivist approach to the policy process? *Journal of European Public Policy* 11, no. 4: 569–592.

Hall, P. 1993. Policy Paradigms, Social Learning and the State. The Case of Economic Policymaking in Britain. *Comparative Politics 25*, no. 3: 275–296.

Halliday, F. 2002. *Las relaciones internacionales en un mundo en transformación*. Madrid: Catarata.

Harvey, D. 2005. *A Brief History of Neoliberalism*. Oxford University Press, USA.

Hasenclever, A., P. Mayer, and V. Rittberger. 1996. Interests, Power, Knowledge: The Study of International Regimes. *Mershon International Studies Review* 40: 177–228.

Hay, C. 2002. *Political Analysis. A critical introduction*. New York: Palgrave.

HCHR. 2002. *Economic, Social and Cultural Rights: Liberalisation of Trade in Services and Human Rights—Report of the High Commissioner*. New York: Commission on Human Rights, Economic and Social Council- UN.

Held, D. 1999. *Global Transformations. Politics, Economics and Cultures*. Oxford: Polity Press.

Henderson, D. 1998. International Agencies and Cross-Border Liberalization: The WTO in Context. In *The WTO as an International Organization*, 97–132. Chicago: University of Chicago.

Henry, M., B. Lingard, F. Rizvi, and S. Taylor. 1999. Working with/against globalization in education. *Journal of Education Policy* 14, no. 1: 85–97.

Hermo, J. P. and C. Pittelli. 2008. Globalización e internacionalización de la Educación Superior. Apuntes para la situación en Argentina y el Mercosur. *Revista Española de Educación Comparada*, 14 (2008), 243–268

Herod, A. 2001a. *Labor Geographies. Workers and the Landscapes of Capitalism.* New York: The Guilford Press.

———. 2001b. Labor Internationalism and the Contradictions of Globalization: Or, Why the Local is Sometimes Still Important in a Global Economy. *Antipode* 33: 407–426.

Heyneman, S. P. 2003. The history and problems in the making of education policy at the World Bank 1960–2000. *International Journal of Educational Development* 23: 315–337.

Hirsch, D. 2002. (Report of the GATS and education debate). OECD/*US Forum on Trade in Educational Services (Washington, DC, U.S.A. 23—24 May 2002).*

Hirst, P., and G. Thompson. 1995. *Globalization and the future of the nation state.* London: Routledge.

Hoekman, B. and W. Martin. 2001. *Developing Countries and the WTO. A proactive agenda.* Malden: Blackwell.

Holm-Nielsen, L. B. 2002. Trade in Education. . . why are we here? In *OECD/US Forum on Trade in Educational Services,* Washington DC, May 23—24 2002.

IATP. 2003. WTO Decision Making: A Broken Process. *IATP White Paper* no. 61623.

IAU. 2005. Compartiendo la calidad de la educación superior más allá de las fronteras: Una declaración en nombre de las instituciones de educación superior en el ámbito mundial. *Perfiles educativos* 27, no. 107: 149–155.

Ikenberry, G. J. 1992. A World Economy Restored: Expert Consensus and the Anglo-American Postwar Settlement. *International Organization* 46, no. 1: 289–321.

Jakobi, A. and K. Martens. 2007. La influencia de la OCDE en la política educativa nacional. In *Globalización y Educación: Textos Fundamentales,* 233–253. Buenos Aires: Miño y Dávila.

Jawara, F. and A. Kwa. 2004. *Behind the scenes at the WTO: the real world of international trade negotiations. The real world of international trade negotiations.* London: Zed Books.

Jessop, B. 1990. *State Theory: Putting the Capitalist State in is Place.* New York: Polity Press.

———. 2000. The State and the Contradictions of the Knowledge-Driven Economy. In *Knowledge, Space, Economy,* 63–78. London: Routledge.

———. 2001. The spatiotemporal dynamics of capital and its globalization—and how they Challenge State Power and Democracy. *http://www.comp.lancs.ac.ik/sociology/soc132rj.pdf* [last retrieved: 23/04/05].

Jiménez, C. 2004. De la Ronda d'Uruguai a Cancun. *dCIDOB* 89: 8–13.

Jobbs, J. 2002. [Oxfam International] Speaking notes for the World Social Forum event "GATS and the future of public services". *World Social Forum,* Porto Alegre, January 31—February 5, 2002.

Johnston, D. J. 2002. Opening Remark by the Honourable Donald J. Johnston, Secretary-General of the OECD. OECD/*US Forum on Trade in Educational Services,* Washington DC, May 23—24, 2002.

Johnes, G. 1995. *Economía de la Educación. Capital humano, rendimiento educativo y mercado de trabajo.* Madrid: Ministerio de Trabajo y Seguridad Social.

Johnstone, D. B. 2004. The economics and politics of cost sharing in higher education: comparative perspectives. *Economics of Education Review* 23: 403–410.

Kapoor, I. 2004. Deliberative Democracy and the WTO. *Review of International Political Economy* 11, no. 3: 522–541.

Karsenty, G. 2000. Assessing Trade in Services by Mode of Supply. In *GATS2000. New Directions in Services Trade Liberalization*. Washington: Brookings.

Keck, M. E. and K. Sikkink. 1998. *Activists Beyond Borders. Advocacy Networks in International Politics*. New York: Cornell University Press.

Kelk, S. and J. Worth. 2002. *Trading it away: how GATS threatens UK Higher Education*. Oxford: People and Planet.

Kelsey, J. 2003. Legal Fetishism and the Contradictions of the GATS. *Globalisation, Societies and Education* 1, no. 3: 321–357.

———. 2008. *Serving Whose Interests?: The Political Economy of Trade in Services Agreements*. London/New York: Routledge-Cavendish.

Kessie, E. K. 1999. Developing Countries and the World Trade Organization. What Has Changed? *World Competition*, 25(2), 83–110.

Khor, M. 2005. GATS negotiators debate "crisis" in WTO services talks. *TWN Info Service on WTO and Trade Issues* 199.

Knight, J. 2002. *Trade in Higher Education Services: The Implications of GATS*. London: OBHE.

———. 2004. Internationalization Remodeled: Definition, Approaches, and Rationales. *Journal of Studies in International Education* 8, no. 1: 5–31.

———. 2007. Cross-border higher education: issues and implications for quality assurance and accreditation. In *Higher Education in the World 2007. Accreditation For Quality Assurance: What Is At Stake?*, 134–158. New York: Palgrave MacMillan.

Koenig-Archibugi, M. 2002. Mapping Global Governance. In *Governing Globalisation*. Cambridge: Polity.

Korzeniewicz, R. P. and W. C. Smith. 2003. Redes Transnacionales de la Sociedad Civil. In *El ALCA y las cumbres de las Américas: ¿una nueva relación público-privado?*, 47–75. Buenos Aires: Biblos.

Krugman, P. 1997. What Should Trade Negotiators Negotiate About? *Journal of Economic Literature* 35, no. 1: 113–120.

Kwiek, M. 2001. Globalization and Higher Education. *Higher Education in Europe* 26, no. 1: 27–38.

Lang, A. T. F. 2006. Reconstructing Embedded Liberalism: John Gerard Ruggie and Constructivist Approaches to the Study of the International Trade Regime. *Journal of International Economic Law* 9, no. 1: 81–116.

Larsen, K., J. P. Martin, and R. Morris. 2002. Trade in Educational Services: Trends and Emerging Issues. *The World Economy* 25, no. 6: 849–868.

Larsen, K., K. Momii, and S. Vincent-Lancrin. 2004. *Cross-border Higher Education: an analysis of current trends, policy strategies and future scenarios*. London: OBHE.

Larsen, K. and S. Vincent-Lancrin. 2002. International trade in educational services: good or bad? *Higher Education and management Policy* 14, no. 3: 2–45.

Laval, C. 2004. *La escuela no es una empresa*. Barcelona: Paidós.

Lavelle, K. C. 2005. Participating in the Governance of Trade. The GATT, UNCTAD, and WTO. *International Journal of Political Economy* 33, no. 4: 28–42.

Lavanchy, S. 2003. La Educación Transnacional y su Impacto en Chile. In *VIII Seminario Internacional 2003. Cruzando fronteras: Nuevos desafíos para la educación superior*. Santiago: CSE/CNAP.

Lemaitre, M. J. 2003. Aseguramiento de la Calidad en la Educación Transnacional. CNAP. In *VIII Seminario Internacional 2003. Cruzando fronteras: Nuevos desafíos para la educación superior*. Santiago: CSE/CNAP.

———. 2005a. *Between privatization and state control: Chile's experience of regulating a widely privatized system through quality assurance.* Paris: IIPE-UNESCO.

———. 2005b. Certificación de Títulos y Grados de la Educación Superior Chilena. Caracas: IESALC/UNESCO.

Levy, D. C. 1995. *La educación superior y el estado en Latinoamerica. Desafíos privados al predominio público.* México DF: Miguel Ángel Porrua.

López Segrera, F. 2003. El impacto de la globalización y las políticas educativas en los sistemas de educación superior de América Latina y el Caribe. In *Las universidades en América Latina: ¿Reformadas o alteradas? 39–58.* Buenos Aires: CLACSO.

Lukes, S. 2005. *Power: a Radical View (Second Edition).* London: Palgrave Macmillan.

Maldonado, A. 2006. Cooperación internacional y visiones sobre la financiación de la educación superior. In *La Educación Superior en el Mundo 2006. La financiación de las universidades, 41–59. Barcelo*na: Ediciones Mundi-Prensa.

Malo, S. 2003. La comercialización de la educación superior. In *El difícil equilibrio. La educación superior como bien público y comercio de servicios,* 101–107. Caracas: Editorial Latina.

March, J. G., and J. P. Olsen. 2005. The Institutional Dynamics of International Political Orders. *International Organization 52,* no. 04: 943–969.

Marginson, S. 1999. After Globalization: Emerging Politics of Education. *Journal of Education Policy 14,* no. 1: 19–31.

———. 2004. Competition and Markets in Higher Education: a 'glonacal' analysis. *Policy Futures in Education 2,* no. 2: 175–244.

Martens, K., A. Rusconi, and K. Leuze. 2007. *New Arenas of Education Governance: The Impact of International Organizations and Markets on Educational Policy Making.* New York: Palgrave Macmillan.

Marquis, C. 2002. Nuevos pro*veedores de Educación Superior en Argentina y Brasil.* Caracas: IESALC-UNESCO.

Mattoo, A., and R. Rathindran. 2001. Measuring Services Trade Liberalization and Its Impact on Economic Growth: An Illustration. *Policy Research Working Paper. The World Bank,* no. 2655.

Meister, J. C. 1998. *Corporate Universities: Lessons in Building a World-Class Work Force.* New York: McGraw Hill.

Merrill-Lynch. 1999. *The Book of Knowledge: Investing in the Growing Education and Training Industry.* New York: Merrill Lynch & Co.

Metzger, J. M. 2000. El papel de la OCDE como impulsro de los nuevos temas del comercio internacional. *Información Comercial Española 785:* 27–35.

Millet, M. 2001. *La regulació del comerç internacional: del GATT a l'OMC.* Barcelona: La Caixa.

MITC. 2004. Guía para la lectura y valoración de los compromisos y las ofertas en el marco del AGCS. *Ministerio de Industria, de Turismo y de Comercio del Reino de España* [Manuscript 11/06/04].

Mollis, M. 1997. The Paradox of the Autonomy of Argentine Universities: From Liberalism to Regulation. In *Latin American Education. Comparative Perspectives,* 219–236. Boulder: Westview Press.

Mollis, M. and S. Marginson. 2002. The assessment of universities in Argentina and Australia: Between autonomy and heteronomy. *Higher Education in Europe* 43: 311–330.

Moos, S. 1951. Is Adam Smith out of date? *Oxford Economic Papers* 3, no. 2: 187–201.

Muhr, T. (2008) Nicaragua re-visited: From neo-liberal "ungovernability" to the Bolivarian Alternative for the Peoples of Our America (ALBA), *Globalisation, Societies and Education,* 6(2): 147—161.

Mundy, K. 1998. Educational Multilateralism and World (Dis)Order. *Comparative Education Review* 42, no. 4: 448–478.

———. 1999. Educational multilateralism in a changing world order: UNESCO and the limits of the possible. *Journal of Education Development* 19: 27–52.

Mundy, K. and M. Iga. 2003. Hegemonic Exceptionalism and Legitimating Bet-Hedging: paradoxes and lessons from the US and Japanese approaches to education services under the GATS. *Globalisation, Societies and Education* 1, no. 3: 321–357.

Naidoo, R. 2007. Higher Education as a Global Commodity: The Perils and Promises for Developing Countries. *The Observatory on Borderless in Higher Education*: 2007–08.

Narlikar, A. 2001. WTO Decision-Making and Developing Countries. *South Centre—Working Papers* 11.

Narlikar, A. and N. Woods. 2003. Sectoral Coalitions: the Case of Services. In *Trade Negotiations in Latin America. Problems and Prospects*. New York: Palgrave Macmillan.

NEA. 2004. *Higher Education and International Trade Agreements. An Examination of the Threats and Promises of Globalization*. Washington DC: National Education Association.

Neave, G. 1988. On the cultivation of quality, efficiency and enterprise: an overview of recent trends in higher education in Western Europe, 1968–1988. *European Journal of Education* 23, no. 1–2: 4–13.

Newman, F. 1999. The Transformation of Higher Education for the New Global Environment. *http://www.nerche.org/futuresproject/news-publications.html* [last retrieved: 08/06/04].

Nielson, J. 2003. A Quick Guide to the State of Play in the GATS Negotiations. In *OECD/Norway Forum on Trade in Educational Services*. Trondheim, November 03–04 2003.

Novelli, M., and M. T. A. Lopes Cardozo. 2008. Conflict, education and the global south: New critical directions. *International Journal of Educational Development* 28, no. 4: 473–488.

Nunn, A. 2001. The GATS: an impact assessment for Higher Education in the UK. www.esib.org/commodification/documents/AUTImpact.pdf [last retrieved: 03/04/04].

Nyborg, P. 2002. GATS in the light of increasing internationalization of higher education. Quality assurance and recognition. *OECD/US Forum on Trade in Educational Services*, Washington DC, May 23—24 2002.

OBHE. 2003. Mapping the Educational Industry (1). Public companies—Share Price & Financial Results. *Briefing Note. The Observatory on Borderless Higher Education* 9.

O'Brien, R., A. M. Goetz, J. A. Scholte, and M. Williams. 2000. *Contesting Global Governance: Multilateral Economic Institutions and Global Social Movements*. Cambridge: Cambridge University Press.

OECD. 1996. *Évaluer et réformer les systèmes éducatifs*. Paris: OECD.

———. 2002. Current Commitments under the GATS in Educational Services. *OECD/US Forum on Trade in Educational Services*, Washington DC, May 23—24 2002.

———. 2004. *Internationalisation and Trade in Higher Education: Opportunities and Challenges*. Paris: OECD-CERI.

———. 2006. *Education at a Glance 2006*. Paris: OECD.

OECD, and WB. 2007. *Cross-border Tertiary Education. A Way Towards Capacity Development*. Paris: OECD.

Olds, K. 2008. Analysing Australia's global higher ed export industry. *GlobalHigherEd*. http://globalhighered.wordpress.com/2008/06/24/australias-global-highered-export-industry/ [last retrieved: 03/02/09].

Olssen, M. and M. A. Peters. 2005. Neoliberalism, higher education and the knowledge economy: from the free market to knowledge capitalism. *Journal of Education Policy* 20, no. 3: 313–345.

Öniş, Z. 2007. Varieties and crises of neoliberal globalization. Argentina, Turkey and the IMF. http://home.ku.edu.tr/~zonis/Argentina.pdf [last retrieved: 22/08/07].

Ortino, F. 2006. Treaty Interpretation and the WTO Appellate Body Report in US—Gambling: A Critique. *J Int Economic Law* 9, no. 1 (March 1): 117–148.

Pardos Martínez, E. 1994. El Comercio Internacional de Servicios y la Ronda de Uruguay del GATT. *Cuadernos Aragoneses de Economía* 4, no. 1: 129–145.

Parker, I. 1992. Discourse *Analysis. Critical analysis for social and individual psychology. London:* Routledge.

Patrinos, H. A. 2002. Promoting Access to Postsecondary Education: Meeting the Global Demand. *OECD/US Forum on Trade in Educational Services,* Washington DC, May 23—24 2002.

Payne, A. 2005. *The Global Politics of Unequal Development.* New York: Palgrave MacMillan.

PCTW. 2003. *El ataque de la OMC contra la educación pública. Lo que debes saber sobre el Acuerdo General sobre el Comercio de Servicios (AGCS).* Washington DC: Public Citizen Trade Watch.

Peet, R. 2003. *Unholy Trintiy. The IMF, WB and WTO.* London: Zed Books.

Peixoto, J. 2007. *Los efectos de las negociaciones comerciales internacionales sobre el marco legal en educación superior: los casos de Argentina y Brasil.* Buenos Aires: Universidad de Buenos Aires.

Pillay, P. 2003. The General Agreement on Trade in Services (GATS): Implications and Possible Ways Forward for the Southern African Development Community (SADC). In *UNESCO Conference on 'Globalization and Higher Education,* Oslo, 26–27 May 2003.

Poblano, J. F. 2004. Los Acuerdos de Reconocimiento Mútuo: La Experiencia de México en el TLCAN. In *Seminario Internacional 2004. Movilidad Internacional de Profesionales: Condiciones para la Confianza Recíproca.* Santiago: CSE/CNAP.

Porter, P. and L. Vidovich. 2000. Globalization and Higher Education Policy. *Educational Theory* 50, no. 4: 449–465.

Putnam, R. D. 1999. Diplomacy and domestic politics: the logic of two-level games. In *Theory and Structure in International Political Economy: An International Organization Reader,* 347–380. Boston: MIT Press.

Ramírez Sánchez, C. 2005. Internationalization of Higher Education in Chile. In *Higher Education in Latin America. The International Dimension,* 149–174. Washington DC: The World Bank.

Reichert, S. and C. Tauch. 2003. *Trends 2003. Progress towards the European Higher Education Area.* Brussels: EUA.

Reid, A. 2005. The Regulated Education Market has a Past. *Discourse: studies in the cultural politics of education* 26, no. 1: 79–94.

Richardson, J. 2005. Policy-making in the EU Interests, ideas and garbage cans of primeval soup. In *European Union: Power and Policy-Making,* 3–30. London: Routledge.

Rikowski, G. 2003. Schools and the GATS Enigma. *Journal for Critical Education Policy Studies.* http://www.jceps.com/?pageID=article&articleID=8 [last retrieved: 09/06/07].

Risse, T. 2000. "Let's Argue!": Communicative Action in World Politics. *International Organization* 54: 1–39.

———. 2004. Global Governance and Communicative Action. *Government and Opposition* 39, no. 2: 288–313.

Robertson, S. 2005. Re-imagining and rescripting the future of education: global knowledge economy discourses and the challenge to education systems. *Comparative Education* 41, no. 2: 151–170.

Robertson, S., X. Bonal and R. Dale. 2002. GATS and the education services industry: the politics of scale and global reterritorialization. *Comparative Education Review* 46, no. 4: 472–496.

Robertson, S. and R. Dale. 2003. This is what the fuss is about! The implications of GATS for education systems in the North and the South. *GENIE—the Globalisation and Europeanisation Network in Education: http://www.genie-tn. net* [last retrieved: 06/11/04].

———. 2006. Changing Geographies of Power in Education: the politics of rescaling and its contradictions. In *Education Studies: Issues and Critical Perspectives*, 221–232. Buckinghamshire: Open University Press.

Rodrigues Dias, M. A. 2002a. A OMC e a Educaçao Superior para o Mercado. In *A educação superior frente a Davos*. Porto Alegre: UFRGS.

———. 2002b. Some aspects of the impact of globalization in Higher Education on developing countries. In *Prometeus Conference*, Paris, September 29 2002.

———. 2002c. Utopía y comercialización en la educación superior del s. XXI. In *Lecciones de la Conferencia Mundial sobre Educación Superior- Perspectivas de la Educación Superior en el s. XXI*, 11–44. Buenos Aires: Siglo XXI.

———. 2003. Espacios Solidarios en Tiempos de Oscurantismo. In *UPC Innaugural course lecture*. Barcelona, September 25 2003.

Rodríguez Gómez, R. 2003. La educación superior en el Mercado: configuraciones emergentes y nuevos proveedores. In *Las universidades en América Latina: ¿Reformadas o alteradas?* 87–107. Buenos Aires: CLACSO.

———. 2004. Inversión Extranjera Directa en Educación Superior. El caso de México. *Revista Educación Superior 33, no. 2.*

Routledge, P. 2003. Convergence Space: process geographies of grassroots globalization networks. *Transactions of the Institute of British Geographers* 28, no. 3: 333–349.

Ruggie, J. G. 1982. International Regimes, Transactions, and Change: Embedded Liberalism in the Postwar Economic Order. *International Organisation* 36, no. 2: 379–415.

———. 1994. Trade, Protectionism and the Future of Welfare Capitalism. *Journal of International Affairs* 48, no. 1: 1–11.

Sáez, S. 2005. Implementing trade policy in Latin America: the cases of Chile and México. CEPAL/Serie Comercio Internacional n° 54. Santiago: CEPAL.

Salazar, J. M. 2003. Convergencia e Institucionalidad en la Educación Superior. In *Cooperación y convergencia en la Educación Superior*. Santiago: CSE.

Sánchez Martínez, E. 2002. *La legislación sobre Educación Superior en Argentina. Entre rupturas, continuidades y transformaciones*. Caracas: IESALC-UNESCO.

Sánchez, H. 2005. Tratados comerciales y de inversión: su impacto en la educación. In *Acuerdos Comerciales y Educación*. San José: IE-AL.

Saner, R. and S. Fasel. 2003. Negotiating Trade in Educational Services within the WTO/GATS context. *Aussenwirtschaft* 11: 257–308.

Santiago, G. P. 2000. El Neoliberalismo en las Reformas Económicas en América Latina. In XXII International Congress of the LASA, Miami, March 16–18, 2000.

Santos, B. de S. 2004. *La Universidad del siglo XXI. Para una reforma democrática y emancipadora de la Universidad*. Buenos Aires: Miño y Dávila.

Sanyal, B. C. and M. Martin. ((2006. La financiación de la educación superior: perspectiva internacionales. In *La Educación Superior en el Mundo 2006. La financiación de las universidades*, 3–23. Barcelona: Ediciones Mundi-Prensa.

Sauvé, P. 2002a. Trade, Education and the GATS: What's In, What's Out, What's All the Fuss About? *Higher Education Management and Policy* 14, no. 3: 1–30.

———. 2002b. Progressing the GATS. *The Evian Group Policy Prief,* April 2002.

Sauvé, P. and R. M. Stern. 2000. *GATS2000. New Directions in Services Trade Liberalization.* Washington: Brookings.

Scherrer, C. 2005. GATS: long-term strategy for the commodification of education. *Review of International Political Economy* 12, no. 3: 484–510.

———. 2007. GATS: commodifying education via trade treaties. In *New Arenas of Education Governance: The Impact of International Organizations and Markets on Educational Policy Making.* London: Palgrave.

Scholte, J. A. 2000. Cautionary Reflections on Seattle. *Millenium. Journal of International Studies* 29, no. 1: 115–121.

Schugurensky, D. 1997. University Restructuring in Argentina: The Political Debate. In *Latin American Education. Comparative Perspectives.* Boulder: Westview Press.

Schugurensky, D. and A. Davidson-Harden. 2003. From Córdoba to Washington: WTO/GATS and Latin American education. *Globalisation, Societies and Education* 1, no. 3: 321–357.

Seoane, J. 2002. Crisis de régimen y protesta social en Argentina. Revista Chiapas, 13.

Shashikant, S. 2005. GATS talks will move only with a "big leap" in mode 4. *TWN Info Service on WTO and Trade Issues, 198.*

Sirat, M. 2008. The impact of September 11 on international student flow into Malaysia: lessons learned. *IJAPS* 4, no. 1: 79–95.

Smith, James. 2004. Inequality in international trade? Developing countries and institutional change in WTO dispute settlement. *Review of International Political Economy* 11, no. 3: 542–573.

South-Centre. 2006. The Development Dimension of the GATS Domestic Regulation Negotiations. *South-Centre Analytical Note,* August 2006.

Suranovic, S. 2005. A Three-Year Review of the World Trade Organization. http://www.internationalecon.com/wto [last retrieved: 09/06/06].

Tarabini, A. and A. Verger. 2007. L'Agenda Educativa Global: Mecanismes i Actors. In *Globalització i Desigualtats Educatives.* Palma: Escola de Formació en Mitjans Didàctics.

Tarrow, S. 1994. *Power in movement: social movements, collective action and politics.* Cambridge: Cambridge University Press.

———. 2001. Transnational Politics: Contention and Institutions in International Politics. *Annual Review of Political Science* 4: 1–20.

Taylor, M. 2003. The Reformulation of Social Policy in Chile, 1973–2001. Questioning a Neoliberal Model. *Global Social Policy 3,* no. 1: 21–44.

Teitelbaum, A. 2004. El ALCA está entre nosotros: Los tratados bilaterales de libre comercio. In III Congreso Internacional—Derechos y Garantías en el Siglo XXI, Buenos Aires, September 8–10 2004.

TFP. 2002. An Update on New Providers. *http://www.nerche.org/futuresproject/news-publications.html* [last retrieved: 12/08/04].

Theiler, J. C. 2005. Internationalization of Higher Education in Argentina. In *Higher Education in Latin America. The International Dimension,* 71–110. Washington DC: The World Bank.

Tomasevski, K. 2005. Globalizing What: Education as a Human Right or as a Traded Service? . *Indiana Journal of Global Legal Studies* 12, no. 1: 1–78.

Torres, C. A. and D. Schugurensky. 2002. The political economy of higher education in the era of neoliberal globalization: Latin America in comparative perspective. *Higher Education in Europe* 43: 429–455.

Tramer, V. 2002. Instrumentos de Prochile para la vinculación. In *Encuentro Nacional Universidades-Empresas. Desafíos y Oportunidades para el Desarrollo.* Valparaíso, November 14–15 2002.

Tsutsui, K. and C. M. Wotipka. 2004. Global Civil Society and the International Human Rights Movement: Citizen Participation in Human Rights International Nongovernmental Organizations . *Social Forces* 83, no. 2: 587–620.

UN. 2007. Enhanced cooperation between the United Nations and all relevant partners, in particular the private sector. http://www.gppi.net/fileadmin/gppi/Enhanced_Cooperation_between_the_UN_and.pdf [last retrieved: 15/03/2006].

UNCTAD. 2005. Trade in Services and Development Implications. http://www.unctad.org/en/docs/c1d71_en.pdf [last retrieved: 23/05/06].

UNESCO. 1998. World declaration on higher education for the twenty-first century: vision and action. http://www.unesco.org/education/educprog/wche/declaration_eng.htm [last retrieved: 12/01/09].

———. 2004. *Higher Education in a Globalized Society.* Paris: UNESCO.

———. 2005a. *Guidelines for Quality Provision in Cross-border Higher Education.* Paris: UNESCO.

———. 2005b. *Convention on the protection and promotion of the diversity of cultural expressions.* Paris: UNESCO.

———. 2006. *Global Education Digest,* Montreal: UNESCO Institute for Statistics.

Uvalic-Trumbic, S. 2002. UNESCO's conventions on the recognition of qualifications: regional frameworks. In *First Global Forum on International Quality Assurance, Accreditation and the Recognition of Qualifications in Higher Education* 63–72. UNESCO: Paris.

Van Damme, D. 2003. Globalisation, liberalisation and the need for international public regulation. In *SG Meeting.* Geneva, January 16 2003.

Vanlathem, J. M. 2003. Education and General Agreement on Trade in Services: preserving public education is the best way to achieve the Education For All program. *Policy Futures in Education* 1, no. 2: 342–350.

Varoglu, Z., and C. Wachholz. 2001. Education and ICTs: Current Legal, Ethical and Economic Issues. *TechKnowLogia,* January/February, 2001: 15–19.

Verbik, L. and V. Lasanowski. 2007. *International Student Mobility: Patterns and Trends.* London: OBHE.

Verbik, L. and C. Merkley. 2006. *International Branch Campuses. Model and Trends.* London: OBHE.

Verger, A. 2008. Measuring Educational Liberalisation. A Global Analysis of GATS. *Globalisation, Societies and Education 6, no. 1:* 13–31.

Verger, A. and X. Bonal. 2008. Education vs Trade: Global Struggles Challenging WTO/GATS. In *Contesting Neoliberal Education: Public Resistance and Collective Advance,* 181–201. New York: Routledge.

Verger, A. and Novelli, M. (2009-forthcoming) "Education Is Not For Sale": Teachers' Unions Pluri-Scalar Struggles Against Liberalising The Education Sector, In *Globalization, Knowledge & Labour,* London:Routledge.

Verger, A. and S. L. Robertson. 2008. The 'other GATS negotiations': domestic regulation and norms. *GlobalHigherEd. http://*globalhighered.wordpress.com/2008/05/19/the-other-gats-negotiations-domestic-regulation-and-norms/ [last retrieved: 23/01/09].

Vidal Villa, J. M. 1976. *Teorías del Imperialismo.* Barcelona: Anagrama.

Villanueva, E. 2003. La Educación Transnacional y la Comisión Nacional de Evaluación y Acreditación (CONEAU). Argentina. In *VIII Seminario Internacional 2003. Cruzando fronteras: Nuevos desafíos para la educación superior.* Santiago: CSE/CNAP.

Vinokur, A. 2006. Brain migration revisited. *Globalisation, Societies and Education* 4, no. 1: 7–24.

Vlk, A. 2006. *Higher Education and GATS. Regulatory Consequences and Stakeholders' Responses*. University of Twente: CHEPS.

Wade, R. H. 2005. Failing States and Cumulative Causation in the World System. *International Political Science Review* 26, no. 1: 17–36.

Wallerstein, I. 1979. *The Capitalist World-Economy*. Cambridge: Cambridge University Press.

Walsh, J. I. 2000. When do Ideas Matter? Explaining the Successes and Failures of Thatchrite Ideas. *Comparative Political Studies* 33, no. 4: 483–516.

WB. 1994. *Higher Education: The Lessons of Experience*. Washington DC: World Bank.

———. 2002. *Constructing Knowledge Societies: New Challenges for Tertiary Education*. Washington, DC: World Bank.

———. 2005. *Global Economic Prospects. Trade Regionalism and Development*. Washington, DC: World Bank.

WB and UNCTAD. 1994. *Liberalizing International Transactions in Services: A Handbook*. Ginebra: UN.

Weiss, F. 2001. Aspectos jurídicos del comercio de servicios en una economia globalizada. In *La Organización Mundial del Comercio y el regionalismo europeo*. Madrid: Dykinson.

Wende, M. C. van der. 2001. Internationalisation policies: about new trends and contrasting paradigms. *Higher Education Policy* 14: 249–259.

———. 2003. Globalisation and Access to Higher Education. *Journal of Studies in International Education* 7, no. 2: 193–206.

———. 2003. Globalisation and Access to Higher Education. *Journal of Studies in International Education* 7, no. 2: 193–206.

Wendt, A. 1999. *Social Theory of International Politics*. Cambridge: Cambridge University Press.

White, L. J. 2002. International Trade in Services: More Than Meets the Eye. In *Handbook of International Trade, Volume 2*. Malden: Blackwell.

Wilkinson, R. 2000. *Multilateralism and the World Trade Organisation: the architecture and extension of international trade regulation*. London: Routledge.

———. 2002a. A tale of four Ministerials. The WTO and the rise and demise of the trade-labour standards debate. *IPEG Papers in Global Political Economy* 3.

———. 2002b. The World Trade Organisation. *New Political Economy* 7, no. 1: 129–141.

———. 2004. The Politics of Collapse: Development, the WTO and the Current Round of Trade Negotiations. *IPEG Papers in Global Political Economy* 15.

Williams, S. 2003. UNESCO in action education: Borderless Education. *The New Courier* 2.

Worth, J. 2000. The threat to higher education. A briefing on current WTO negotiations. www.peopleandplanet.org/tradejustice. [last retrieved: 24/11/03].

WTO. 1996. Guidelines for arrangements on relations with Non-Governmental Organizations. Geneva: WTO.

———. 1998. Education Services. Background note by the Secretariat. Geneva: WTO.

———. 1999. *Introducción al Acuedo General sobre el Comercio de Servicios (AGCS)*. Geneva: WTO Trade in Services Division.

———. 2000. *Guide to the GATS. An Overview of Issues for Further Liberalization of Trade in Services*. The Hague: Kluwer Law International.

———. 2001. *GATS- fact and fiction*. Geneva: WTO.

———. 2002a. *Diez malentendidos frecuentes sobre la OMC*. Geneva: WTO.

————. 2002b. Director-general of WTO and chairman of WTO services negotiations reject misguided claims that public services are under threat. *WTO News: 2002 Press Releases Press/299,* 28 June 2002.

————. 2004. *The Future of WTO.* Geneva: WTO.

————. 2005a. *Understanding the WTO.* Geneva: WTO- Information and Media Relations Division.

————. 2005b. Council for Trade in Services, Special Session. Education Services. Information Note by the Secretariat. Geneva: WTO.

————. 2005c. Initial and Revised Offers. A factual assessment of the sate of play. http://docsonline.wto.org [last retrieved: 21/07/06].

————. 2005d. *WTO Annual Report 2005.* Geneva: WTO.

————. 2008. *10 benefits of the WTO trading system.* Geneva: WTO.

WTO-Australia. 2001. Communication from Australia. Negotiation Proposal for Education Services. http://www.wto.org/English/tratop_e/serv_e/s_propnewnegs_e.htm [last retrieved: 21/01/09].

WTO-NZ. 2001. Communication from New Zealand. Negotiation Proposal for Education Services. http://www.wto.org/English/tratop_e/serv_e/s_propnewnegs_e.htm [last retrieved: 21/01/09].

WTO-Switzerland. 2005. Comunicación de Suiza. Los servicios de enseñanza y el AGCS: la experiencia Suiza. http://www.wto.org/English/tratop_e/serv_e/s_propnewnegs_e.htm [last retrieved: 21/01/09].

WTO-US. 2000. Communication from US. Higher (Tertiary) Education, Adult Education and Training. http://www.wto.org/English/tratop_e/serv_e/s_propnewnegs_e.htm [last retrieved: 21/01/09].

Yin, R. K. 1994. *Case study research: design and methods.* Thousand Oaks: Sage Publications.

Zdouc, W. 1999. WTO dispute settlement practice relating to the GATS. *Journal of International Economic Law* 2, no. 2: 295–346.

Zhang, C. 2003. *Transnational Higher Education in China: Why has the State encouraged its Development?* Stanford: University of Stanford, School of Education.

Ziguras, C., L. Reinke, and G. Mcburnie. 2003. 'Hardly Neutral Players': Australia's role in liberalising trade in education services. *Globalisation, Societies and Education* 1, no. 3: 359–374.

Authors Index

Subject Index

Printed in the United States
by Baker & Taylor Publisher Services